Robert Alston Jones

COMMON BLOOD:

The Life and Times of an Immigrant Family in Charleston, South Carolina

This book was printed in the United States of America.

Cover design by permission of Historic Urban Plans, Inc., Ithaca, New York, USA.

To order additional copies of this book, contact:
Xlibris Corporation
1-888-795-4274
www.Xlibris.com
Orders@Xlibris.com
119236

COMMON BLOOD

CONTENTS

For my grandchildren
Lily, Loey, Mae, Piper, Walden, and Winnie
And theirs to come

ACKNOWLEDGEMENTS

I have lived with these ancestral family members so long that they have come, and are, alive to me. In their virtual presence, I acknowledge and thank them for everything they endured in establishing the ancestral lineages that I have written about in the chapters that follow, and which I confidantly assert became part of the fabric of Charleston—that unique city on the South Carolina coast. I owe particular gratitude to those whose stories seemed eminently illustrative of the intersection of individual lives with the historical context of their times—my great-great-grandfathers Peter Weber and Johann Wilhelm Friedrich Struhs, my great-grandfathers Bernhard Heinrich Bequest and Seaborn Jones, my great-great-grandmother Jane Thompson—and not least, their spouses and their children who carried each ancestral heritage into a future that has now become the past.

In the present, my thanks go to the many who helped me in this endeavor. Much of my research was done in the South Carolina Room at the Charleston County Public Library: the librarians there were wonderfully resourceful accomplices who more often than not led me out of cul-de-sacs into other, more productive avenues. Marianne Cawley, Molly French, Dorothy Glover, Elizabeth Newcombe, Alicia Thompson, and Christine Shedloch never tired of my questions and responded with admirable patience to my insistent efforts to find alternate routes to my genealogical destinations. Also in Charleston, Nancy Kruger, who manages the St. Matthew's Lutheran Church Archives, helped me access those carefully inscribed historical records of the German ethnic community and graciously arranged her volunteer schedule to accommodate my periodic visits to Charleston.

At the University of Wisconsin-Milwaukee Library, my research was greatly facilitated by Kim Silbersack, who granted me workspace close to the books I needed, and the Interlibrary Loan staff, who followed through on my every request for sources that were unavailable locally. UW-Milwaukee houses the world-renowned American Geographical Society Library's collection of maps and other resources, and the staff there, particularly Jovanka Ristic and

Lisa Sutton, provided invaluable assistance in all matters geographical, both hard copy and digital.

In my efforts to read and decipher original handwritten German church records, I depended on my colleagues Johanna Moore and the late Professor Emeritus Gerhard Rauscher for clarification, translation, and interpretation. Without their help, any number of linguistic and orthographical riddles would have remained unsolved.

I am indebted also to my Aunt Ernestine, whose ninety-eight-year-old memory served willingly to relay to me much of the lore I have about the Thompson and Jones families. She never tired of being interviewed by a fair-weather nephew who could visit her only occasionally in Charleston.

Lastly, I thank Mary, who stood by patiently while I researched, read, wrote, and was—seemingly forever—engaged with the life and times of this immigrant family in Charleston.

I

INTRODUCTION

I initially intended to write this family history for my children and their children—in the hope that at some point in their lives they would be interested in their cultural heritage. That interest, I appreciated, sometimes takes a while to develop: early maturity is too busy with life in the present to find time to think about life in the past. I was nonetheless firmly convinced that where and from what one has come often influences where one heads in the future: the lucky ones discover this perspective early enough to appreciate that a certain foundation marks their lives whether they wish to admit it or not. At some point, however, I thought the stories I had discovered were worthy of a wider audience—readers who appreciate that history does indeed repeat itself, and who find social, cultural, and political history fascinating in its ability to provide a vision of both the past and the future.

The particular cultural heritage that I delineate interweaves European and American strands of [primarily] nineteenth-century history by looking at an immigrant community that was in many ways unique and that has been largely overlooked. I was born in Charleston, South Carolina, a descendant of post-colonial English and German immigrants, and it is their story that I want to tell. Charleston by almost unanimous consent has always represented a unique cultural context, a city then and now characteristically not like any other on either coast or in the middle. Charlestonians have always talked differently, thought differently, and acted differently than the rest of the state, the region, and, for that matter, the entire country. The city's Lowcountry blend of elegance, arrogance, lethargy, mixed with its architecture, cuisine, and geography has forestalled any attempt to replicate it anywhere else. It is unto itself—ask anyone from Charleston!

Of course, Charleston was not always the beautiful city that is now a tourist destination. It is famous for its colonial heritage, and its current state of historical preservation is a twentieth-century phenomenon that imparts to its environs the character of an open-air museum. Between its colonial past and its current vitality lies a century or more of development that often was not pretty, not healthy, not admirable, nor forward-thinking. It was during that period from the early 1800s to the turn of the twentieth-century that an extended family of English and German immigrants evolved into Charlestonians of a slightly different character than those citizens who gained fame of one sort or another and whose names appear in the history books as Charleston notables. These immigrants were never the blue-bloods who populated the Charleston peninsula "below Broad", although they may have lived in that area before it accrued its snob status. These were the European settlers who took up residence carrying lots of cultural baggage, and if light in worldly possessions and wherewithal, were laden with determination and backbone. They were the common blood that played a significant role in transforming a patriarchal planter society mired in itself into a southern culture that somehow managed to save itself.

The character of the immigrant community in Charleston is generally not well-known.[1] It is not that it wasn't diverse—there were the English, the Irish, the Italians, the Germans, and the Jews—but it seems not to have been of sufficient interest or significance to anyone to warrant serious consideration. While Charleston was of major importance during Colonial and post-colonial times, it declined in importance as other cities expanded and as the original East Coast territory moved westward. In most cases, post-colonial English newcomers weren't even thought of as *immigrants*, although they streamed in throughout the nineteenth century along with numerous others from continental Europe. For that matter, we rarely think of any colonial settlers as *immigrants*. From the pilgrims onward, however, those arriving on newly found shores were as much representatives of migration, emigration, and immigration as any who left Europe in the later century to establish themselves in a new land. In the nineteenth century, however, those who came and lived in Charleston were not in the mainstream. One can find numerous studies of ethnic immigrant communities in cities to the north and west—the Irish and Italians in the northeastern cities, the Germans in Missouri, Texas, and Wisconsin, the Scandinavians in the Upper Midwest. The immigrants in Charleston, although

---

[1]   A recent work by Andrea Mehrländer, *The Germans of Charleston, Richmond, and New Orleans during the Civil War Period* (Berlin/New York: DeGruyter, 2011), cites a number of articles and monographs on the German immigrants in Charleston, but there are only eight items in her list, including one dissertation. Her study acknowledges that the relatively small percentage of immigrants who chose the states of what would become the Confederacy, compared to those who migrated to the northern states, represents in general a neglected ethnic population. None of the works she cites could be expected to have a wide readership.

a significant percentage of the population,[2] failed to attract much attention. So as Charleston evolved from its somewhat singular beginnings into its peculiar Lowcountry, charming—if rather elitist—character, its immigrant community grew and established a solid middle class that based itself on its European roots and values, and which modified the character of the older city into what we know today.

My intent is to relate how typical my immigrant family's lives and experiences were relative to the nineteenth century cultural evolution of Charleston. The English and German stock of this extended family populate the period from about 1820 to the turn of the century. Although there are contemporary descendants of these families still living in Charleston, I have not created fictitious names to hide identities. These were real people who lived documented lives and who passed into and out of the historical record. In most cases, these persons are embodied through my interpretation of that historical record since there are precious few personal documents to give expression to the past and to actually record what went on in their lives. But there are few secrets to hide and very few remarkable feats to showcase. The family is of the most ordinary sort, and it is in their ordinariness that I find their significance. I try to explain who they were, where they came from, what they brought with them, how they managed to put down roots in the sandy soil of the South Carolina coast, how they were buffeted by all the winds of historical change that blew after their arrival, how they transformed themselves from immigrants to residents, what legacy they left behind as Charlestonians.

---

[2]   Ira Berlin and Herbert Gutman state that "the peculiar pattern of European migration and settlement in the slave states gave immigrants importance far beyond their numbers and projected foreign-born workers into a place in the Southern working class that rivaled the role played by immigrants in the North. Although a comparatively small number of Europeans migrated to the South during the nineteenth century, those who did generally settled in cities. South Carolina, Georgia, and Alabama had few immigrants, but Charleston, Savannah, and Mobile had many. At mid-century, the foreign-born population of these states reached 3 percent only in the case of South Carolina. But more than a fifth of Charleston's residents, more than a quarter of Savannah's, and almost a third of Mobile's had been born outside the United States" (Berlin and Gutman 1983, 1177-78).

II

THE FAMILIES

I view my German heritage as book-ended by my English forebears. Both English lineages were in evidence in the Charleston area before the German families immigrated. The one English line was distinctly *urban*, the other *rural*. They ultimately merged to interact with their continental counterparts to extend the family in both directions. It turns out they were not so different from each other, and not at all surprising that they came together as an extended family. They were neighbors in a relatively small community whose parallel experiences destined them to relate to each other.[3]

If the reader were a Charleston resident anytime during the 1900s, a summary outline of the family connections could be readily acknowledged: the English families were Thompson and Jones; the Germans were Weber, Struhs, and Bequest. The English-born Thompsons were there first; the English-descended Jones family came to Charleston much later from thirty miles to the north, from Moncks Corner. The remarkable thing about the family Germans is that they were virtually all from a small area of what is now northwestern Germany—as were most of the German immigrants who settled in Charleston. Struhs married Weber, and Weber married Bequest. Then Bequest married Jones, who had married Thompson. By the time the last connection was made, the family had transitioned out of the nineteenth into the twentieth century. The untangling of that family knot into the separate, but

---

[3]   Frederick Luebke makes the point that the perceived social distance between the ethnic group and the culture of the host or receiving society plays a role in how easily the two relate to each other. "In the United States the core culture may be described as having emerged from English and pietistic Protestant origins" (Luebke 1990, 150). This would have definitely been the case in Charleston, such that the German immigrants and the English, both native and immigrant, could be expected to find communality.

related, strands outlining the course each family took constitutes the chapters that follow.

If we look at the family picture delineated with a broad brush, it is a great-great-grandmother, Jane Thompson, who begins the story. She landed in Charleston in the 1820s with her sister and parents from Lancashire, England. She was married in her twenties to an Irishman who had immigrated to Charleston about the same time as her parents. Soon after her young husband's untimely death, she married a Charleston Englishman, had six children by him, and died in 1877. She witnessed the major events in Charleston's nineteenth-century history, including the Civil War and Reconstruction, and her heirs still living in Charleston are numerous. She was the only one who might have thought she had risen to a status a little higher than the middle, although that may have been wishful thinking on her part.

Jane Thompson had not yet married her second husband when Johann Rosenbohm, in his twenties, took leave of his North German village and embarked on a sailing vessel bound for the United States. He was the first on the German side of the family to emigrate, and it was his presence in Charleston that would subsequently serve as a draw for others. He was naturalized already in 1830, purchased several properties in Charleston, and returned to Germany in 1837 to get married. He tried his luck operating a grocery store on the corner of Queen and Meeting Streets, but left in 1839 to move to New York. Other members of his family, however, would find their way to Charleston by the time Johann died in New York in 1843. He had three sisters, each of whom ended up in Charleston: his sister Adelheid had married a Bequest descendant in the small town of Geestendorf in the northwest of what is now the German state of Lower Saxony. She came to Charleston as a widow with her daughter Adeline, who would subsequently marry Frederick Schroeder at St. Matthew's Lutheran Church. Another of Johann's sisters, Anna Maria, and her husband from the Black Forest, Nicholas Fehrenbach, emigrated shortly after their first child was born in Geestendorf. They had seven other children in Charleston. Johann's third sister, Catharina, married Hermann Knee, who figured prominently in the establishment of the Lutheran community in Walhalla, SC. It would be Adelheid Bequest's husband's nephew, Bernhard Heinrich Bequest, who would immigrate at the close of the Civil War and establish the Bequest family in Charleston.

The Weber ancestors are the family's only representatives of Germans who emigrated from another area: Johann and Peter Weber were from the town of Billigheim in the northern part of Bavaria. Johann's wife, nonetheless, was from Wulsdorf, a village within the jurisdiction of Geestemünde,[4] the same

---

[4]   In 1888 the villages of Geestendorf and Geestemünde were united as Geestemünde. Both towns derived their names from their proximity to the river Geeste where it flows into the Weser.

area from which virtually all the other relatives originated. Johann and his wife were married in Charleston in 1844, a match made after both had emigrated independently. Peter and his wife were natives of neighboring South German villages and were likely married before they came to Charleston. They had six children, but both Peter and his wife were dead by 1859. The Webers left one scion who would later marry the Walhalla-born daughter of Johann Wilhelm Friedrich Struhs.

The Struhs line had its origin just a little north of where the other North German families came from. Resident ever since the seventeenth century along the northwestern coastal area of Germany south of Cuxhaven, the Struhs family's first to emigrate was Johann Wilhelm Friedrich, born 1829. He arrived in the United States in 1851 and was naturalized in Walhalla, SC in 1856. The fact that his naturalization occurred in Walhalla marks him as well as one of the early settlers of that German community in upstate South Carolina, a *mission* undertaken by the Lutheran congregation of St. Matthew's *German* Lutheran Church in Charleston. The granddaughter of Johann Wilhelm Friedrich would tie the Weber and Struhs families to that of John Frederick Bequest after the turn of the twentieth century. By then, the German family members could be described as acculturated German-Charlestonians.

The other English bookend adds the Jones lineage to the composite family picture. A Bequest daughter would grow up in Charleston next door to a family that had merged with the first bookend—the Thompsons. In 1890, Jane Thompson's granddaughter, Ida Thompson, had married Irving Little Jones, a 32-year-old man from Moncks Corner, a small town to the north of Charleston. His family had lived in that rural area since at least the early 1800s, and might have been considered less *cultured* than the urbanized Charleston Thompsons. By the end of the nineteenth century, Charleston had been through Reconstruction and a middling decline, and if the Thompson family had earlier thought itself part of the the city's Episcopalian establishment, the union of Ida and Irving had a moderating effect on the family heritage. Ida's mother, in fact, was a German whom her father had married in defiance of what the family thought proper. But that's another German and a later chapter in the story! Ida and Irving Jones's seventh child was born in 1904 and was a teenager of 15 when his family moved next door to the Bequests on East Bay Street just south of Calhoun. With the Bequest and Jones union in 1935, the five family lines were tied together. By the close of the nineteenth century, the extended, interrelated family had integrated the Germans with the English and had acculturated and assimilated itself into the Charleston society. It, however, was never *society*, but rather a family of ordinary citizens, most of whom had brought Europe to Charleston and put their heart and soul into the melting pot on the coast of South Carolina. That common blood still courses through Charleston's veins.

III

EARLY HISTORY BEFORE THE MOVE

Those broad strokes depicting the families and their interrelationships conceal many a detail. Each family had its own trajectory even while crisscrossing and merging with the path of the others. While the family's earliest immigrants were not in Charleston until the second decade of the nineteenth century, all of their stories start further back in time. Everyone came from somewhere and left behind a home with all its familiar associations. While this is not the place to rewrite European history for the nth time, at least a cursory review of the conditions in Europe that precipitated the decisions to seek life anew in a different place is warranted. It will provide a perspective on what the immigrants undertook in coming to Charleston,

The paths begin in the middle of the seventeenth century. The Struhs lineage is documentable back to 1651 when the earliest direct forebear, one, Marten Struß, was born in the village of Flögeln. Flögeln lies in the extreme northwest of present-day Germany, south of the city of Cuxhaven, in an area between the Elbe and the Weser Rivers. Flögeln's history goes back to the middle ages when the town belonged to the Archbishopric of Bremen. In 1648, just shortly before the estimated birth of Marten Struß, the area became part of the Duchy of Bremen. This was the result of the Peace of Westphalia, the close of the Thirty Years War that had ravaged most of Europe for more than a generation. The village/town would pass through the eighteenth century being *owned* by the crowns of Sweden, then Denmark, then Hanover; in the nineteenth century it would belong to Napoleonic France, then to the Electorate of Hanover, to the King of England, and finally to Prussia after 1866. It still exists—now as a town in the northern corner of the modern state of Lower Saxony.

Area of Germany that was home to so many of the immigrants to Charleston. From the American Geographical Society Library, University of Wisconsin-Milwaukee Libraries.

Within three generations, Borchert Struß, a grandson of Marten Struß, was born in the town of Cappel, just slightly to the north and west of his grandfather's birthplace. Cappel lies within the small North Sea coastal area [only about 45 sq. miles] that was earlier known as *Land Wursten*. Approximately twelve miles southwest of Cuxhaven and nine miles north of Bremerhaven, it was from there that Johann Wilhelm Friedrich Struhs—another three generations later—would immigrate to Charleston. In the one hundred and seventy-eight years between the birth of Marten and that of his great-great-great-grandson, the family would have weathered the changing conditions of that part of Europe and experienced enough turmoil that the ultimate move to the west would seem the only recourse.

The Bequest heritage can be traced almost as far back as that of the Struß family. Just to the south of the area of Land Wursten, closer to the mouth of the Weser, lies the town of Geestendorf. During the Middle Ages it too belonged to the Bremen bishopric, and after the Peace of Westphalia underwent the same territorial changes as its neighbors to the north, ultimately becoming a part of the Kingdom of Hanover. It was here that the daughter of a local farmer and blacksmith, Johann Nohrden, married a corporal of the French navy and started the Bequest line. The Nohrdens are traceable back to a generation born before 1700, and together with the Struß family establish this northern area of Germany as the main source of the family's German immigrants.

The point was made earlier that this North German heritage is characteristic of the Charleston immigrant community. If one walks through the oldest sections of Bethany Cemetery in Charleston—one of the city's three largest cemeteries—one cannot help but notice that the headstones seem to take special note of the individual's birthplace, and there are relatively few that do not specify a town within the area surrounding Bremen. Many are indeed from Geestendorf [usually spelled *Gestendorf*] itself or from its immediate neighbor Lehe. This northwest corner of Lower Saxony bordering on the North Sea anchored one end of the chain of migration, the other, Charleston. While other German settlements in the United States also enjoyed a similar kind of cohesion within their respective ethnic communities, there is none other than the one in Charleston that stemmed so exclusively from this particular area of Germany. Regional differences invariably manifest themselves in individuals, and in the case of those immigrants who settled in Charleston a close look at the history and nature of their origins gives some sense of who they were and what they were about.

The approximately eighteen-mile coastal strip of Land Wursten gets its name from the Low-German *Wursaten* or *Wursasses*, terms descriptive of "people sitting on dwelling mounds." (http://www.lancewadplan.org/Cultural%20atlas/LS/Land%20Wursten/land_wursten.htm). These dwelling mounds were used by the inhabitants of the area since the Stone Age and were devised to provide living space above the ever-changing sea level. The land to the east of the shoreline is predominantly marshland that has been changed over the years into arable land protected by dikes and shoreline management. By the time the self-governing area became part of Bremen in the sixteenth century [1525], it was primarily farmland of somewhat limited quality, and peopled by individuals living in nucleated and more dispersed villages. There would have been no paved roads throughout the seventeenth and eighteenth centuries. A network of paved roads was not in evidence until the end of the nineteenth century, and Cuxhaven to the northeast and Bremerhaven to the south were not connected until 1863. A train route through the coastal strip itself was not in effect until 1896.

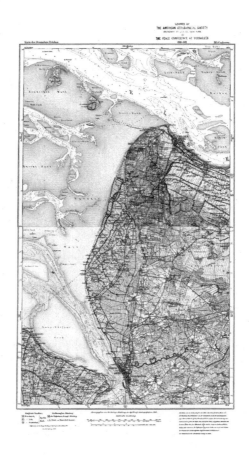

The area of Land Wursten along the coast north of Bremerhaven. From the American Geographical Society Library, University of Wisconsin-Milwaukee Libraries.

The majority of the inhabitants of this entire northern area of German lands were of Saxon heritage,[5] with an infusion of Friesian the closer to the neighboring and related tribe to the west. By virtue of their location and the region's topography, the inhabitants have been described as *cut off*, *courageous*, *adventurous*, *pugnacious*, and *independent to a fault*. One needs to think in small numbers when describing the course of much of the area's history: these were small villages in a sparsely—by today's standards—settled rural setting,

---

[5] There may be some dispute about claiming tribal heritage, but there is little doubt that these northern peoples evolved into inhabitants whose characteristics can be differentiated from those whose lineage derives from other regional sources.

with customs and traditions bearing heavily on the individual.[6] According to Willy Klenck's account of Mulsum (Klenck 1959, 21), one of Land Wursten's villages, the old church records indicate that the population was not all that indigenous, but rather transient, as individuals moved within a restricted area in search of a sustainable existence. Many operated as seasonal workers or tenant farmers, so that there was little to hold them in place. The Strußes may have been one of the few families in neighboring Flögeln and later in Cappel who could trace a lineage back for a hundred years. Marriages were usually with someone from a neighboring village—one could travel only so far—and the small number of inhabitants of one's own village limited the selection at any given point in time. One's class, moreover, determined the marriage prospects: there was little chance of moving out of one's *Stand*, not likely *up*—for man or woman—and all too possibly *down* if one did not own property. Until more modern times, lives were short: in the period between 1700 and 1819 the life expectancy for men was 33.5 years, for women, 33.6. Death occurred according to the conditions of the times: although most church records indicate the cause of death only from about 1780 on, it was usually smallpox, dysentery, scarlet fever, measles, tuberculosis, pneumonia, or the endemic "marsh fever" that took most lives. (Klenck 1959, 82) The infant mortality rate was high, and many women died in childbirth. As a consequence, second and third marriages were common—a widowed parent could almost never maintain a family and an occupation alone.

The social structure of these North German villages was regimented and resistant to change. Those who were nothing more than laborers (*Häusler*) owned no property and were considered the equivalent of rabble with little, if any, rights in the community. Above them were those literally on the *edge/brink* of social legitimacy, the *Brinksitzer*, the lower category of farm laborer, akin to a tenant farmer, but working primarily uncultivated areas. Above them were the *Kötner* (cottager) who were tenant farmers working small parcels of land. There were those known as *Großkötner*, working larger parcels but who were tenants of less than a large and independent *Hof* or farm. All of these categories of individuals owed taxes of time [labor] and harvest—of whatever size—to the entity above them, so that in each instance they were indentured in every sense of the word—distinctly not "free". (Klenck 1959, 82) At the very top of the pyramid were royalty and *government* in its several classifications—both of which lived off such peasant communities within their jurisdictions.

---

6   A village like Flögeln could support only about 250-300 inhabitants. According to one study of a typical 18th century *Geestdorf*, in 1677 there were 36 occupied farms, 8 unoccupied; in 1735 the number had grown to 54, and remained constant until 1825. The increase was due largely to allowing a type of farmer [*Brinksitzer*] at the lower level of society to be counted among the village's *legitimate* citizenry. (Pech 1981, 51-53)

The inhabitants of Land Wursten had been building dikes since the eleventh and twelfth centuries—primarily to increase the yield of the marshland that surrounded them and to enable them to plant winter grains. They also harvested peat and used it for heat. What had developed was a closed agrarian society that existed virtually unchanged since the Middle Ages. Cattle and sheep were the main animals that were grazed on public and royal lands. Grazing areas were very limited and not very good, and fertilizer other than manure was not developed or used. For individual use, there was flax, vegetables [cabbage] and some fruit. Fishing was supplemental, although each third fish had to be given to the pastor who headed the community. The usual drink was water or watered-down milk. Most townspeople could not afford beer. Seasonal work did not support all that many and was practiced mainly by the unemployed and the *Häusler*. Except for the heir, most young men left at age fourteen to work in the marshes. The farming system was dependent on the number of animals that could provide manure; these in turn depended on the amount of grazing land or land that could be cultivated for animal fodder. Any increase in population required more land to raise more animals to feed on more fodder. Overgrazing led to deterioration of the land, less nourishment for animals, and thus for the population, decline. Bad harvests and other disturbances, to say nothing of war and pestilence, led to a very precarious existence.

While the focus thus far has been on the area of Land Wursten, the scene for Geestendorf just to the south would not have been very different. This small village, the home of the Bequests, would later be merged with other small communities to become Geestemünde, ultimately to form part of the major port city of Bremerhaven. At one point it too was ruled by Sweden, then Denmark, and in 1715 sold to the Duchy of Braunschweig-Lüneburg. It was not until the mid-nineteenth century that it was destined to become a place on the map that anyone considered of any importance. A summary Wikipedia history credits it with only 59 citizens living in 15 houses in 1848. It would become part of a more urbanized area than the villages to its north, but earlier it too would have supported primarily an agricultural society that had not changed much from earlier times.

As stated earlier, the Bequest line can be traced back to the early eighteenth century, and that story really begins after the French Revolution at a time when this area was occupied by Napoleonic France. What life was like in Geestendorf during this early period is revealed in the occupations that the Bequest family members held. We find them working as: ferryman (*Fährmann*); inn keeper (*Gastwirt*); seaman (*Seemann*); cottager (*Baukötner*); cottager (*Kötner*); workman (*Arbeitsmann*); ship's carpenter (*Schiffzimmermann*); boatman, later ship pilot (*Jollenführer, später Lotse*); sailor/skipper (*Schiffer*); ship pilot (*Lotse*); apprentice pilot (*Lotsenlehrling*); sailor (*Matrose*); caretaker

(*Hausmann*); smith (*Schmied*); blacksmith (*Grobschmied*); master smith (*Schmiedemeister*); church legal spokesman (*Kirchjurat*); highway toll collector (*Chausseeeinnehmer*). (Friedrichs 2003)

With almost every Bequest family member working in multiple capacities, it is clear that many of them—like other inhabitants of Geestendorf—worked at maritime jobs. Three Bequests, in fact, died at such jobs, drowning by virtue of storms or accidents at sea. While most families farmed small land holdings, Geestendorf offered some diversity in ancillary work, some of it seasonal, some a steady aspect of the agrarian-based community life. The specification of a *master smith* and an *apprentice pilot* suggests that the guild system was to some extent still in effect. It can be noted that inheritance also played a role: in several instances, the son carried on the same occupation of the father. Bohl Nohrden worked as smith or master smith in 1815; his son functioned similarly in 1870. Michael Böse took over as inn-keeper from his father-in-law. Johann Graefer's father was a ship pilot, he, an apprentice pilot in 1845 and pilot by 1852. There were not all than many options, and if one could step into already-filled shoes, there was continuity in the family and in the community. As for inheriting real property, this area of North Germany still operated according to the tradition of undivided property passing to the heir, while in areas to the south and southwest, land partibility led to smaller and smaller holdings passing to subsequent generations with the result that the inherited property was often too meager to sustain an individual family. These traditions affected the migration patterns of the various areas within Germany, and ultimately had something to do with the trends of emigration that swelled in the nineteenth century to unparalleled levels.

Both the area of origin of the majority of the Charleston German immigrant community and the nature of life typical of the village communities where two of the lineages originated were under the influence of larger forces. James Sheehan (Sheehan 1989) articulates these forces against the broader background of what he terms "traditional life" in Europe in general, that is, life during the eighteenth and nineteenth centuries. In his chapter on the politics of the eighteenth century, he acknowledges the *new* instability that manifested itself around 1740 in the tensions between old Austria and rising Prussia and which, by the end of the Seven Years War in 1763, had set two antagonistic poles in place as these two states took on roles independent of the other players in what was left of the *Reich* still called the *Holy Roman Empire of the German Nation*. The Napoleonic regime's control of German areas "radically transformed Germany's map in response to two principles: 'mediatization' and secularization. The former signified the subjugation of lesser territorial units to stronger states, while the latter meant the annexation of ecclesiastical principalities by larger secular states. [One] decree eliminated 112 small states, mostly free cities and ecclesiastical units. Of the 511 free cities, only six survived, and of the ecclesiastical states, only three endured. More than three million inhabitants changed rulers" (Grob 2003, 88).

The political times were dealing with traditions, laws, and institutions teasing out the concepts of sovereignty and authority, as well as rulers who were challenging the populace and other rulers in their insular worlds with visions of both secular and ecclesiastical power and glory. Most of the action on all these fronts took place on a level high above the heads of the common folk. They had little time to notice the machinations of the mighty and had only to deal with the forces that impinged on them at a much more local level.

After mid-century, however, the consensus was that things had begun to change: some rulers became more enlightened, their governments more attuned to the social orders and the need for reform. Improvements were made in infrastructures, increasing commercialization changed economies, and growth pushed everything haltingly forward. Sheehan cautions, however, not to "overestimate the rate or extent of change in the German countryside. Even where the traditional social order was no longer intact, the influence of traditional values and élites persisted. The restrictive web of institutions that kept the vast majority of central Europeans on the edge of subsistence was just beginning to unravel. Nevertheless, many thoughtful observers recognized that population growth, state efforts at social reform, and increases in the value and productivity of the land had begun to transform rural society and to reorder the relationship between agriculture and manufacturing, between city and countryside" (Sheehan 1989, 105).

By the end of the eighteenth century then, the march of history would have affected the inhabitants of the area around Geestendorf. Land Wursten was part of the Kingdom of Hanover, and in 1803 when Napoleon resumed hostilities with England, he ordered the occupation of the country that still belonged to the English crown: "Hanover's army was dismantled, its arms and revenues were transferred to France, and it was forced to maintain a French occupation army and close its borders to English commerce" (Grob 2003, 89).[7] Then in the aftermath of Napoleon, the Congress of Vienna in 1815 had the task of putting Humpty-Dumpty Europe back together, realigning its composite parts once again, some states gaining territory, some losing, and some remaining as they had been, but all confronting new challenges that new times had brought into play. In general, it was a period of transition from the traditional political and social order to more modern ways, transforming the old into the preconditions for a "capitalist, legally equal, religiously tolerant and rationally governed bourgeois society" (Grob 2003, 111).

---

[7]   This is precisely what would bring a certain Frenchman to Geestendorf—the beginning of the Bequest story.

This essentially marginal area of Europe would have maintained a conservative view of changing political and social conditions. Anyone alive at the time would have sensed in the air the tensions between the classes as early revolutionary ideas buzzed throughout the realm in one form or another; would have breathed easier after the cessation of successive hostilities; would have been sensitive to any impositions on religious practices, whether by a governing authority or by believers of a different creed; would have known that the revolution in France had upset pretty much everything and that again there were foreign troops occupying the region; would have been aware of rumors suggesting that things were [more] prosperous elsewhere, that mercantilism and industrialization were changing things, sometimes for the better, sometimes for the worse, but changing nonetheless. And by the first decades of the nineteenth century, they would have known that the population itself was growing and that their communities were facing economic and social issues they had not faced in the past.[8]

The unparalleled growth in population functioned to instigate the wide-spread movement of people in Europe that culminated in unprecedented rates of emigration—mostly to the United States—during the nineteenth century. Already in 1803 the state of Baden had recognized the right of its citizens to move freely. Other states followed suit. The Charter of the German Confederation of 1815 established freedom of emigration for its member states, and it took no time for individuals under the stress of economic, social, and political pressures to exercise their options. By 1816 there was significant emigration from southwest Germany as the result of crop failures and hunger.[9]

---

[8]   Sheehan's statement on the increase in homelessness speaks succinctly to this point: "In the second half of the eighteenth century, the fear of homelessness increased, largely because the most immediate and manifest impact of the vital revolution was to swell the ranks of those on the fringes of the social order. From the middle of the eighteenth century until the middle of the nineteenth—an era of unparalleled social turmoil almost everywhere in Europe—the population grew faster than the economy . . . As populations expanded, local communities found it more difficult to control their members. This weakening of social controls is apparently behind the dramatic increase in illegitimacy, another mysterious demographic phenomenon that occurred throughout Europe. Rare in traditional society, illegitimacy became more and more common after 1750" (88-89). The Bequest line was not immune to this issue.

[9]   Despite what appeared to be a liberal approach to emigration, it was not until 1867 that the requirement for official permission to emigrate was abolished, and not until 1870 that one no longer had to prove fulfillment of military service. Until these later dates, those inspired for one reason or another to seek relief by emigrating were met with a "semi-official" negative attitude toward emigration on the part of governments in the various states seeking to exercise some control over concerns on the one hand with overpopulation and unemployment, and on the other with inadequate labor pools and faltering economies.

The first wave of emigration would last roughly until just after the American Civil War, during which there was a kind of hiatus before a second wave would begin about 1865 and last until the end of the century. The two periods of intense immigration to the United States [and elsewhere] are sometimes referred to as the "old immigration"—predominantly by populations from Germany, Scandinavia, Ireland and Great Britain, and the "new immigration" by populations from southern and eastern Europe. (Hoerder and Knauf 1992, 12) According to Michael LeMay, "German immigration reached nearly 7 million, making it the largest single source of immigrants to the United States after that from the British Isles." Writing in 1987, he claims that "roughly 40 million persons in the U.S. today claim some German ancestry." He sees three major currents in the pattern of German migration to the U.S.: (1) the colonial period, "when they immigrated mostly for religious and economic reasons"; (2) from 1848 to the Civil War, "when they came for political and economic reasons"; and (3) the post-civil War period, "when they came mostly solely for economic opportunity, often having been actively recruited by one of several major industries, various state governments, the railroads, or friends and relatives already living here" (LeMay 1987, 21-23).

Now some of this pertains to the nineteenth-century immigrants in Charleston, but in many ways the group of interest falls outside this scheme. There certainly was an earlier German community in Charleston. Indeed, they were there in substantial numbers by the middle of the eighteenth century. St. John's Lutheran Church was established already in 1743, and by 1766 those early immigrants had founded the German Friendly Society in support of German interests in the city. By the middle of the nineteenth century when the members of this extended family were arriving or were recently settled, the Colonial-era German immigrants had become acculturated and integrated into "old Charleston" society. These citizens had never congregated in a separate ethnic community, and by the end of the 1700s they would have considered themselves more as Charlestonians rather than as Germans. The later immigrants, in contrast, would have to find their way in a southern city of a particular character, not a *little Germany* into which they might transplant themselves. There was little continuity between the earlier and the later groups, and the experiences of the one had little to do with those of the other: the earlier group had originated in a different area and found their cause in religious freedom. The later group derived from elsewhere and came for different reasons. Beyond that, there was no concept of a common *German* ethnicity through which either group might identify with the other. The German Friendly Society's acculturated members were not immediately open to receiving the newcomers landing on their doorstep. Thinking in terms of a heavy influx of immigrants during a pre-Civil War period between 1848 and 1861 [*old* immigration], and another wave of heavy immigration during the post-Civil War period into the Nineties [*new* immigration], also does not apply to this particular group of Charleston immigrants: most of them had come before the 1848 revolutionary era in Europe, and it was only a Bequest relative who arrived when the war had come to a close. No matter exactly when they arrived, German immigrants to Charleston would have been representatives of *old immigration* with little or no connection to the *new* immigrants from southern and eastern Europe who came in the latter years of the century.

The immigrants to Charleston in the nineteenth century must of course be viewed against the background of the larger parameters of the European population explosion and the resulting waves of emigration. That it was a predominantly rural population moving because of a general decline in the standard of living is indisputably a factor of the chain-migration that brought so many from the German state of Hanover to Charleston. And that the nineteenth century was the "Century of the Common Man" supports the thesis about the nature of the Charleston immigrant families. In a 1950 journal article, Merle Curti and Kendall Birr's very general statements lend substance to the emphasis on the ordinariness—and therefore representativeness—of this family's lineages:

> Despite the great emigration and all the efforts of the federal government, the states, railroads, steamship companies, and commercialized emigration companies, despite firsthand reports from immigrants in letters or on visits home, America remained only partly discovered, only partly understood. There was an inadequate appreciation of the great variety in this country, a failure to understand the changes incident to the shift from a predominantly agricultural to a predominantly industrial economy. Yet this very limitation of knowledge helped to maintain the aura of dream and fancy which contributed to making this period part of the "American Century" in the eyes of Europe's masses. And, of course, in spite of the limitations, exaggerations, and distortions in the predominant image of America, there was a solid core of reality beneath it. The ability of the European masses to achieve, through emigration, in part at least the life they had dreamed of made the nineteenth century "the Century of the Common Man" (Curti and Birr 1950, 230).

Further, it can be noted that the "leaven of democracy" that had taken effect in every state in Western Europe worked to awaken hopes in the general population for personal freedoms that could only be imagined in a different society: As Marcus Hansen, in his *The Immigrant in American History*, puts it:

What poor people wanted was freedom from laws and customs that curbed individual economic enterprise. In the cities they wished to escape the regulations of guilds and trade unions; in the country they sought exemption from traditional restrictions upon the transfer of land, the working at a trade, or the conduct of agriculture. In other words, they wanted the freedom to buy, sell and bargain, to work or loaf, to become rich or poor . . . . To enjoy the opportunities of free enterprise and to preserve the fruits thereof—this was the aspiration of the rank and file of immigrants. Republicanism and monarchism were only shadowy backgrounds to something more personal and vital (Hansen 1940, 81-82).

It would be possible to add additional general statements about nineteenth-century immigration to provide context for what lured immigrants to, of all places, Charleston. They would all apply to a broad-brush portrait. But from the beginning it was recognized that the situation in Charleston was not the usual one, as Charleston itself was not the usual city to accept an immigrant population. It is rather the small-brush details that should now command attention.

Despite the fact that Charleston had once been among the five largest cities in young America, it was not quite what it had been earlier by the time the English and German immigrant family members began to arrive in the early decades of the nineteenth century. It was nonetheless a city with a unique history and one that was distinctly not like any other southern city. Although it was no longer the capital, the city had enjoyed prosperity during the plantation-dominated economy of the post-Revolutionary years. The invention of the cotton gin had enabled the production of this crop to the point that it had become the state's number one export. Cotton production depended on slave labor. According to George Rogers Jr.'s *Charleston in the Age of the Pinckneys*, in 1761 there had been 4,000 white persons and 4,000 Negro slaves in the city. In 1790 there were 8,089 whites, 7,684 slaves, and 568 free Negroes—a total of 16,341. In 1820 there were 11,229 whites, 12,652 slaves, and 1,475 free Negroes—a total of 25,356. And by 1850 there would be 20,012 whites, 19,532 slaves, and 3,441 free Negroes for a population total of 42,985. (Rogers 1969, 141)

Although German and English immigrants also relocated themselves in other cities in the South, e.g. New Orleans, Savannah, Mobile, or Richmond—to be sure in fewer numbers than in northern cities[10]—those who

---

[10]   "At mid-century, when fully one Northerner in seven had been born outside the United States, only 5 percent of the Southern free population was foreign born, and a disproportionate number of these resided in the border states. Ten years later, the margin had widened as European migrants surged into the North, while they continued to dribble into the South.

went to Charleston stepped into a patriarchal planter society that ruled over an economy based to a unique degree on an enormous slave population. It was a financially top-heavy society with a broad base of the poor and enslaved supporting an aristocracy of the wealthy. In Michael Johnson's analysis, "the strength of the patriarchy rested ultimately not just on the quantity but on the nature of the estate: land and slaves. The Charleston planters were among the nation's largest landowners; their mean real estate value of $27,300 easily put them among the top 1 percent of landowners in the nation. Even the planters' $13,000 median real estate value was more than that owned by the top 2 percent of American men. In fact, a full 60 percent of the Charleston planters owned more real estate [in dollar value] than 97 percent of their countrymen. Slightly less than 7 percent of the planters were grandees with more than $100,000 worth of real property, a level attained by just under five American men in ten thousand-a disproportion in favor of the Charleston planters by a factor of 137" (Johnson 1980, 53).

Beyond this chasm between the wealthy and the less affluent, Charleston early on became a tense environment. In the social environment of a majority ruled by a minority, the Denmark Vesey slave "insurrection" in 1822 transformed the city into something like a police state. John Radford writes: "The white community viewed the slave conspiracy of 1822, apparently led by a free Negro, Denmark Vesey, as a direct threat to its existence. The immediate repercussions were trials, mass public hangings, meetings of outraged citizens and ensuing legislation, but the conspiracy also marked the beginning of a new and extended era of repression. The city . . . never again relaxed the outward forms of vigilance. To supplement its sizeable police force the city now established a town guard, a force of 100 men. They were uniformed, trained and heavily armed, being issued with muskets and bayonets as well as alarming devices such a rattles. Whites as well as blacks were dealt with at the guardhouse, but the list of offenses for which blacks could be held liable was much larger" (Radford 1976, 331).

On a more personal level, what living in Charleston was like during the years from the beginning of the century until about the mid-1830s, what conditions the immigrants met, can be culled from Walter J. Fraser, Jr.'s book *Charleston! Charleston! The History of a Southern City*, and a census undertaken by the city in 1848 "exhibiting the condition and prospects of the city". (Dawson and DeSaussaure 1849) Consider the following indicators as descriptive of the pre-1850 Charleston *scene*:

On the eve of the Civil War, when fewer than one free Southerner in fifteen had been born outside the United States, immigrants composed nearly a fifth of the population of the free states" (Berlin and Gutman 1983, 1176).

- In 1797 there was undeclared naval war between the United States and France. This was the time Charleston began building its fortifications because of the fear of invasion. Castle Pinckney in the harbor was built as part of the city's defense.
- In 1800, the city was still fifth in size after New York (60,515), Philadelphia (40,220), Baltimore (26,514), and Boston (24,937). "By the United States census of 1840, the white population of the City and Neck [the area of the peninsula north of Boundary St. not incorporated into the city until 1849] conjoined, amounted to 15,711. If the present white population of the Neck be added to that of the City, as determined by the enumeration made in 1848, the number will amount to 19,053, giving an increase of 3,342 in nine years, or 21.27 per cent" (Dawson/ DeSaussure, iv-v).
- In 1848, 21.28% of the persons living in the four wards of the City were not born in the U.S.
- "At the time of the taking of the first United States Census, in 1790, the white exceeded the slave population by about 3 per cent. During the next decade, the slaves increased with more rapidity than the whites, and at the commencement of the present century, slightly exceeded them by about .89 per cent. From this period up to 1830, the increase of the slave population was both absolutely and relatively greater than that of the whites" (Dawson/DeSaussure, 10).
- From 1801 on, Charleston underwent a number of boom and bust times, as the economy and conditions changed. There seemed to be no "steady state" that could be relied on to last for very long, a condition that must have resulted in a pronounced sense of insecurity on the part of the citizenry.
- Most citizens relied on shallow wells and cisterns for water. Storms such as the 1804 hurricane mixed privy wastes and drinking water, partly explaining the outbreaks of cholera, diarrhea, and dysentery.
- Already in 1807 there was the Trade Embargo Act that closed U.S. ports to the export-import trade, as well as slave importing. "Planters, merchants, mariners, slave-auctioneers, professional people, and artisans all felt the economic effects of the trade restrictions" (Fraser, 192).
- In 1812 a catastrophic fire swept along Church to Queen St. and into Broad St., destroying nearly 200 houses. "In the period of 60 years, comprised between 1780 and 1840, the number of houses recorded to have been destroyed by fire in Charleston proper, equals very nearly the number of houses now existing in the city" (Dawson/DeSaussure, v).

- After the War of 1812 ended, Charleston—primarily its wealthy planters—enjoyed a boom time. This was the period when Charleston became known as the "Capital of the Plantations".
- By 1820, there was a "bust". At the time, some 58 % of the population of Charleston was black, and the Denmark Vesey episode caused the whites to live in constant fear of the black population, despite the fact that they played such an important role in the economy of the city, and were an essential part of the picture for an elite who relied on them as servants.
- Antebellum Charleston was known for its sophisticated, cosmopolitan, and scholarly clergy who were ardent defenders of the status quo. The Reverend John Bachman of St. John's Lutheran Church had been referred to as the 'chief religious spokesman for slavery', and Bishop Gadsden, grandson of the Revolutionary leader and rector of St. Philip's Church from 1814 to 1852, frequently reminded blacks that they should 'fear God, obey the civil authority . . . be subject unto their own masters, and be contented in that state of life to which God hath called them' (Fraser, 204).
- "The slave population was never without suspicion for seditious activity. Beginning on Christmas eve 1825 and for the first several months of 1826 fires broke out almost nightly; the City Council offered a $1,000 reward for the capture of arsonists; furious mobs attempted to lynch suspected incendiaries, and several Negroes were convicted and apparently executed. Hardly a year passed in antebellum Charleston without reports of attempts by arsonists to fire the city. Of 204 fires reported in the Courier between 1825 and 1858, the editors labeled 91 as arson" (Fraser, 206).
- In 1828 the city shipped its greatest rice crop and the second largest cotton export ever, 214,000 bales, but that same year the Chamber of Commerce reported: 'Charleston has for several years past retrograded . . . . Her landed estate has within eight years depreciated in value one half. Industry and business talent . . . have sought employment elsewhere. Many of her houses are tenantless and the grass grows uninterrupted in some of her chief business streets' (Fraser, 206).
- Charleston endured its first epidemic of Asiatic cholera in 1832, and the following year the author of a widely read travel book wrote: 'The people of Charleston pass their lives in endeavoring to escape from . . . the . . . fever. This continual dodging with death strikes me as very disagreeable.' In 1835 a lazaretto was built on James Island to provide a more effective quarantine, but despite this precaution a cholera epidemic ravaged the city the next year and nearly 400 people

died. A state-owned pest house was constructed on Morris Island in 1838. (Fraser, 211)

- From 1807 to 1817 . . . there was nearly a complete exemption from epidemics of this disease [Yellow Fever]. In this latter year it re-appeared, and caused 270 deaths, of which a large number were children. In 1819, it again prevailed epidemically, causing 176 deaths. In the next year if prevailed slightly, but did not become epidemic. In 1824, another serious epidemic occurred, which carried off 231 persons. From this period, 1824-1838, no serious visitation of yellow fever occurred, although several cases of it existed in each of the years 1827, 1828, 1834, 1835. In 1838, the most serious epidemic occurred which has been known in the annals in Charleston, and causing the largest mortality which has ever resulted from the disease in this city. In 1839, it was again epidemic, but to a much less extent, than during the former year. From 1839 to the present time, nine years have elapsed during which the city has been exempt from the visitation of the scourge, and it is a question vitally important to her interests. This problem can be solved by time only" (Dawson/ DeSaussure, 201-02).

- In 1848, "the sums annually devoted to benevolent purposes is large, if it be considered that it is contributed by a white population of only 14,187 persons, and is destined solely for the relief only of the whites and free colored, whose number only reaches 15,679. The slave population requires no relief from public charities; in old age and decrepitude they become a charge upon the master, by whom it is borne with alacrity and cheerfulness" (Dawson/DeSaussure, 40).

For the immigrant, then, Charleston presented particular challenges—social, economic, and personal. As it turned out, those challenges also offered opportunities, and it was up to the immigrants to find those opportunities wherever they could—that was, after all, why they had come. If within Charleston society's pyramid there was somehow space between the high and the low to accommodate those vying to create a middle—that was a role for the immigrants, the English and the Germans, and somewhat later, the Irish. Some did it better than others.

The English immigrants in this family story were the first to immigrate to Charleston. In general, English immigrants found it not too difficult to settle in any of the original colonial states; they had no new language to learn and would be relocating themselves in a relatively similar culture. Many left England because of the effects of the fast-moving industrial revolution and its concomitant displacements of one kind or another—because of poor harvests, or rising food prices, or because of the lure of new opportunity. It was during the first half of the nineteenth century that there were waves of emigration from England, and Charleston would have presented as English-oriented a society as a British subject might have wished—whether or not one could claim actual relatives among the city's aristocracy.[11] The Church of England was well represented by the congregations of St. Michael's and St. Philip's, both there since the late 1600s. As for Ireland, it had been united constitutionally with Great Britain in 1801, but there were very few Irish who thought unification to be a step in the right direction: the English had quickly transformed the Irish agricultural landscape, enclosing most of the arable land and leaving little for the non-moneyed to farm. Anti-English sentiment ran high. Escape from what was becoming no more than a British colony to one that had earlier been a colonial holding but which was now a land of new opportunity and freedom from English oppression would have been sufficient cause to bring a young Irish man like John Michael Murray—Jane Thompson's first husband—to Charleston by 1820.

For the German immigrant, the story is a little different. All the ideas, many of them illusions or based on misinformation, about the freedoms that America offered—the unlimited opportunities that could be had in the cities or the countryside, the chance to farm one's own land or pioneer new territory unencumbered by laws and rules—were likely overruled by the pull of the unique long-standing connections that Charleston had with the North German communities in the vicinity of Bremen and which engendered the chain migration pattern that set up in the 1830s.

Charleston had long had a significant trade relationship with Bremen, with ships crossing the Atlantic taking Charleston exports, e.g. cotton and tobacco, to northern Europe through one of its major ports, among them Bremen.[12] That German port had developed in competition with neighboring Hamburg and other European trading centers, and by the early decades of the nineteenth century it undertook to enlarge its role and to secure its existence as a port. By 1827 the Hanseatic city had secured a treaty with the government in Hanover to purchase land on the Weser estuary to develop a more navigable harbor. The acquisition of an area of land between the Geeste and the estuary of the Weser in the district of Lehe led to the creation of the city of Bremerhaven. The founding of Bremerhaven coincided with the significant increase in the rates of emigration during the late 1820s-early 1830s, and the Bremen authorities

---

[11]   Agnes Bretting (Bretting 1992, 28) cites the peak years in the century's first half as 1819, 1827, the early 1830s, and 1842.

[12]   The city's dynamic commercial link with northern Europe was undercut somewhat in 1793 when Baltimore assumed priority in trade with Bremen.

sought out the emigrant trade in support of the city's new port capacities. In his *Germany and the Emigration 1816-1885*, Mack Walker points out that "in its competition with Hamburg, which was entrenched with a near monopoly of the British trade, Bremen turned to North America, especially to tobacco; Auswanderer were exchanged for American goods. Inland freighters, on water or land, brought emigrants to Bremerhaven, where they picked up merchandise for their return to the interior. Steamships appeared on the Weser in 1843; then railroads became significant, and eventually special emigrant trains arrived regularly at Bremerhaven, on the first and fifteenth of the month during the season, from marshaling points inside Germany" (Walker 1964, 88). The city of Bremen and its port of Bremerhaven, encompassing the earlier communities of both Geestendorf and Geestemünde, almost immediately passed legislation aimed at protection of the emigrants who waited there to board ships to take them to their U.S. destinations. In 1832 and 1834 laws were passed that regulated inns and other accommodations providing temporary shelter, and requiring ships leaving port to provide adequate space for passengers and to carry sufficient food supplies for a crossing that could take up to three months. Shipping companies were required to carry insurance in the event of shipwreck on European shores. In the mid-forties, the authorities in Bremen undertook to comply with new American regulations stipulating an increase in the amount of space per passenger and "forbidding the embarkation of a criminal or a deserter on pain of a hundred-thaler fine imposed upon the captain." By 1849 an emigrant hostel, the *Auswanderungshaus* had been built, a facility able to feed 3,500 emigrants and to sleep 2,000 at a time. According to Walker, in 1853, 37,492 of 58,551 emigrants passing through Bremen and Bremerhaven made use of the *Auswanderungshaus*. (Walker 1964, 89) While Bremerhaven became the most popular embarkation point for the majority of nineteenth-century emigrants from northern and central Europe, it was literally on the doorstep for the emigrant families living in this northwest corner of Hanover, in Geestendorf or Geestemünde itself, or in Land Wursten just to the north.

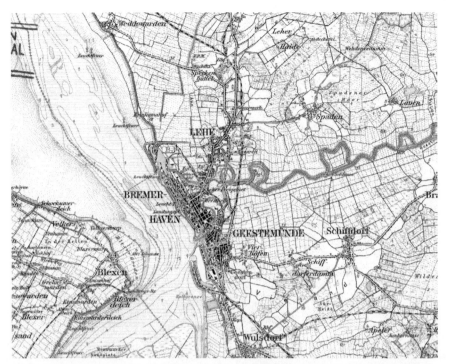

The close proximity of the *doorsteps* of Bremerhaven—Lehe, Geestemünde, Wulsdorf, and Land Wursten to the north. From the American Geographical Society Library, University of Wisconsin-Milwaukee Libraries.

There was another factor that heavily influenced the link between Bremerhaven and Charleston and that effectively anchored the chain at both ends: Captain Heinrich Wieting. In the employ of the Bremen shipping company of N. Gloystein Söhne, he commanded three ships, the *Johann Friedrich*, the *Gauss*, and the *Copernicus* from the 1840s to the late 1860s, usually bringing twice a year on average some 200 emigrants to Charleston each trip. The record of Wieting's correspondence with his employer is the subject of a recent volume, *"Was fernern vorkömmt werde ich prompt berichten": Der Auswanderer-Kapitän Heinrich Wieting Briefe 1847 bis 1856*, edited by Jörn Bullerdiek and Daniel Tilgner. From available records they have compiled a list of Wieting's departures from Bremerhaven and arrivals in Charleston and New York as follows (Bullerdiek and Tilgner 2008, 285):

SHIP	DEPARTED	DESTINATION	ARRIVED	#PASS	#DAYS
JFriedrich	4 Nov 1843	Charleston	—	6	—
JFriedrich	29 Apr 1844	Charleston	14 Jun 1844	23	46
JFriedrich	6 May 1845	New York	19 Jun 1845	140	44
JFriedrich	7 Oct 1845	Charleston	25 Nov 1845	131	49
JFriedrich	5 Oct 1846	Charleston	—	116	—
JFriedrich	19 Mar 1847	New York	1 May 1847	140	43
JFriedrich	8 Oct 1847	Charleston	15 Nov 1847	135	38
JFriedrich	19 Mar 1848	New York	30 Apr 1848	126	42
JFriedrich	10 Nov 1848	Charleston	—	122	—
JFriedrich	19 Apr 1850	New York	16 May 1850	126	27
JF/Leontine	20 Oct 1850	Charleston	—	125	—
Copernicus	6 May 1851	New York	19 Jun 1851	217	44
Copernicus	7 Nov 1851	Charleston	—	135	—
Copernicus	6 May 1852	New York	10 Jun 1852	249	35
Copernicus	12 Oct 1852	Charleston	28 Nov 1852	190	47
Copernicus	21 Apr 1853	New York	30 May 1853	229	39
Copernicus	6 Oct 1853	Charleston	21 Nov 1853	242	46
Copernicus	5 Apr 1854	New York	18 May 1854	238	43
Copernicus	8 Oct 1854	Charleston	24 Nov 1854	258	47
Copernicus	9 Oct 1855	Charleston	—	176	—
Copernicus	6 Mar 1856	Charleston	27 Apr 1856	14	52
Copernicus	7 Oct 1856	Charleston	24 Nov 1856	223	48
Gauss	12 Oct 1857	Charleston	23 Nov 1857	233	42
Gauss	9 Apr 1858	Charleston	16 May 1858	36	37
Gauss	10 Oct 1858	Charleston	18 Nov 1858	197	39
Gauss	7 Mar 1859	Charleston	4 May 1859	18	56
Gauss	8 Oct 1859	Charleston	19 Nov 1859	161	42
Gauss	11 Feb 1860	Charleston	20 Mar 1860	7	37
Gauss	14 Oct 1860	Charleston	4 Dec 1860	227	51
Gauss	14 Mar 1861	Charleston	—	11	—
Gauss	6 Oct 1867	Charleston	—	158	—
Gauss	6 Oct 1868	Charleston	29 Nov 1868	278	54

An analysis of the record provides a good sense of the traffic across the Atlantic during those years, and particularly the role that Charleston played on the receiving end. While Wieting sailed on occasion to other ports, his transatlantic passages carrying immigrants and goods was only between New York or Charleston and Bremerhaven. Some of the passengers were undoubtedly immigrants returning from visits back in the homeland. The majority disembarking in New York or Charleston, nonetheless, would have been immigrants, not travelers, following the pattern of those relatives or friends who had preceded them. The eight crossings to New York carried a total of 1,465 passengers, while the twenty-five trips to Charleston brought 3,350 individuals to their southern destination. The average length of the trip on these sailing ships was more than a month, sometimes almost two months, under conditions that were trying, in spite of everything Wieting and the Bremen authorities had done to make the passage tolerable. Looking at the list, one cannot help but notice the hiatus in the Bremerhaven-Charleston traffic after the departure from Bremerhaven of the *Gauss* on March 14, 1861: the Civil War would begin in Charleston a month later, and the eleven intrepid souls who set off in March arrived just after the first shots had been fired at Fort Sumter. The political situation in the U.S. was a hot topic in Europe, and the more timorous would have had second thoughts about emigrating at that point—to Charleston for sure—since the outcome of South Carolina's secession the previous year would shortly precipitate military action there between the southern Confederacy and rest of the Union.[13]

In Bullerdiek and Tilgner's list, the October 1850 joint *Johann Friedrich/ Leontine* entry hardly describes the traumatic tale than lies in the background: the shipwreck of the *Johann Friedrich* on a sandbar off the coast of England at Harwich. The group was rescued and returned to Bremerhaven, then safely delivered to Charleston by Captain Thormann of the *Leontine*. On January 26, 1851, an address expressing the public's gratitude was given by Pastor Müller of St. Matthew's German Lutheran Church, and on the 28th the Charleston German newspaper, *Der Teutone*, published a notice of thanks to both captains and Wieting's *Gloystein Söhne* for saving the lives of the 125 passengers on board. It was signed by sixteen passengers in the name of all the others. The same notice was subsequently published in the *Weser-Zeitung* on 22 February, as was Pastor Müller's sermon. The German and the American readers/audiences obviously felt the close personal connections that existed between the two communities. The episode is further detailed in a small diary held in the manuscript collection

---

[13] By the time the war was over, steamships had begun to overtake transatlantic routes and offered shorter and safer passage: in 1868 sixty-four steamships brought 36,279 passengers from Bremerhaven to New York, while sixty-two sailing ships carried 15,451 on the same route. (Bullerdiek and Tilgner 270)

of the University of South Carolina: it is the diary of Alexander Melchers, one of the passengers on the voyage of the *Johann Friedrich* that ran aground. He was the younger brother of Franz Adolph Melchers, who had established himself as the editor of the Charleston *Deutsche Zeitung* and who, together with Wieting, would become part of a triumvirate of influential men giving direction to the community of German immigrants gathering in Charleston. After Alexander's harrowing passage to Charleston, he would also become a leader in the Charleston German community. He became a captain in the Palmetto Riflemen, was president of the German Rifle Club [1868-1873], as well as president of the German Friendly Society from 1874 to 1875.

Although other ships traveled regularly between Charleston and Bremerhaven [it was relatively inexpensive—a third-class ticket was less than forty dollars], it was Wieting's caring and personalized concern for the well-being of his passengers, as well as his regular schedule, that helped to establish the chain of migration from Bremerhaven to Charleston. Those whom he had brought were a magnet for those friends and relatives in the communities close to Bremen still contemplating emigration. Besides, Wieting was a *local*. He had been born 1815 in the village of Rönnebeck, not far from Bremen, where his father had moved the family from Vegesack, an area of Bremen proper. The father had been a ship's captain and in Rönnebeck had taken over a brewery he inherited from his brother-in-law. Prior to Wieting's birth, the entire area had been occupied by French troops, and Wieting's father is believed to have been an active participant in the smuggling operations which the German natives undertook in defiance of the French troops in residence. There is something of this personal past that seems to have carried over into Wieting's role in personally leading emigrants from the land they had reasons to leave into a less authoritative country that offered opportunity to all. He himself lived in Geestemünde, and his name would have been a household word in the surrounding communities. When waiting in Charleston for his ship to be readied for departure, he participated in the life of the German community like a local citizen. His veneration by the Germans he had been instrumental in bringing to the city was known on both sides of the Atlantic, and his death in 1868 was a heartfelt loss to the Charleston community. On his last trip from Bremerhaven Wieting had contracted typhus and died in Charleston on December 2, 1868. He is buried in Bethany Cemetery in Charleston. A notice of his death was reported in the *Wochenzeitschrift für Vegesack und Umgebung* [Weekly for Vegesack and Environs] and stated: ". . . denn wohl selten gab es einen Capitain, der im Kreise aller derer, die ihn kannten, hier sowohl wie jenseits des Oceans sich einer größeren Popularität erfreute." [. . . for only rarely was there a captain who enjoyed as much popularity among those who knew him, here as well as on the other side of the ocean.]

Captain Heinrich Wieting's prominent monument in Charleston's Bethany Cemetery.
One side of the monument's base in English names the three ships that brought the
immigrants to Charleston; the opposite side in German indicates
his birth in Rönnebeck and his death in Charleston.

That Wieting's sailings would serve to encourage so many emigrants from
the area is attested in the lists of passengers who traveled with him. The list of
passengers embarking in Bremerhaven was usually published in the German
newspaper in Charleston approximately two weeks before the expected arrival
date, furnishing the names of the passengers as well as the towns they came
from. While in any given list there are many citations of localities in other

29

German states, the majority of the names and places of origin consistently indicate that Wieting's passengers were from towns and villages in Hanover, Oldenburg and Holstein, i.e. from areas close to Bremen and Bremerhaven.

Another *local*—the third member of the triumvirate mentioned above—who was instrumental in starting the chain of migration to Charleston was Johann Andreas Wagener. Wagener was born in 1816 in Sievern, a town of about 500 located north of Bremerhaven in Land Wursten.[14] Gertha Reinert has edited and translated a letter Wagener wrote to his teacher back home telling of his life in the United States. (Reinert 1999, 51) From that letter we know that he came to Charleston in 1833 or 1834 after first landing in New York. He was one of twelve children, and his father operated a general store and an inn in Sievern. Ten of those children lived to maturity, and five sons and four daughters emigrated, leaving Johann Andreas's younger brother Hanke the only descendant of Johann Andreas Wagener, sen. in Sievern. In addition to young Johann Andreas, Charleston became the home to the following of his siblings: (1) Jürgen, born February 2, 1818, married Becka Mehrtens, born 1823 in Ritterhude, on April 5, 1846; Jürgen died in Charleston in 1847; (2) Georg Heinrich, a twin, born July 6, 1822, immigrated shortly after his elder brothers to Charleston where he died of yellow fever in 1840; (3) Maria Elisa, born April 11, 1824, immigrated 1838 to Charleston where she married Heinrich Mehrtens from Lehe in 1852; (4) Rebecka Margarethe, born February 2, 1826, immigrated to Charleston in 1840 where she married Johann Köster from Beverstedt in 1851; (5) Johann Christian, born February 26, 1828, immigrated 1843 to Charleston where he died in 1861; (6) Maria, born April 4, 1830, immigrated 1848 to Charleston where she married Christoffer v. Hadeln from Misselwarden in 1856; (7) Friedrich Wilhelm, born October 29, 1832, emigrated 1848 to Charleston; in 1859 married Johanne Sophie Kranz, and died in Charleston in 1925 at age 93; (8) Beta Lisette, born July 17, 1841, immigrated to Charleston where there is a record of her being there in 1855. (Friedrichs 1997, 565-66)

The 33-year-old Johann Andreas moved with alacrity as soon as he came to Charleston to become possibly the main culture broker in the city until his death in 1876. In outline, within twenty-five years he "founded the German Fire Company (1836), St. Matthew's Lutheran Church (1840) . . . the German newspaper *Der Teutone* (1844), the German colony of Walhalla, Pickens District (1848), and a number of beneficial clubs and societies for mutual support and interaction" (Reinert 1999, 51). In addition, "after a successful

---

[14]   And thus close to Flögeln and Cappel where the Struhs family originated, and not far from Geestendorf/Geestemünde where the Bequests were located. The proximity is apparent in the geographical coordinates: Sievern is at 53° 39N 36E; Geestemünde is at 53° 32N 35E; Cappel is at 53° 44N 35E.

career in some of Charleston's flourishing militia organizations, [he] became a respected, successful officer in the Civil War. In 1861 he commanded the German artillery in the bombardment of Fort Sumter. During the same year he equipped a company commanded by Captain Bachmann and composed entirely of Germans for the Virginia campaign. Also in 1861 his regiment built and defended Fort Walker on Hilton Head Island at the battle of Port Royal. In 1863-64 he commanded the militia forces in the defense of Charleston. In 1866 Governor Orr commissioned him a brigadier general of South Carolina militia. After the Civil War [he] began to participate in South Carolina politics . . . . In 1865 he was a member of the constitutional convention and the first legislature after the adoption of the new constitution. In 1871 he was elected mayor of Charleston, and in 1876 he was a delegate to the Democratic convention in St. Louis and chosen elector-at-large from South Carolina . . . . He died suddenly on August 27, 1876 in Walhalla" (Reinert 1999, 51-52). The body was brought back to Charleston with great ceremony to be interred in Bethany Cemetery. His widow, Maria Elise Hesse, whom he had married in 1837, survived him for almost twenty years, dying in Charleston in 1897.

No question but that Johann Andreas Wagener exerted a kind of centrifugal force in both ante- and postbellum Charleston, both within and beyond the German immigrant community. He is undoubtedly the North German immigrant model of success *par excellence.* And as if one Wagener were not enough, John Andreas's two younger brothers were also of some notice in the Charleston community, although less prominent than their elder brother. Don Doyle, in his book looking at the "new" traditions in the South gives an account of the career of Frederick W. Wagener, the younger brother born in 1832. According to Doyle, Frederick, "another German, began a small grocery and liquor business in Charleston before the war. He served as captain of the Confederate German Artillery of Charleston during the war. In 1865 the firm Wagener, Heath, and Monses was described as without 'much means,' but the proprietors were 'said to be industrious and honest men of families,' with $20,000 to $25,000 worth of capital invested in the firm by 1869. 'Active pushing fellows,' a later report warned, 'but not cautious enough and blow too heavy.' By 1876 Wagener had built a large warehouse on East Bay—'one of the finest buildings in the South'—and expanded into the cotton business. The firm's new assets rose from $195,000 in 1876 to $415,000 by 1880, but R.G. Dun and Company still warned that 'they are too much extended or too liberally.' The firm continued to deal in groceries as well, claiming the largest business among all Charleston firms in that line by 1881. Wagener invested heavily in land on the Charleston Neck and in the Royal Bag and Yarn Manufacturing Company, one of the city's few ventures into the textile industry. Wagener also launched a prosperous tourist resort for northern visitors in Summerville, outside Charleston. In 1901 he was the moving spirit behind the South Carolina Interstate and West

Indian Exposition." But Doyle makes the point that this Wagener brother, despite all his efforts for the Exposition and his financial success, did not hold any directorships in the business community and "was not even a member of the Charleston Chamber of Commerce until 1883" (Doyle 1990, 127-28). He remains a rather obscure figure in the city's history, as does another of John Andreas's immigrant brothers, Jürgen Wagener. He was just two years younger than John Andreas and in Charleston was known as "George". He was secretary of the newly founded [largely at the instigation of brother John Andreas] St. Matthew's German Lutheran Church 1841-42 and organized the German Artillery in 1842. The 1840 Charleston city directory lists him simply as a bookkeeper and transfer clerk at the South Carolina State Bank. (Reinert 1999, 51-52) He died in his youth at 29 in 1847 while his older brother still had much of his career ahead of him. One can posit that had he lived longer, he might have risen to greater heights in the trail of his brothers' leadership in the German community and in Charleston's history.

This, then, sets the stage for how the Charleston German immigrant community would develop by the middle of the century. It would already have several movers and shakers working on its behalf who would function in leadership positions within the ethnic community and whose work would register positively with the Charleston native population.[15]

Those who came by the 1820s would precede what would become a growing tide of newcomers starting already in the 1830s. Those who would become instrumental in the community's evolution would be there by 1835, and when Captain Wieting began his regular transatlantic deliveries there would be a regular infusion of new German blood. By mid-century things were well underway and the immigrants would become a recognized force in the social, political, and cultural scene of the city.

---

[15]   Doyle cites the success of John C. H. Claussen as another success model among "Charleston's 'industrious' and 'pushing' German entrepreneurs" (127-28). Claussen had established a flour mill on Anson Street in early 1860, and according to Doyle, supplied bread to the Confederate troops during the war. He was such a pillar of the German community that there was a grand civic celebration of his and his wife's 50th wedding anniversary in 1898. The event was written up and published in book form by F. Münch. (Münch 1898)

With his financial resources Claussen supported the interests of numerous North German immigrants; in 1859 he adopted several boys from the Charleston Orphan House and employed them in his bakery; more relevant to this story, he and his wife were sponsors for the marriage in 1875 of H. D. Schumacher and Gesine Wiers at their home in Charleston; it was the Schumacher daughter, Marguerita Josephine, who married Charles William Henry Weber in 1913 and became a beloved member of the composite—and further extended—family. Claussen was also later instrumental in recruiting Germans to Charleston after the war. Claussen's bakery was supplying bread to Charleston citizens into the 1950s.

In conjunction with the earlier set of indicators that were cited to characterize the nature of the pre-1850 Charleston community, a somewhat more specific backdrop against which this local ethnic community would develop is described in Andrea Mehrländer's study about the Germans of Charleston, Richmond and New Orleans. Her work provides interesting statistics, although her focus is on the somewhat later period between 1850 and 1870:

- At the beginning of the 1840's the German population had increased to about 1,200 persons, so that in April 1844, the first German newspaper appeared and was issued twice weekly.
- Among the foreigners in the city of Charleston, after the Irish, the Germans formed the second largest group in 1850 and amounted to 9.1% of the free white population of the city. Ten years later, in 1860, their population had sunk to 8.3%, although about 66% of all the Germans in the state of South Carolina lived in Charleston; with 1,944 persons the Germans were still the second largest group of foreigners (30.8%) after the Irish.
- Between 1850 and 1860 the entire population of Charleston declined by almost 2,500 persons (=6%).
- German immigrants were distributed throughout all the wards of the city in 1850 and also in the area known as the "neck" north of the old city limits that was incorporated into the city in 1849. With the exception of the 2nd ward, the Germans comprised more than 10% of the white population in every district; in the "neck" they accounted for more than 15%. The majority of Germans in 1850 were male (86%) and unmarried (66%).
- The number of Germans in Charleston's poorhouse was far lower than that of the Irish after 1830; in 1855, when the "neck" area was included in the poorhouse area and a large wave of immigrants arrived in Charleston, the number of Germans needing welfare in the pre-Civil War era peaked at ninety-eight persons.
- In 1850 one third of all German men in Charleston were employed in trade; 20% worked in crafts, mainly in those in which they had the least possible competition from free blacks and hired slaves. In 1860 the occupations diversity remained unchanged; only the category of grocers grew considerably (by 143%): the number of 147 shops increased to 210 in 1860. In 1870 Germans still owned almost 80% of all Charleston groceries.
- In 1850 a little over 330 Germans in Charleston owned slaves, possessing 583 of them; in 1860 only 8.9% (c.170 Germans) owned a total of 325 slaves. The number of slaves in Charleston decreased during the last decade before the Civil War by 5,600 persons. The

Germans joined their American neighbors and sold their "human chattel." Most of them owned one or two slaves, although there were exceptions. (Mehrländer 2011, 38-40)

Many of these statistics will come to bear weight when looking in detail at the lives of individual members in this family to see how they fared as their lives intersected with Charleston's history and the events that molded both the city and the immigrants until the end of the century.

IV

EARLY ARRIVALS GET ESTABLISHED: 1810-1840

By the beginning of the nineteenth century, on the eastern seaboard of the North American continent the American Revolution had happened, and the former colonies were now a set of united states. In Europe, Napoleon had come to power and had ushered in a new order for most of the continent. By the time the Napoleonic Wars were at an end, the Holy Roman Empire had been dissolved, and Western Europe was distinctly not united, but rather a patchwork quilt of regional royalties vying for control and/or stability after the Congress of Vienna in 1815. By 1810, the U.S. population had grown to 7.2 million, with 1.2 million slaves and 60,000 immigrants. Within the next five years, the War of 1812 between the United States and Great Britain would end, Francis Scott Key would write the words to *The Star-Spangled Banner* after the battle of Baltimore, and the British would finally leave North America.

On a more personal scale, by the time Jane Thompson arrived with her parents in South Carolina, the Charleston Anglican community—native and English-born—which they would join was well established. That community dominated the entire lower Charleston peninsula, a neighborhood designated since 1751 as the Parish of St. Philip's and St. Michael's. The dual designation allotted the area south of Broad Street to St. Michael's, the area to the north, to St. Philip's. The congregations of both churches were thus almost a century-and-a-quarter old, and among the members were the pillars of society. It was a society still very much oriented to its English heritage, and despite the fact that Jane did not arrive until well after the revolution that separated the colonies from their English governance, the British, relatively speaking, had only just recently left, and their shadows were thus perceptible, their influence pervasive, and their presence still redolent. It was not exactly a foreign land onto which the English immigrant set his or her foot as late—or as early—as the second decade of the nineteenth century.

Four gravestones in St. Michael's churchyard on the southeast corner of Broad and Meeting Street—Charleston's so-called four corners of law—mark individuals in the family as members of this established Charleston congregation. The gravestones lie about midway down the stone path closest to the wall along Meeting Street. To the left of the path there is a stone for Mrs. Catherine Cunliffe, another for Mrs. Jane M. Thompson, a third for Jane's daughter, Adeline Lewis. The stones for Catherine and Jane are quite large [about 3 feet high] but barely legible because of erosion. Both inscriptions, however, were recorded by Clare Jervey more than a century ago. (Jervey 1906) For Catherine Cunliffe the inscription reads: "Sacred to the Memory / of / MRS. CATHRINE CUNLIFFE / Who departed this life on the morning / of the 18th of August 1828 / Aged 48 years / She has left a husband and two / daughters to bemoan their irreparable / loss." A short poem follows: "When sorrowing o'er some stone I bend, / Which covers all that was a friend / And from her voice her hand her smile / Divides me for a little while, / If e'er my heart forget—/ Her welfare or her wo—/ Let every joy this heart forsake / And every greif [*sic*] o'erflow / For her my tears shall fall, / For her my prayers ascend / To her my cares and toils be given / Till toils and cares shall end. / I praise her heavenly ways, / Her sweet communion and solemn vows / Her hymns of love and praise. / C.C. / 1828".

**Cathrine Cunliffe's inscribed, but barely legible,
headstone in St. Michael's Churchyard.**

For Mrs. Jane M. Thompson: "Sacred / To the Memory of / MRS. JANE M. THOMPSON, / Daughter of / Richard and Catherine[16] Cunliffe, / of Bolton Lancashire England / Who departed this life / on March 8th, 1877, / Aged 69 Years, 2 Months / And 12 days". Then the statement: "She leaves Four sons and / Three daughters to mourn / Their loss", followed by the verse: "Blessed are the dead that die / in the Lord for they rest / from their labours." The stone for Jane's daughter Adeline is smaller and lies to the left of that of her grandmother. Adeline is identified as the "wife of Greene Lewis", with her birth and death dates [1835-1928] inscribed.[17] No verse.

Jane Thompson's headstone to the right of her sister and brother-in-law.

---

16 On her mother's stone the spelling is "Cathrine". I have used the spelling as here on Jane's headstone.

17 This first daughter of Jane Thompson was confirmed at St. Michael's in 1848. The dates on her gravestone suggest that she was the second daughter, born almost exactly a year after her sister, Sarah Jane. Those gravestone dates are likely in error; she is always named first in the list of children, e.g. in her mother's will, and was named executrix of her mother's estate, suggesting that she was the eldest of the three daughters. The 1850 census shows her at age 17, one year older than Sarah Jane, and therefore born in 1833.

Genealogists would normally be grateful for such definitive information as contained on these gravestones, i.e., age, date of death, number of children, place of origin, etc. For Catherine Cunliffe, however, there is no confirming evidence of anyone by that name in any other source: nothing in the records of St. Michael's or St. Philip's; no such name in the 1820 or 1830 census; nothing in the Charleston city directories; no legal records, e.g. in the Office of Judge of Probate or at the Register of Mesne Conveyance Office. It is as if the Cunliffes did not exist as citizens or as members of the congregation in whose churchyard some of them are buried. The headstone for Jane suggesting that Cunliffe was the surname of Richard and the married name of his wife is contradicted by other evidence revealing that the parents of Jane Thompson lived in Charleston as Richard and Catherine Connolly.[18] On the basis of that evidence, it appears that when Catherine died in 1828, her survivors thought it proper to have her maiden name inscribed on her headstone, and when her daughter Jane died some fifty years later, it was then also appropriate to confirm the maternal heritage and very specifically identify the place [Bolton/Lancashire] of the family's origins. Identifying Jane's parents as a couple named *Cunliffe* from an identifiable location suggests that the Lancashire Cunliffes had assumed another name when they immigrated to Charleston: perhaps as immigrants they wanted a genuinely new identity; perhaps they left Lancashire under some kind of civil or criminal duress; or perhaps there were debts that could not be paid, and emigration was a kind of bankruptcy whereby obligations could be left behind. But it is questionable that *Connolly* was an assumed name: it was doubtless Richard's surname, and *Cunliffe*, as just suggested, Catherine's maiden name. In death, as it were, the couple's earlier separation could be revealed without consequence. Nothing was admitted in 1828 since no survivor is identified by name, and by 1877, the parental divorce would have long ago become part of a past history. For whatever reason(s), on both occasions the survivors responsible for the headstone inscriptions were all too ready to abandon the Connolly name.

Thus begins, on a somewhat muddled note, what may be called the Thompson *line*. As identified on her gravestone, Catherine Cunliffe, the author's paternal great-great-great-grandmother was an early nineteenth-century English immigrant. Exactly when she arrived is not known. As for her husband Richard, the fact that he is not buried at St. Michael's suggests that the couple had separated when Catherine died. His death was announced in a notice in the *Southern Patriot* of April 7,

---

[18]   The name is spelled variously, whether in legal documents or other documentation: it appears as Connoly, Connolley, Conolley, or Connoly. I have opted to use "Connolly" unless quoting a source verbatim.

1836, indicating that he was to be buried on the 8th after a 3 o'clock funeral at the home of Mr. and Mrs. James L. Murray, corner of King and South Bay Streets. (Wilson and Grimes 1986) The death record suggests that he died a pauper since it specifies that he was buried in the city burial grounds—essentially in an unmarked grave. That record indicates his age as 54 and lists his birthplace as Ireland. No local marriage record exists, so it is safe to assume that Richard and Catherine arrived in the U.S. as a couple, she from England and he an Irishman.[19]

The fact that the Connollys [or at least Catherine] were members of either the St. Philip's or the St. Michael's congregation does not reveal very much since those were the primary Episcopal congregations in Charleston.[20] And that she was buried in the churchyard of St. Michael's does not indicate that the Connollys were prominent in some way, or that they were wealthy, although they must have been to some degree more than anonymous members of the congregation.[21] The records of St. Michael's verify that a Richard Connolly

---

[19]   Federal records show that Richard—as Richard Connolly—became a citizen in 1832—after Catherine had died. That record states that he was from England. There seems frequently to be an easy confusion between the two countries when immigrants stated their nationality for authorities in the U.S. In the case of Richard Connolly, the name Connolly lends weight to the Irish side of the argument.

[20]   According to a small brochure available in the Church Office, St. Michael's is "the oldest church edifice in the City of Charleston, standing on the site of the first Anglican Church built south of Virginia. In the 1680's a small wooden church, the first in the new town of Charles Town, was built on this spot for the families of England and named St. Philip's. By 1727, the town had grown too large for the small church and a more spacious one was built on Church St., later destroyed by fire in 1835. By 1751 St. Philip's had again proved too small for the incoming population, and another church was authorized by the General Assembly of the Province, to be built on the old site and to be known as St. Michael's. The cornerstone was laid in 1752 and in 1761 the church was opened for services. Except for the addition of the sacristy on the southeast corner, the structure of the building has been little changed."

[21]   George Williams' *St. Michael's Charleston, 1751-1951, with Supplements 1951-2001* (Charleston: College of Charleston Library, 2001), describes how the churchyard was almost from the beginning too small for the number of grave sites the congregation needed. By the early 1800s, the number of parishioners was increasing, and "transients and members of other churches which did not have burial grounds were filling the churchyard much too quickly." Earlier, in 1798, the vestry had "resolved that no persons—excepting the proprietors or renters of pews and their relatives residing in the families—shall under any pretense whatever, be interred in St. Michael's Church Yard, unless by the consent of the Vestry." The intent was difficult to honor, and non-members continued to be granted exceptions to the rule. In 1812, "equal burial rights with the parishioners of St. Philip's were agreed to by the vestries, and in 1828 this accommodation was extended to the members of St. Paul's, so that any family might secure interment on equal terms in any of the churchyards."

paid his rental fee as a pew holder [pew #105] in September 1829 and again in October 1833, and that the fee was paid again on August 9, 1841 and October 2, 1842 by his "estate", with a cross reference ["see"] to "Mrs. J. L. Murray". Clearly the family belonged to the congregation as *Connolly* and would have enjoyed status as citizens and church members who had already established themselves prior to the waves of immigrants who would arrive later. Catherine's death in 1828 at age 48 takes the Charleston Thompson line back to about 1780 in northern England's Lancashire.

The Lancashire town of Bolton, Catherine's purported native town, has a long history as a textile manufacturing site that boomed during the English industrial revolution. The town and its neighbors in the vicinity of Manchester specialized in the production and export of cotton cloth, and it is not unlikely that the Cunliffe/Connollys immigrated to Charleston because of that cotton connection—whatever their personal circumstances might have been, or whatever the immediate cause(s) for their departure. Richard Connolly might well have thought his opportunities to be greater in the port shipping the cotton than in the mill town spinning it into thread and fabric.

The English immigrant experience represented in the Thompson story really begins with Jane, Catherine's daughter. Whether or not her story can be considered entirely typical, it certainly describes the context in which a young Englishwoman grew to become the matriarch of a Charleston family of immigrant origins. She left no personal written account, but much of what she experienced as a newcomer to the city can be pieced together from her Charleston record.

Significant information can be gleaned from Jane's will, which was filed January 5, 1877, two months before she died the following 8 March. The document carries the usual opening statement, then moves to her first bequest: "I give and bequeath to my son, Captain Lawrence M. Murray, the sum of twenty-two Dollars to buy a mourning ring, and in token of my maternal regard, feeling rejoiced that by the goodness of Providence he is so well supplied with the material blessings of life, as to be beyond standing in need of any other thing, that I could give him, than a blessing, and therefore I give, devise, and bequeath all the rest and residue of my estate, both real and personal . . . . unto my children . . . in fee simple . . . and absolutely equally between them share and share alike."

Now while other records reveal the names of Jane's six other children—three daughters and three sons—it is only this late, legal acknowledgment of a son by the name of Lawrence Murray that clarifies the statement on her gravestone that she left "four sons and three daughters to mourn their loss." The Murray name of this legatee helps to explain the fact that another large headstone sits in St. Michael's churchyard between that of Catherine Cunliffe and Jane M. Thompson. That stone reads: "In Memory of / James L. Murray / died 9th

December 1850 / aged fifty years / And of his wife/ Elizabeth Murray / died 7th April 1855 / aged forty-nine years." What might have appeared as a randomly placed headstone in a crowded church cemetery reveals instead an important family relationship.

The three headstones in St. Michael's Churchyard for Cathrine Cunliffe and her daughters, Jane Thompson, and Elizabeth Murray (and son-in-law James L. Murray).

Jane's pieced-together records attest that she was born in England about 1807 and was married in Charleston when she was a young girl of 14 or 15 to John Michael Murray in May 1821. She bore him a son in early 1823. That child, John R. Murray, died March 27, 1823, aged 57 days, of croup. (King 2002, 239) Two years after a second son, Lawrence Michael Murray, was born in 1827, Jane's husband John made out a will that was signed April 18, 1829. In it he makes his wife, Jane M. Murray, the executrix of his estate consisting of "my three story brick house on South Bay the lot of land & premises thereunto belonging, as also my two story wooden house now occupied by me as a Dwelling House and Grocery store at the lower end of King Street . . . After payment of my just debts and funeral expences I give to my beloved Wife Jane M. Murray all my real and personal estate . . . for & during her natural life & after her decease I give the same to my son Michael Murray an infant, to him and his heirs forever, but should my said son Michael die before his mother, then I desire that my estate both real and personal should vest in my Wife and her heirs Executors administrators & assigns forever." John Michael Murray died three days later on April 21, 1829 and is buried in the cemetery of St. Mary's Catholic Church in Charleston. His gravestone inscription reads: "Sacred to the Memory of / John M. Murray / A Native of Waterford, Ireland / who departed this life on / the 21st of April 1829 / Aged Thirty Two Years

Eleven Months and nine days / ALSO In memory of his Son / John R. Murray / who departed this life on / the 3rd of April 1823 / Aged 2 months."[22]

In light of the information on the Murray headstones, it becomes evident that Jane Murray—as the married daughter of Richard and Catherine Connolly—had an elder sister Elizabeth. It is indeed Elizabeth and her husband James L. Murray who are buried in St. Michael's churchyard between Elizabeth's mother (Catherine Cunliffe) and her sister (Jane M. Thompson). Elizabeth's husband James was the younger brother of John Murray. As the gravestone indicates, Elizabeth died in 1855 at age 49—her birth year thus 1806, at least one year older than Jane; James at age 50 in 1850 would have been born in 1800, some four years after his brother John[23]. Thus two sisters married two brothers, and Jane Thompson lies in St. Michael's next to her sister and her brother-in-law twice over. It is less than certain that these two women chose to marry these men, or whether—as was customary at the time—they were not *given* in marriage *to* them by virtue of their father's wishes and design. It will become clear that Richard Connolly was instrumental in arranging the lives of his two daughters to his own advantage, further, that he considered them the same as property—in good English fashion. In more than one instance he reveals himself capable of manipulating his wife and daughters—and their husbands—as he tried to establish himself in the South Carolina Lowcountry.

There are a number of documents relating to John Murray and Richard Connolly that show the course of their—and their children's—connected lives while the two immigrant families were working to integrate themselves in their new context. From the record contained in Charleston city directories, Richard Connolly and his wife Catherine arrived between 1819 and 1821. John Murray can be confirmed as a resident by 1822. The 1824 directory lists John M. Murray as a grocer at 1 King Street, with Mrs. R. Murray[24] operating a grocery at 18 South-Bay. James Murray is listed as a clerk in the post-office, but without an address. The same directory shows Richard Connolly as a grocer

---

22   There is an obvious discrepancy between the date of the child's death on the gravestone and the earlier one cited by Susan S. King. The death card in the Charleston County Library gives the date of death as "Thursday, April 3, 1823" but the age is generalized "2 mo."

23   John Michael Murray's headstone states that he was exactly 32 years, 11 months, 9 days old when he died on April 21, 1829: his birthdate would thus be May 12, 1796.

24   John Murray's address at 1 King Street. suggests that his house was on the corner of King and what is now South Battery. The latter street was initially known as South Bay Street. The two addresses seem to indicate a north-south and an east-west enumeration for the grocery on that corner property. The only explanation for Mrs. Murray to be listed as "Mrs. R." is either the inaccuracy for which the city directories were known or the duplicity of the informant.

at 14 South-Bay and Mrs. Elizabeth[25] Connolly at 10 Stoll's Alley. Five years later, the 1829 directory shows "J.M. Murray, store, 4 King near South-Bay", and for the Connollys, only "Catherine, 26 South-Bay" and "Elizabeth, store, 26 South-Bay". No mention of Richard. By 1831, James is listed with a grocery on South Bay. Catherine Cunliffe Connolly had died in 1828, John Michael Murray in 1829. [26]

It is possible to assemble a fairly good picture of Jane Thompson's early years in Charleston as the daughter of Richard Connolly. Married in 1821 and widowed in 1829, her eight-year marriage to John Murray is of secondary consequence to the lineage she established with her second husband, James Thompson. Nonetheless, certain aspects of those early years helped to form her for the role she would later play as matriarch of the Thompson clan. It will be seen that with very little to say about it she was under the control of one man or another, either her father or her husband. When she married both Murray and Thompson, Jane became a *feme covert*—"a wife under the cover of her husband, who gained the right to control her property, among other things, in return for his protection" (Gordon-Reed 2008, 57). Only after her father's death was she rid of one controlling element but still officially under the thumb of the remaining one.

The documentation relating to Jane's early period in Charleston can best be reviewed chronologically, going back to when Richard Connolly and John Murray were, so to speak, just off the boat. How the two men knew or met each other is unknown: Murray was for certain an Irishman and a Catholic,[27] and Connolly suspiciously so.[28] Whatever the circumstances of their first meeting, Connolly was likely the one to have seen some advantage in aligning himself with the younger Murray, either as fellow countryman or as a potential husband for one of his daughters. Perhaps it was the daughters who attracted the Murray men and brought them to the attention of their father. At any rate, it was not long after they were in Charleston that their relationship was cemented through

---

[25] This is Richard's wife Catherine [Elizabeth?] at a different residence, suggesting that perhaps the couple occupied more than one property. Stoll's Alley is close to the South Bay locations.

[26] The fact that Catherine is listed in the 1829 directory does not contradict the fact that she died in 1828. The information for the directory was gathered a year in advance of the publication year.

[27] John Murray became a citizen in October 1828; James Murray filed a notice of intention only in March of 1843.

[28] English, if we take his wife's gravestone citing Lancashire as the place of origin, or his naturalization papers stating that he was an Englishman, or Irish, if we accept Ireland as his birthplace as in his death record.

the marriage of Connolly's daughters to the brothers Murray. From that point on, the plot thickened.

As soon as Richard Connolly was in South Carolina, he set about to acquire slaves. In March of 1821 he purchased two slaves, Sidney and Peggy, from J. A. and Samuel Woolfolk in Augusta, GA. In August of 1822, he sold the slaves Lydia and Sidney [bought the previous year] either to his wife or his daughter Elizabeth.[29] This was likely only the first of his efforts to secure something for himself by arranging *ownership* by a family member over whom he had ultimate control. In October of the same year he bought a slave named Louise from one, Jean Dufort.

Meanwhile, John Murray had married Richard Connolly's daughter Jane and was planting himself in the swampy area at the bottom of the Charleston peninsula. On March 1, 1823 he purchased two parcels of land on lower King Street and South Bay [South Battery] from two sisters, Mary Lamboll Beach and Elizabeth Lamboll Gilchrist, for $3,333.00 each. The mortgage deeds outline the installment payment program he was to follow to pay off the note. The first transaction was for the corner lot measuring 46' x 34'4", the 34'4" dimension being on South Bay; the second lot measured 34' x 50' and was adjacent to the corner parcel with the 50' bordering on King Street. It was these properties that Jane Thompson believed she inherited as John Murray's widow and which she tried to hold onto during her lifetime.

Two weeks later, Murray conveyed the corner parcel just purchased from the Lamboll sisters to Catherine Connolly, "wife of Richard Connelly", through an attorney [for Catherine], Steven Terry, for $1,000, with the provision that she could do with it what she would, and that Murray's wife Jane (Catherine's daughter) had renounced her right to dower. This particular transaction—by which John Murray arranged to put property into the hands

---

[29] Catherine's death record gives her name as Elizabeth, suggesting that she used both names. The possibility of confusion with her daughter Elizabeth sometimes appears intentional [on Richard's part] and can only be clarified on the basis of the date. In this instance, the date is of little help. It is interesting to note here that the slave Lydia belonged indeed to Elizabeth the daughter. According to *The Private Register of the Rev. Paul Trapier* (Jervey 1957), the son, James [Murray], of Lydia and her partner Nat, "slaves of Mr. James Murray", born 2 April 1832, was baptized at St. Michael's on May 17, 1842. On the same day, two daughters of "Harry and Lydia, slaves of Mr. James Murray", Sophia Eleanor [Murray], born 9 October 1834, and Elizabeth [Murray], born 19 March 1833, were baptized (p. 103). The latter, "slave of Mrs. James Murray", was married to Robert, "slave of Mrs. Bonneau", on 25 October 1849, "at her mistress' house, before many witnesses and consent of owners" (p. 182). Lydia could have been given to Richard's daughter directly in 1822, or to his wife, through whom Elizabeth would have inherited the female slave and her offspring.

of his mother-in-law—suggests that the two men were actively and legally merging the families in a way that went beyond intermarriage alone.

Or so it would appear on the surface. This merged family was subsequently involved in two suits argued before the South Carolina Court of Appeals. The first one in 1833 reveals interesting detail as to what was in play in the Connolly-Murray-Thompson circle and is related to the sequence of events mentioned above. The plaintiffs were "James Thompson and Jane, his wife, and Michael Murray, an infant by his next friend, the said James Thompson, v. Stevens Perry, James Murray, and Elizabeth, his wife, Robert W. Seymour, and Richard Connoly." The case was filed March 27, 1832—some nine years after the 1823 property transfer between John Murray and Catherine Connolly: Catherine Connolly and John Murray were both dead, and the latter's widow Jane had remarried [1829]. She was now the wife of James Thompson. The case was heard by the Court nine months later, in January 1833.

A summary of the case reveals that the two sisters, Jane and Elizabeth, were arguing about the purchase and subsequent disposition of the lot and building on the corner of King Street and South Bay, as well as who should be held responsible—and to what extent—for a debt of their father Richard. Catherine Connolly's right to will/devise property was questioned, and as a consequence, whether the property could in fact be claimed by her daughter Elizabeth and be entrusted to Richard as part of the daughter's marriage settlement with James Murray. Jane Murray and her second husband brought suit to have restored to them what, in their opinion, was rightfully hers [*theirs,* now that she was the wife of a second husband] through her first husband's will, and to compel her sister Elizabeth and her husband to share equally in covering the debt of the two women's father. From the depositions that were put before the court, the following facts emerged: (1) James and Elizabeth Connolly Murray claimed that Catherine Connolly (Elizabeth's mother) paid John Murray $2,750 for the lot he conveyed to her, and that she (Catherine) had funds separate from her husband Richard that enabled her to enter into the transaction. Elizabeth claimed that her ownership of the lot and the negroes was legitimate and safely protected by her marriage settlement "as a purchase for valuable consideration without notice of any equity or lien";[30] (2) Richard Connolly claimed that the

---

30   Annette Gordon-Reed provides an explanation for the significance of the so-called *marriage settlement*: "Wealthy families very often had great concerns about losing property that could have been in the family for generations simply because one of its female members got married. Marriage settlements, essentially prenuptial agreements usually entered into before the couple wed, provided a way out of the bride's and her family's predicament. The couple, or typically their fathers, negotiated a contract that allowed the wife to maintain control over specified property that she held before she married. The prospective bride, in

purchase of the lot by John Murray was made with *his* funds, advanced by his wife to Murray without his knowledge in an effort to secure the property to their family; further, that his wife executed her will without any authority from him, and without his knowledge or consent, and although he was a party to the marriage settlement of his daughter, he did not intend to waive any of his rights. He argued that since the property was paid for with his funds, the court should restore it to him; further, that his wife loaned $1,000 to Murray without his knowledge and the plaintiffs [his daughter and her husband] should "account to him for his money." "He denies that at the time the release was executed, the plaintiff, Jane, was under age; on the contrary, he believes she was then twenty-one";[31] (3) In 1826, Richard had *given* to his two daughters five slaves: to Elizabeth, he gave three, to Jane, two, in exchange for $150 and $100 respectively. One of Jane's slaves was subsequently sold in order to pay a debt owed by her father Richard. Part of her suit as plaintiff was that this action was unfair, and that her sister Elizabeth should be made to contribute equally toward satisfaction of the father's debt.

The case brought by the Thompson plaintiffs was ultimately dismissed. In the Court's opinion, Catherine had indeed used funds realized from the grocery business to launder the funds for the lot which she received from John Murray, but that she was perfectly within her rights as a *feme covert* to will that property to her daughter Elizabeth—with or without the express permission of her husband. The Court found that Richard could not claim innocence of the transaction alleged to have been with *his* funds, since he acknowledged it in his arranging the marriage settlement of his daughter. It was decided further that Jane and James Thompson had no standing to require equal contribution toward the debt of Richard. The sale of Jane's slave to pay for Richard's debt

---

turn, often gave up the right to the dower interest that would have given her a life interest in one-third of her husband's freehold estate upon his death" (Gordon-Reed 2008, 57). Here the "marriage settlement" is between James Murray and Richard Connolly, Trustee with Robert W. Seymour, of Elizabeth Connolly, whom James L. Murray intends to marry. That marriage was indeed performed by the Rev. Dr. Dalcho and announced in the January 9, 1830 issue of the *Charleston Observer*. (Holcomb 1980) Dr. Dalcho was assistant at St. Michael's from 1819 to 1836, during which time there was no rector of record. The "settlement" speaks of the corner property at King and South Bay, as well as of Elizabeth's plantation, Three Pine Islands, and further establishes a trust whereby both James and Elizabeth can enjoy the proceeds/rents of the property and the benefits of the labor of the slaves held [the 1850 slave census reports five slaves held by James L. Murray], without binding Elizabeth to any debts that James has made or will make.

[31]   Here Richard Connolly is arguing against his own daughter and her second husband. That he should be so unknowing about the age of his daughter does not put him in very good light: if she was indeed 21 in 1823, she would have to have been born c. 1802, and her age as attested on her gravestone would be off by some five years.

was improper in the first place because Richard had not been proven to be insolvent,[32] but the rectification of this was not appropriately part of this case. Thus Jane and James Thompson got no satisfaction from sister Elizabeth and brother-in-law James Murray on this score. Additionally, it was questioned whether John Murray in his will in 1829 had left anything to Jane and Michael [his son by Jane] other than his two houses—one his dwelling house, the other his store, and the one lot he held in his name. It would end up the case that Elizabeth Murray ultimately held the lot and house on the corner of King and South Bay willed to her by her mother, while the adjacent lot on King belonged to Jane through the will of her husband John Murray.

There were undoubtedly hard feelings by the time the whole affair was over: the Thompsons had gotten the short end of the stick and little satisfaction. But as it turned out in the long-run, Jane outlived her sister and brother-in-law. Both Elizabeth and James Murray died intestate, and after their deaths Jane assumed possession of the corner lot and house on South Bay and King. After Elizabeth's death, Jane devised the corner property in 1/6 portions to her six children, and after a series of sibling buy-outs, George J. Thompson finally sold the property in August 1881 to Rudolph Siegling.

What unfolds in the larger story and the period preceding the filing before the Appeals Court is the following: In January of 1827 Richard Connolly

---

[32] During the proceedings, Elizabeth made reference to her father *removing* himself to his plantation. *His* plantation is one and the same with the property "entrusted" to him through his daughter's marriage settlement. Records show that Elizabeth bought a "plantation" known as Three Pine Islands from the neighbors, Mary Beach and Elizabeth Gilchrist, in 1828. It was located in "Charleston District" and was a 65-acre area of islands and marsh originally granted to William Raefael in 1710. The purchase occurred on August 27, 1828, nine days after her mother had died. Her father had been "trustee" of this plantation since her marriage to James Murray in 1829, and undoubtedly had removed himself there after a dispute with his wife. The ownership, one way or another, of a plantation property, seems a clear indication of Richard Connolly's attempt to become a member of Charleston's leading class. Jane and William Pease (Pease and Pease 1981) explain in their analysis of the economic and political ramifications of the nullification crisis of 1832 that "plantation ownership was the form of wealth most associated with upper-class position in South Carolina. Consequently, professionals and merchants, who had made their money in the city, frequently bought plantations for themselves or their children. Thus, although rural landholding was neither a necessary nor sufficient measure of upper-class position, plantation ownership when coupled with membership in the urban South Carolina or Hibernian societies or the rural Agricultural Society of Jockey Club or paired with service on an Episcopal church vestry was indeed a significant measure of upper-class standing"(351). Richard Connolly managed to get himself the rural property, but not the membership in a club or a position on a vestry, and thus failed to establish himself or his family as members of Charleston's *upper class*.

transferred a 3-year-old slave named Charles to John Murray as trustee for Michael Murray. If one wanted to give Richard Connolly the benefit of the doubt, this transaction could be viewed as an acknowledgement of his grandson Michael's birth. Yet it seems Richard always had a purpose in mind. Recorded on the same date is another transaction ("bill of sale") that would have consequences long after the fact: Connolly sold two slaves, Jim and Neptune, to John Murray. In a few years the slave Neptune would become something of a *cause celèbre* and involve Jane's second husband, James Thompson. The drama that swirled around Neptune lasted for a good six years and again put Jane Murray Thompson before the South Carolina Court of Appeals two years after she had earlier been a plaintiff.

The second time around, James and Jane Thompson brought suit against J. W. Schmidt to recover the full cost of the slave Neptune whom Schmidt had purchased five years earlier in 1830. The case centered on the fate of Neptune—who stole him, bought him, sold him, owned him—over a period of some six years. It involved John Murray, Richard Connolly, the sheriff, an auctioneer, and the defendant Schmidt, who—it turned out—was Richard Connolly's personal physician to whom Connolly owed money. Schmidt pleaded "not guilty", and the crux of the matter ended up a matter of the statutes of limitation involved—one for Jane as a *feme covert*, the other for James as her husband.[33] The case was ultimately decided in favor of the Thompsons, but

---

[33]   In the course of the several hearings, it was revealed that Jane Thompson had taken out a loan from the Fellowship Society for $4,000 in July 1829 [her husband John Murray had died in April]. She had done this with her father as co-signer, since she was unable to do so by herself. As executrix and legatee of John Murray's estate, she had only a life estate in the property, and was unable therefore to borrow money against it on her own. The loan was collateralized with another property owned by John Murray which he had purchased in early 1826 from Sam S. Saylor. It, in fact, was on this property that the "Brick House" of John Murray stood and this property that he references in his will as part of his real estate, "to wit my three story Brick House on South Bay the lot of land and premises thereunto belonging" [in addition and separate from his "two story wooden house now occupied by me as a Dwelling House and Grocery store at the lower end of King St."]. It was explained to the Court that Jane had effected some $400 worth of repairs to the brick house, and, additionally, there was an outstanding mortgage on the property of $1,400. She, together with her father, sought to borrow additional funds from the Fellowship Society, pay off the debts, and with the small remainder, she would stock the [grocery] store [the wooden structure] and operate it as a business. She would not have to sell the female slave who had been left to her. The brick house could be rented for $500 per annum. With this plan, she could support herself and her minor child. The loan was obtained, and after their marriage in November, the Thompsons were "in the entire possession and enjoyment of the real property and stock in trade." The 1831 city directory in fact shows Joseph [*sic*] Thompson "blacksmith & grocery" at 1 King Street. It was this property that Jane and

appealed by Schmidt—not once but twice. In the end, the basis for the legal arguments was viewed as having changed between the first and the second hearing, and again between the second and the third, but not so much as to warrant overturning the original decision.

It becomes apparent that the second case brought in 1835 [extended by appeal to 1836] was a continuation of the first, heard in 1833. The unnamed slave who was sold from under the feet of Jane and James Thompson to satisfy the debt of her father in the earlier case was the same slave Neptune who was the crux of the matter in the second case when James Thompson tried to force the issue which the earlier Court had left unresolved. Thus Richard Connolly can be seen as exploiting his own daughters and his wife and capable of legal and financial machinations to satisfy his own interests. And in James Thompson we see a man who did not hesitate to litigate in securing the property of his wife for his own benefit.

These suits before the Court furnish only some aspects of what appears to have been the rather contentious nature of Jane Murray Thompson's early life in Charleston. As a young English woman accompanying her immigrant parents, she could not easily divest herself of the customs and traditions that prevailed in her former homeland. She was under the control of her father insofar as that was the custom in England and, as well, a carried-over custom in the young United States at this point in history. She was married off before she was out of her teens to a man almost eleven years her senior and was widowed in her early twenties. She was the younger of two daughters and could expect little in terms of equity with her older sister with regard to inheritance or distribution of family property or wealth. There was no marriage settlement for Jane when she married John Murray in 1821. Both families were newly arrived and there was insufficient property to control and defend. If John Murray was indeed "a poor young man", he was in no position to expect much in the way of a dowry from Jane's father. And Richard Connolly was likely only too happy to divest himself of responsibility for his younger daughter. As second in line, Jane was pretty much on her own in Charleston, as she would have been in England. Her removal to Charleston brought her no personal advantages. She would have felt pressure to remarry after the death of her first husband, since the prospects for a young widow with an infant son were not encouraging, no more in Charleston than in England. Her 1829 plea to the Fellowship Society displays her efforts to eke out a living from rental of an inherited property added to the small profit she could expect from running a corner grocery.

John Murray's son, Lawrence Michael Murray, living in Brooklyn, N.Y., claimed as his legacy and sold in 1880. The Fellowship Society loan story is documented, although the information about the circumstances necessitating her mortgaging the property is known only from the explanation given to the Appeals Court some six years later.

A second marriage to any qualifying suitor would have been the preferable option to remaining an unmarried widow: a *feme covert* enjoyed significantly more protection than an independent woman of no means. It took Jane less than a year to marry James Thompson, another husband of English heritage, who would provide a measure of security in the Charleston she was still getting used to. And although only recently arrived, the young English immigrant Jane Thompson almost immediately became a slave owner. This was clearly the result of her having moved into the Charleston slave-owning community and the fact that her father [and husband] had readily partaken of the customs of the city and state to which they had immigrated, bought slaves as chattel property, and had seen advantages in owning and exchanging this property as financial security in the welter of uncertainties facing the newly unsettled. The readily accepted role of slave owner suggests that these Irish or English immigrants were accustomed to the idea of having servants in their household and were themselves not members of the servant class that supported and served the mountain of English society above them. Jane Thompson tried to borrow funds in 1829 so she would not have to sell her slave, suggesting that she was convinced that she could not survive without the servant, or that in the least it would be a serious insult to her dignity to be deprived of the slave. She and her new husband subsequently fought tooth and nail to recover a slave they desperately wanted to have in their possession.

With regard to the matter of slave ownership, it is interesting to note that Richard Connolly was dealing in slaves at approximately the same time that Charleston experienced the 1822 Denmark Vesey uprising. That insurrection would put Charlestonians on notice that vigilance was needed if the majority represented by the slave population was to be successfully managed by the minority of whites whose livelihood and success depended on control of the laboring class. The Vesey incident would not have escaped notice—certainly not by anyone trying to establish membership in the community. The fire of rebellion by blacks was quickly smothered, but the embers continued to glow: Alan January quotes a contemporary recollection that claimed never to forget "the feeling of alarm and anxiety that pervaded the whole community from the time the danger became known, until all risk appeared to be over." The court that was called into session executed thirty-five blacks, among them Vesey, who supposedly masterminded the insurrection. January writes that "although the extent of the danger was undoubtedly exaggerated, most Charlestonians were sincerely convinced that they had barely escaped a horrible massacre. During the next several months Carolinians speculated at length about ways to avoid a repetition of this harrowing event" (January 1977, 192). The Vesey crisis was the stimulus for the founding of the South Carolina Association, a society initiating and enforcing the Negro Act of 1823, the essence of which prevailed until the Civil War. The Association was chartered by the South

Carolina Legislature in 1828, re-chartered in 1849, and succeeded in 1850 by the Charleston Vigilant Association. As January summarizes, "for nearly thirty years the . . . Association served as the most influential and effectual of the many extralegal vigilance organizations which assisted the police in keeping a tight rein over the Negro in South Carolina" (January 1977, 201). On a more personal level, the "Neptune affair" at the center of the Thompsons' 1833-35 litigation efforts reveals how tenuous the relationship between slave and slave owner was during this time. It also demonstrates how far the Thompsons, as recent immigrants, had come in assimilating the cultural and social context of the city they were now a part of. This, however, would not have been all that difficult for the English immigrant. Barbara Bellows points out that the English had for a long time been accustomed to the kind of unequal relationships endemic to slavery. "During the Tudor period, the English defined slavery in terms of power relationships rather than race; those unable to defend their liberty did not deserve to enjoy it. As liberty emerged as the 'central idea' during the colonial period, southerners made mastery over others rather than self-control a key element in their interpretation of the ideal citizen . . . . As poverty and slavery became increasingly conflated, so did labor and subjection . . . . In a slave society, the aristocratic ideal considered work degrading rather than ennobling. Freedom meant freedom from labor" (Bellows 1993, 69). Richard Connolly would have fully subscribed to this kind of relationship with a ready-made underclass. By acquiring slaves as he attempted to ground himself and his family in Charleston, he would have elevated himself in his own eyes and those of others to the degree that he would be viewed as the master over the *property* he *owned*. His daughters would be similarly empowered by owning slaves, and the daughters themselves appreciated the extent to which their ownership facilitated their status within the acculturation process.

By the time the widow Jane Murray married the blacksmith James Thompson in November of 1829, she had been in Charleston hardly a decade, and as the immigrant daughter of a rather devious immigrant father, a deceased immigrant mother, and a more-favored immigrant elder sister, she faced an uncertain future—her own and that of Charleston. There would be unsettledness at the city, state, and national levels: Charleston had already experienced economic depressions in the early 1820s, the number of free blacks in the city was on the increase and a threat to any sense of cultural stability, and the issue of nullification would come to dominate South Carolina politics. Charleston would undergo a period of stagnation in many sectors, as other areas—in the north and the west—took on the glow of expansion and development. Opportunity would be harder and harder to come by, and Charleston would dig in its heels and become more defensive of its sectionalist orientation. In John Lofton's analysis, "[a]s time passed, South Carolina's behavior was to show how solidly the state had welded itself to the slave system. With her commerce declining, with her own soil exhausted from overplanting in a single crop, with her population drifting to the west where fertile new fields were being cultivated in effective competition with the worn out land of the east—South Carolina refused to face the changed conditions. The state ignored warnings against wasting her soil, advice to fight tariff discrimination by adopting varied industry. Instead South Carolina clung to the vision of a one-crop economy based on slaves and supporting an aristocracy of planters in baronial splendor" (Lofton 1964, 211-12). Jane Thompson, one could predict, would not have an easy time in the next few years.

But would this also be the case for the other family members who would be immigrating to Charleston to begin new lives? How would the German immigrants fare in meeting the challenges Charleston presented?

V

THE FOLLOWERS IN CONTEXT: 1840-1860

While Jane and James Thompson were fighting in the courts for possession of their slave property during the 1830s, the State of South Carolina was in the thrall of the nullification crisis that pitted the State against the Union in alleged defense of its rights. In the midst of all this personal, local, and national commotion, new immigrants were arriving and trying to find their place in the Charleston community. Within the framework of this particular family, the English members had already opened the door. The German members would follow in their footsteps, although along a slightly different course.

As noted earlier, a German community was long established in Charleston since the mid-1700s—so that by the 1830s, there had been time for two or more generations to become acculturated. While still very conscious of their German heritage, the members of this group would now think themselves less German and more Charlestonian—established citizens—in contrast to the immigrants who would come during the nineteenth century. That older ethnic community had organized itself sufficiently to be represented by a militia organization—the German Fusiliers—that would display its loyalty to the adopted country through participation in the Revolutionary War, the War of 1812, the Seminole War of 1836, and subsequently, in the Civil War. The German Friendly Society had been founded already in 1766 and its members had become pillars not only of the German community but of Charleston's society itself. It has been noted that ". . . next to the English the German people have unquestionably had the greatest influence in determining the character of this city. Since the second quarter of the eighteenth century they have constituted numerically a large portion of the population. In commerce, in civic affairs, in religion, and in music their part has been particularly significant. German is the only language other than English which had ever had wide usage in Charleston" (J. B. Easterby in Gongaware, Lesemann, and Cotton 1999, 78).

When the Duke of Saxe-Weimar visited Charleston in December of 1825, the German Friendly Society received him royally. At the dinner given in his honor, his response to toasts in his honor included references to "so many of my countrymen representing my native land in so gratifying a manner," while the Governor of South Carolina offered praise to "the German associations in the United States—founded on the principles of usefulness and benevolence, whilst they conform to the institutions of the Country" (Gongaware, Lesemann, and Cotton 1999, 112-13). The Society made the Duke an honorary member on December 21, 1825 and had the certificate of membership hand-carried by one of its members for presentation to the Duke after the latter had returned home. But while the Society was obviously enthralled with its members' heritage, it had matured since its founding to effectively represent the members' *conformity* to the larger issues affecting American society and their inclusion in it. In the minutes of the Society in 1826, much attention was paid to the announcement of the deaths of John Adams and Thomas Jefferson: a motion was adopted to provide for the "participation by the Society in the community observance of the death of these two distinguished American citizens" (Gongaware, Lesemann, and Cotton 1999, 116-17).

So both the Fusiliers and the German Friendly Society might be seen as representative of the first German ethnic community that contributed to Charleston's evolution up to the first quarter of the nineteenth century. Both the Fusiliers and the Society ultimately absorbed many of the immigrants who came in the nineteenth century so that those newcomers—the followers—did not, in effect, step onto *terra nova* when they set foot in the Lowcountry. The way had been prepared so that the later German immigrant would not be viewed by native Charlestonians as a newfangled foreigner. Nonetheless, the immigrants of the second wave could not for the most part assume they would be warmly welcomed into an already-settled family.

This separation between the earlier and the later group is of course not meant to suggest that immigration to Charleston occurred at two separate and distinct times. Immigration was continuous, but it was not until the 1830s that there was a noticeable increase in the number of Germans emigrating from their native lands to the United States: in 1832 the count was roughly 10,000; in 1834, roughly 17,000; by 1837 the number had grown to 24,000, and from 1845 to 1881 an average of 80,000 came each year. As for Charleston, the second wave began in the late 1820s and early 1830s and was closely linked to the development of the port of Bremerhaven and the efforts of the city of Bremen to become the "embarkation-point-of-choice" for the increasing numbers of emigrants leaving Europe for America. As noted above, Charleston had long had a direct trade association with the North German city, and it was the proximity of its newly developed port, as well as Bremen's ordinances directed toward protecting the interests of emigrants, that encouraged so many emigrants from the area immediately surrounding Bremen to come to Charleston. As suggested earlier, once the first ones had ventured forth, other members of the family would follow, so that the effects of *chain-migration* were well established in Charleston before the middle of the nineteenth century.

—JOHANN ROSENBOHM—

The first of the German family members to settle in Charleston was Johann Heinrich Rosenbohm. He is listed as a 19-year-old passenger [one of ten, all ranging in age between 18 and 26] on the *Constitution* that arrived in New York from Bremen on June 21, 1824. Exactly when he made his way south to Charleston is not known, but he was naturalized as a U.S. citizen in Charleston in October of 1830. The listing in the 1830 census confirms that his birth year was around 1800.[34]

Johann Heinrich Rosenbohm's story is important in that he represents the first link in the chain between Charleston and Geestendorf/Geestemünde, although he was not the individual who would establish one of the family's German lineages.[35] That individual would not arrive until almost forty years later and, at best, could count Johann Rosenbohm a distant relative by marriage. That extended relationship nonetheless demonstrates just how strong an influence the chain could have after it had been established.

---

[34] The Rosenbohm name appears in other Charleston records, but it is not known whether or how they were related to Johann: the 1840 census shows a Theodore Rosenbohm in a large household of sixteen persons, male and female of various ages, doubtless not all of them Rosenbohms. No records have been found for a Rosenbohm immigrant prior to Johann, nor any further record of Theodore. The records of the German Lutheran congregation in Charleston, St. Matthew's, mention the death of Meta Adelheid Rosenbohm from Weissenberg, who died in 1858, aged 20, of yellow fever, as well as a G. Wilhelm Rosenbohm, a bachelor, likewise from Weissenberg, who died that same year, aged 20. Weissenberg is only a stone's throw from the villages where one of Johann's sisters was born, so it is likely that this pair (probably brother and sister) were related in some way to Johann's family.

[35] There is every reason to claim that Johann Rosenbohm and/or his wife were *from* Geestendorf. The marriage in 1837 of Johann Hinrich Rosenbohm "from North America" to Caroline Louise HUHNE on the 24th of July is recorded in the Geestendorf church record. And the *Staatsarchiv Stade* (Rep 72/172 Geestemünde Nr. 09104) holds the will of Johann's parents, Caspar and Adelheid Rosenbohm, although Caspar's gravestone in Bethany Cemetery in Charleston states his birthplace as Burg Steinfort, Husum. Husum in Lower Saxony lies southeast of Bremen (52.56° N/9.25° E). Johann's mother (née Büggeln) died and is buried in Geestendorf.

Johann Rosenbohm would come to Charleston in the same decade that Jane Connolly Murray would become a widow and then remarry. Jane's first husband, the immigrant from Ireland, had run a grocery store at his property at the foot of King Street, and she, after his death, did the same. Johann set foot in Charleston and incidentally determined to follow the same course. The *Constitution*'s passenger manifest lists his occupation as "Sugar Baker" [*Zuckerbäcker*] or confectioner: of the ten passengers, six of them were similarly classified; two were merchants, one a baker, and one a blacksmith. Shortly after he became a citizen, he purchased a house at 306 St. Philip Street and sold it in 1833. The Charleston city directory for 1835-36 shows him operating a grocery store at 88 Meeting St [on the corner of Queen and Meeting Streets]. He was granted a U.S. passport in 1836. His passport application gives his age as 29—if accurate, his birth year is closer to 1804 than 1800—and describes him as having a "high and full" forehead, blue eyes, a "long and sharp" nose, a "full" mouth, "round" chin, and "ruddy" complexion. He returned to Germany that same year to marry Caroline Huhn.[36] That year he also bought a house on the northeast corner of Stoll's Alley and Church Street.

By 1839, however, the German-American grocer had decided to leave Charleston. He left his grocery store and its stock worth $2,849.35 to be disposed of by his legal representative, Henry Humberg, who would retain half of the sale monies. Rosenbohm went to New York, taking his wife and children. The family must have had sufficient means to make a return visit to Germany in 1841. Passenger-ship records show a party of four Rosenbohms arriving in New York from Bremen on the *Charlotte* on June 1, 1841: John Henry, 37 [again suggesting that his birth year was c.1804]; Caroline Louise, 22; Catherine, 2 1/2; and Auguste, a 1-year-old infant. They were cabin passengers—not in steerage—and arrived with "seven boxes and beds". The same ship would return the following November to bring Johann's widowed father, Caspar Rosenbohm, to America. He did not stay with his son in New York, but came instead to Charleston, where he took up residence in his son's house on Church Street and Stoll's Alley. John Henry returned that same November to Geestendorf: New York City Lutheran church records indicate that he was a witness to a marriage in Wurffleth, the village near Geestendorf where his sister, Anna Maria, was born. John Henry Rosenbohm died in New York in May of 1843. In his will he left the property on Church Street to his widow, but after his death Caroline remarried [Jurgen Skriefer] and relinquished

---

[36] In the *Staatsarchiv Stade* (Rep 72/172 Lehe Nr. 4723) there is a *Depositenschein* [legal transaction receipt] for Johann Hinrich Rosenbohm and his wife, where her name is given as *Caroline Lucie, geb. Huhn*. One might suppose that the legal record is the more accurate, but it is difficult to explain the variance in her maiden name by deciding between the church and the legal record.

her inheritance. The house was put up for auction in 1845 to satisfy the debt John Henry owed to his executor, Luder Rust ($1119.82). It was purchased by John Henry's brother-in-law, Herman Knee, married to Rosenbohm's sister Catherina. John Henry's father Caspar lived in the house until his death in 1852.

**Caspar Rosenbohm's headstone on the Schroeder family plot at Bethany Cemetery.
His stone includes the names of two of his grandchildren, Clarence Knie and
Caroline Fehrenbach. Caroline's name is engraved incorrectly.**

That Johann Heinrich/John Henry Rosenbohm undertook to make his fortune as a grocer is indicative of a pattern that would become typical of German immigrants to Charleston—a city characterized by a wealthy planter/plantation elite to whom manual labor was anathema, a black majority/slave laboring class which served the white population in almost every capacity, and a small class of free laborers and artisans who practiced the service functions that the composite society relied on.

A disproportionate number of tailors, shoemakers, and smiths came from Europe; four out of five shoemakers in Charleston came either from Germany or England. On the other hand, unclean occupations such as barber or butcher were considered 'negro work' and were carried out by free blacks: 78% of all the barbers in Charleston in 1860 were free blacks. The black and white competition in craftsmen's occupations was looked upon with justified suspicion; in competition with blacks, white laborers were seen as inferior persons. Indeed, the slave-holding elite of Charleston feared for social peace in their city; free white laborers were unreliable, and were met with deep suspicion. Thus Charleston was one of the few southern cities that prevented the displacement by immigrants of free blacks from their typical workplaces, because Charleston employers refused to give up their preference for free black employees. Instead a radical racial division continued in specific occupations (Mehrländer 2011, 41, citing Berlin and Gutman).

An analysis of that society indicates that immigrants would astutely find niches where they could operate without displacing and antagonizing what was already in place. "As a group, immigrants entered Southern society at the bottom of the free social hierarchy and made up a large part of the lower ranks of urban society." In the thirty years after J. H. Rosenbohm became a grocer, "native-born white men composed better than two-thirds of the male merchants, political officials, and professionals in Mobile, Charleston, and other Southern cities, while foreign-born men equaled a similar proportion of petty proprietors—grocers, restauranteurs, stable keepers, and the like" (Berlin and Gutman 1983, 1178). Rosenbohm's early attempt to find an occupation in his new-found home was consistent with his earlier experience as a confectioner and indicates an effort to establish a business he could expect to be patronized by his fellow immigrants, serve an existing neighborhood of both native and foreign-born, and which would not exhibit a competitive arrogance that a smart newcomer would try to avoid. While he did not establish the trend to become an innocuous grocer, he was nonetheless an early representative. "In 1850 one third of all German men in Charleston were employed in trade; 20% worked in crafts, mainly in those in which they had the least possible competition from free blacks and hired slaves. In 1860 the occupational diversity remained unchanged; only the category of grocers grew considerably (by 14.3%): the number of 147 shops increased to 210 in 1860. In 1870 Germans still owned almost 80% of all Charleston groceries" (Mehrländer 2011, 40).

One might wonder why young Rosenbohm would abruptly leave Charleston in 1839, abandoning his store to have it liquidated by someone else. Absent any personal record, it is speculative to reason why, but some aspects of the following might have affected his decision. Shortly after he had disembarked in New York and made his way to South Carolina, Johann would have seen

Andrew Jackson elected President of the United States in 1828. But by 1832, the German immigrant's adopted South Carolina would become politically and economically embroiled in the nullification crisis which the state created with its 1832 Ordinance of Nullification. This crisis dominated South Carolina and Charleston politics and ultimately put South Carolina as a state in a category by itself, brought forth the volatile career of John C. Calhoun, and was ultimately precedent to the secession of the state from the Union thirty years later. The state's and city's population was almost evenly divided on the issue, and no individual could count on a neighbor of any variety to hold the same opinion on these political matters. One can easily imagine how disconcerting it would have been to be a foreigner in this context, to know which side to take, to know what it all meant for one's future—a future that was supposed to be free of the political discord and instability rampant in Europe: the *old* life in Europe after all had been exchanged for a new, more peaceful and stable existence in a place that had put its revolution to rest. For a German it might have been possible to see the handwriting on the wall and to realize that the adamant defense of states' rights against the imposition of laws designed for the good of a united country was a cover-up for an increasingly divisive sectionalism that had to justify the *peculiar* institution of slavery on which it depended. Rather than fall in with the nullifiers and risk offending the other half of the community over a policy which he could hardly have fully understood, discretion might have helped Johann Rosenbohm decide to abandon his efforts in Charleston and seek refuge in the North.

On the other hand, perhaps Johann Rosenbohm's efforts as a grocer were not sufficiently rewarded. The German immigrants who were there at the time would not yet have had a chance to benefit from the boost that John Andreas Wagener would stamp on the German ethnic community with his dynamic personality, beginning with his founding the German Fire Company in 1836. Another possibility is that Rosenbohm was spooked by the sequence of destructive fires that ravaged large sections of the city, all but missing his store on the corner of Queen and Meeting Street. St. Philip's Church nearby was destroyed by fire in 1835, and the great fire of 1838 took away a large section of the lower city.

These conjectures on the reasons for Johann Rosenbohm's departure, while they do not establish anything as fact, provide insight into the Charleston framework that the early nineteenth-century German immigrant met prior to the 1840s. And even though their paths undoubtedly never crossed, the Rosenbohms in Charleston were running a parallel course with the Thompsons depicted earlier. When Johann Rosenbohm acquired his first property in 1831—the house on St. Philip Street—and had either previously, or would shortly thereafter, set himself up in business as a grocer, the English, newly married widow Jane Murray was starting her new existence as the wife of

James Thompson. How would the Charleston scene unfold for her, without an escape hatch to New York?

The 1830 Charleston census shows the Thompsons as a childless couple. Jane then had six children—starting with Adeline in 1833—so that a decade later the 1840 census shows James Thompson as head of a household of seven: himself, Jane, her son, Michael Murray, their daughters Adeline, Sarah Jane, and Annastatia, and a son, Joseph E. S. By 1850, the census [the first census that enumerated individuals living in a household by name] shows all the Thompson children, Adeline, 17; Sarah Jane, 16; Annastatia, 10; Joseph E. S., 11; George J., 9; and John G., 5. Michael Murray is absent. For whatever reason, he had left the Thompson household and was living with his uncle and aunt, James and Elizabeth Murray.

The 1850 census identifies James Thompson as a blacksmith and states that he was born, like Jane, in England. One can suppose that they met each other in Charleston, in all likelihood within the St. Michael's congregation. St. Michael's records indicate one pew holder as James Thompson in 1833, suggesting that the couple's financial status was sufficient to enable them to pay the required rent on a St. Michael's pew along with other members of that Anglican congregation, including Jane's father, Richard Connolly.

The Thompsons would be consumed during the 1830s with their legal entanglements before the South Carolina Appeals Court. Their efforts to regain their slave property may be an indication that their financial status was threatened and not all that secure. Very early in the marriage Jane became a member of the newly established congregation of St. Stephen's Episcopal Church. The church had been established in 1822 as a *free* church for those who could not afford to rent a pew as was the practice at the other churches. In November 1834, the Rev. Paul Trapier and Rev. P. H. Folker were the ministers, and in 1835 the church was destroyed in the same fire that destroyed St. Philip's. A lot on Anson Street was purchased that same year, and the cornerstone for a new church was laid on St. Stephen's Day. The ministry of Paul Trapier at St. Stephen's was dynamic enough that he received the call to become rector of St. Michael's in 1840. Jane was a staunch member of St. Stephen's under the leadership of Paul Trapier by the time her second and third daughters (Sarah Jane, 1834; Annastatia, 1836) and her eldest son (Joseph E. S., 1839) were born, and her life became anchored in her membership in this slightly renegade Episcopal congregation as her marriage to James Thompson unraveled.

When Paul Trapier became the rector of St. Michael's in 1840, the dynamic John Andreas Wagener and his immigrant German compatriots were making preparations to establish St. Matthew's German Lutheran Church. The original congregation from which the St. Matthew's founders split was at that time housed in a structure on the corner of Hasell and Anson Streets [now St. Johannes Lutheran Church], only a few blocks south of St. Stephen's.

The English, German, and other immigrants who populated that area created the neighborhood that came to be called Ansonborough—struggling members of a community that would begin to have a significant impact on life in Charleston. And although Johann Rosenbohm had thought it better to relocate elsewhere, other German immigrants would follow him to take their place in a city whose complicated character became more intense during the decades that followed.

Ansonborough neighborhood at the turn of the century.
By permission of Gini and Richard Steele of antiquepix@aol.com.

—THE FEHRENBACHS—

Johann Rosenbohm was undoubtedly responsible for the immigration of his three sisters to Charleston, and each of their stories represents a telling chapter in the development of the immigrant German community there prior to the Civil War. Johann's sister, Anna Maria Rosenbohm, had married a watchmaker from the Black Forest. How the native of Baden and the young woman from the environs of Bremen met is not known, but Nicholas Fehrenbach would likely have come north, probably down the Rhine, and met Anna Maria in Geestendorf.[37] They were a couple by 1830, and the baptism of their first child,

---

[37]   As Michael Bell explains, emigration from the German-speaking parts of Europe in the first half of the nineteenth century was a complex of causes. Despite the fact that some regions of Germany had difficulty with food crops—as had Ireland with the potato blight—"famine alone was not the cause of their emigration. Other forces were at work pushing Germans to America. While there were a myriad of factors contributing to the

Wilhelm Eduard, is recorded in the Geestendorf church record in May 1831. That baptism record is in fact the first mention of the Rosenbohm name in the church ledger and suggests that the Rosenbohm clan resident in Geestendorf may have originated elsewhere before moving to Geestendorf. Anna Maria was born in neighboring Wurffleth, and her father Caspar, as noted earlier, in Burg Steinfort near Husum: it was not uncommon, however, to move among neighboring villages to find opportunity in one place that was missing in another. In any case, the young Fehrenbach couple emigrated shortly after the birth of Wilhelm Eduard: their second son, Nicholas, jun., was born in Charleston in 1833. The family in Charleston grew with the birth of Johann Premos in 1835, Richard in 1837, Adelheid in 1840, Caroline in 1842, Herman Heinrich in 1844, and Adeline Catherina Mariane in 1846. An additional son was born in 1851, not in Charleston, but in Sheboygan, Wisconsin, where the family later lived for a while. Nicholas Fehrenbach, sen. became a naturalized citizen in 1838.

If Nicholas Fehrenbach had left his native Baden because of economic hardship and come to Charleston—where his wife had a brother who had become a U.S. citizen and established himself as a grocer—hoping for opportunity to practice his artisanal talents as a clockmaker, he and his wife appear to have been dealt a bad hand. The Fehrenbach name would become a well-known one in the Charleston German community, but the family's fame—if it ever amounted to that—rested on the shoulders of their second son, Nicholas, jun., who became a successful restauranteur and a well-known figure in the ethnic community. The immigrant parents, Nicholas, sen. and his wife Anna Maria, struggled mightily.

The evidence is that Nicholas could not make a go of it as a clock/watchmaker in Charleston, nor was he successful in establishing himself in another occupation. On the contrary, as the family was increasing in size during

---

exodus (such as overpopulation, a market revolution, political and religious persecution, and sometimes famine), all were not present in all German-speaking regions of Europe at the same time." Nonetheless, "the first German areas to be hardest hit by these difficulties were those in the southwest: Baden, Bavaria, Hesse-Darmstadt, the Palatinate, and Württemberg. The age-old inheritance practice of dividing land among heirs (*Realteilung*) so subdivided individual holdings in this region that it became economically detrimental following the end of the Napoleonic wars. As more persons grew into adulthood (due to the absence of war as a natural limiting factor), the population increased greatly. In these regions, emigration occurred 'on a scale comparable to that of Ireland.' Between 1840 and 1859, almost 40 percent of all emigrating Germans came from Baden, Bavaria, and Württemberg. Peasant-farmers and artisans left the region because 'they could no longer support themselves and their families'—even with the combined income from farming and cottage industries" (Bell 1996, 110).

the decade after their immigration, their situation deteriorated to the point that they were all but destitute. In her book cited earlier [*Benevolence Among Slaveholders: Assisting the Poor in Charleston 1670-1860*], Barbara Bellows actually uses the case of Anna Maria Fehrenbach as an example. Bellows's study analyzes the benevolence exhibited by Charleston's elite in taking care of the indigent among its citizenry, including its efforts at educating the children of the less fortunate. The founding of the Charleston Orphan House already in 1790 emanated from that sense of civic responsibility:

> As Charleston's elite became increasingly self-conscious about the need to demonstrate their dedication to public stewardship, the orphan house served as a useful tool. Rather than merely warehousing derelict children or leaving that task to religious or private societies, Charlestonians transformed a social problem into a political opportunity. The two thousand white children who passed through the asylum's doors from 1790 to 1860 not only had their basic needs met but also learned about their place in the urban community and their role in a biracial society. The patronage of some of the town's wealthiest and most influential men and women gave the abandoned and homeless a place in a society traditionally based upon the ties of blood, race, and kinship . . . . The orphan house served as a workshop where three generations of the urban elite formulated, clarified, honed, and refined their theories of class relations in a patriarchal world . . . .
>
> In Charleston, the orphan house commissioners represented the interest of children in family conflicts. They assumed roles in the life of the poor most closely resembling some amalgam of magistrate and secular priest. They even took turns holding Sunday-evening services at the orphan house and teaching in the Sunday School. Their statutory control over the city's children provided a mighty lever over the personal morality of poor parents. As nineteenth-century Solomons, they served as mediators in family disputes, took away children from the abusive, and returned them to the penitent (Bellows 1993, 122-27).

That institution would in fact come to play a role in the lives of several members of this particular immigrant family. But it was the Fehrenbachs who were the first to throw themselves on Charleston's mercy, and it is in the context of educating the poor that Bellows subsequently cites Anna Maria Fehrenbach's plea to the Commissioners of the Charleston Orphan House. In Bellows's account,

The abandoned wife of Nikolas Ferenbacher, unemployed watchmaker from Baden and father of six . . . pressed her claims upon the town. Mary Ann Ferenbacher assumed control of the family finances, became the disciplinarian for her six children, and borrowed money from relatives to open a small dry-goods shop. She put food on the table through 'rigid economy and ceaseless industry,' but her sons ran riot, totally beyond her control. The young Ferenbachers spent their days absorbed in side-street amusements and petty crimes with ragtag gangs of street urchins. Frequent absences expressed their contempt for the tedium of the 'paupers' school.' When the town fathers agreed to receive only one son, Ferenbacher, pressed by a 'burden she could not bear,' reminded the city officials of the implications of southern patriarchal tradition: 'My children are yours. They are natives, they are Southerners, and though their Father has forgotten himself, and deserted them, this is their country. And though poor and friendless, shall my son not be heard because a Mother's tongue alone urges his claim . . . Oh, save him from being a curse to the soil that gave him birth, and spare the Mother from the anguish which this Mother must endure at the mere debasement of her child.' So it was that Johann Himrick Richard Ferenbacher, the southern boy with the German name, was brought under the mantle of Charleston's elite (Bellows 1993, 129).

Bellows has embellished the story a bit, has spelled the surname incorrectly, and christened the Fehrenbach son *Himrich* instead of *Hinrich*. The full story on the Fehrenbachs is more accurately as follows:

Anna Maria Fehrenbach made application for her son Nicholas to be admitted in August 1844 [born in May 1833, he was just over 11 years old]; on 29 August the case was referred to the Visiting Commissioner; a report dated 5 September was favorable—admitted "upon being bound by the Commissioners of the Poor." An undated letter accompanied the mother's application, signed by both John Phillips and W. Heemsoth, "pastor of the German lutheran congregation in Hasell Street, residence George Street Nr 3," [Heemsoth was the pastor of the original St. Matthew's congregation housed in the structure on Hasell and Anson Streets] and reads as follows [unedited]: "Nicolaus Fehrenbach the father of the good boy came from the Grandduchy of Baden (Germany) and has resided in Charleston S.C. till last spring, when he left for New orleans; since when his wife never heard from him. Shortly before the time of his leaving the whole property was sold for the benefit of creditors; but by the assistance of some friends, the wife opened again a small retail dry goods store, by which she tries, although with great difficulty to support a large family of six children, the smallest of whom is an infant of three weeks: Unable therefore to superintend and educate the children, the aforesaid boy Nicolaus is at present in great danger to become a bad member of the society. For this reason the Committee of the Orphan House is respectfully solicited to receive the said boy under their protection."

An undated certificate states in columns across the page: *Name of the Applicant*: Ann Marie Fehrenbach—*Settled Place of Abode:* Charleston S.C. corner of Church and Tradd strs—*Name of the Child*: Nicolaus Fehrenbach—*Age*: 11 years 3 months—*Sex:* Boy—*Place of Nativity*: City of Charleston S.C. Meeting Str.—*Time of residence in the city*: since his birth—*Property*: none—*Religious denomination:* Lutheran. Across the bottom of the certificate is the recommendation on behalf of Nicolaus Fehrenbach, signed by John Phillips and [illegible]: "We recommend the boy Nicolaus Fehrenbach as one peculiarly and particularly a subject for the charity of the Orphan House of Charleston. His parents are very poor and his Father has deserted his Family. His Mother is unable to afford him support or educate him properly. The boy if now taken may become a good and useful citizen." The formal Indenture shows the date of September 5, 1844 as the beginning of the legal transfer of Nicholas Fehrenbach, jun. to the Charleston Orphan House for ten years—until September 5, 1854.

With her one son successfully accepted, Anna Maria then wrote [in a clear hand] on October 16, 1844 the following letter [unedited]: "To the Chairman of the Commissioners of the Charleston Orphan House / Gentlemen / You will allow to express the grateful feelings of my heart for that kind sympathy you partook in my bereaved circumstances and that benevolence you bestowed upon my second son Nicolaus in giving to his youth an asylum in the Charleston Orphan House. But alas! though my heart in somewhat is raised, that now one of my children is under the care and guidance of faithful tutors, it nevertheless gets depressed when I look on the other children, bereaved of the parental care and the means for their support, for their are left to me five more. I therefore, encouraged by your kindness, take once more my refuge to you, gentlemen, trusting and fully assured you will exert all means which a benevolent community bestowed upon you to save poor children from want and destruction against me and my children, and confer upon one of them: Johann Hinrich Richard born in Charleston S.C. 8th of July 1838 the great favour which now so richly enjoyes the above named in giving him too an asylum in the Charleston Orphan House. I remain with sincere gratitude/ Gentlemen/ your obedient servant/ Mary Ann Fehrenbach/ corner Tradd and Church Street."

An Orphan House note reads: Mary Ann Fehrenbach application for the admission of her son John Henry Richard Fehrenbach aged 6 years October 22 1844 // Referred to the Visiting Commissioner // Oct 31 1844 Report of the

Visiting Commissioner unfavorable to the reception of the child—// Report of the Visiting Commissioner adopted—child rejected".

The Orphan House Commissioners then received a two-page letter from A.M. Fehrenbach, undated, in perfect penmanship, different from her earlier hand and thus likely written *for* her by someone else, bearing what is possibly her signature. Whosever hand, it was a German who was the scribe: the orthographical convention of the old German *Sütterlin* script [ß] shows up at every instance of *ss*. The letter is the poignant plea of an abandoned immigrant mother, and is the source for some of what Bellows quoted. It is worth reading in its entirety:

> To the Honorable the Commissioners of the Orphan House/ Gentlemen/
> I have heard with deep regret the decision you have recently made in refusing to admit John H. F. Fehrenbach my son to the benefit of the Orphans Charity. I do not wish to vex your attention with complaining. The complaints of the poor and friendless are too important to excite attention, and I would be untrue to my feelings if I entertained other than the kindest regard for those who are sheltering and properly educating an older child who I was unable to support and over whom I was losing all control. If you shall do no more for me and mine you have my gratitude, the gratitude of a heart stricken by misery and misfortune, and the mother's prayers that neither you nor yours shall ever require that public charity over which you preside. My object Gentlemen is to entreat that you would reconsider your determination-a determination which must have resulted from a mistaken apprehension of the facts. At least hear my story and then decide whether the boy is not entitled to this charity. My husband Mr. Fehrenbach was unfortunate and about the beginning of this year the Sheriff seized and sold out everything he possessed for debt leaving us destitute. To save his family from begging or starvation he consented that I should by the assistance of my brother in law Mr. Herman Knee open a small dry goods shop. Discontented however at being unable to obtain work he suddenly left the State about eight months ago leaving his wife and six children in want and wretchedness to [illegible] for themselves. I believe he went to New Orleans. I have heard so to my knowledge he has never been back since, and if has made any enquiries respecting his family I have never heard of them. I had and have no credit. Mr. Knee buys goods in his name and I repay him from the sales I make one half of the premises which I rent and let out and thus by a rigid

economy and ceaseless industry I have scarcely been able to shelter and feed my children. I have never received nor will I as long as I can work receive charity for myself. It has however never been offered, unless the suggestion made I presume in kindness by Mr. Loundes that I could apply to the poorhouse for bread may be considered an offer of Charity. I do not know that my feelings are more sensitive than others. I do believe the remark was meant not to offend but if I have prayed to you to take my boy to aid a deserted wife in living honestly, to assist a mother in saving her child from the ruin of a neglected education, to relieve her from a burden she felt she could not bear. Oh do not think that it was for the purpose of enabling her to seek charity for herself. It was to escape this mortification. It was to avoid this shame that I have solicited your charity towards my children. In my native land I was taught that poverty was not crime that to beg when one could work was dishonest and that the bread of charity was very bitter. I am now too old and too unwilling to unlearn this lesson. My children are yours. They are natives, they are southerners: and though their Father has forgot himself and deserted them this is their country. And though poor and friendless shall my son not be heard because a mothers tongue alone urges his claims. If poverty if destitution if perfect friendlessness avail my childs rights are they not great. Oh save him from being a curse to the soil that gave him birth and spare the mother from the anguish which the mother must endure at the moral debasement of her child. Be not offended at my language I am filled with anxiety: Again reject him and to whom shall he go. It has been said I have been supported by the contribution of german friends. No one ever loaned or offered to loan much less gave me a dollar since Mr. Fehrenbach left. Take my boy let him go with his brother and although I have myself and three children to support this relief will be encouragement to live in the fear of God.

Gentlemen excuse what has here been written which may be considered boldness and be assured/I am with consideration/of profound respect your/Petitioner/A.M. Fehrenbach

Even without punctuation, the letter reveals the desperation of an immigrant mother trying her level best to enable the survival of her family beset by hostile conditions she would never have envisioned. Her plight is confirmed by another letter, a second recommendation from John Phillips, who is now revealed as the Fehrenbach's landlord. It is dated November 5, 1844 and reads:

To the Commissioners of the Orphan House/ Gentlemen/

Having been requested by Mrs. A Fehrenbach to state for your information all that I know respecting her family and circumstances, I very cheerfully comply. My acquaintance with the Fehrenbachs commenced some six or eight years ago, Fehrenbach becoming the tenant of a house which was under my control as Agent for Mrs. Mills. He was in the habit of frequently consulting me respecting his affairs. During the last eighteen months he complained of the great difficulty he found in supporting his family and I thought he was often tipsy. In the early part of the year after he had been sold out by the sheriff, I urged him to leave the house as I appreciated he was not able to pay the rent. He refused to go, declaring he had no place on earth to which he could carry his family and his credit would not enable him to own a room. Soon after he called and told me he was going to run away. That he was miserably poor, that he could get no work and he could not endure the misery of seeing his children starve. He wept very bitterly and said as I was his only friend he trusted I would be kind to his family. He did not exactly know where he was going. He however spoke of going on the guard in New Orleans and of working at his trade, that being the watch making. I have never seen him since. I am confident that if he had ever returned he would have called on me. Mrs. Fehrenbach still continues to occupy the house, the rent having been greatly reduced from the fall of rents and at her earnest solicitation I see her often and I take great pleasure in expressing the high opinion which I entertain of her integrity and industry, and intelligence. She has six children, the eldest boy is bound an apprentice to Mr. Stein the watch maker, her second is in the Orphan House and she had four living with her. She hires or underleases the greater part of the premises and with the proceeds of her little shop and Mr. Knees assistance she is enabled to exist. She is miserably poor and with the exception of Mr. Knee friendless. If her son John Henry Frederick Fehrenbach was admitted into the Orphan Asylum it would be a great relief. It would certainly enable her to support herself and her other children with less slaving than what she is now compelled to undergo. It would however in a moral point of view be of still greater consequence. The boy is getting above her control and he will soon be selecting his associates and taking amusements where neither a mother's influence is felt or will be acknowledged. It is now that education is to establish his principles or if neglected he is to incur the fearful consequences resulting from allowing his pleasure to be ["the only" stricken out] law for his government. I have felt and still feel an interest in this family. I have always found Mrs. Fehrenbach a worthy woman: and her boys if not neglected will become useful citizens."

Another certificate is on record for John Henry Richard Fehrenbach, age 6, signed by John Phillips, [?] Biehling, and W. Heemsoth, pastor of the German congregation. A note reads: "Mrs. Fehrenbach/Nov 6. 1844 requesting the Board reconsider their decision in rejecting her application for the admission of her second son.// Nov 7 1844 Referred to Mr. [illegible] for special Inquiries // Nov 14 1844 Report of Mr. [illegible] favorable; Report adopted, and child admitted upon being properly bound by the Commissioners of the Poor." Anna Maria Fehrenbach's pleas thus did not fall on deaf ears.

But a year later, things changed dramatically. In a letter dated "Charleston October 30th, 1845" in a hand which does not resemble either of the other two letters signed by Anna Maria F., the abandoned mother wrote: "To the Hon. Commissioners of the Orphan House / Your Hon. Body had the kindness about a year ago to admit into the Orphan House two of my sons Nicholas and Richard, at a time when I was unfortunately reduced to needy circumstances. These circumstances having been greatly improved by the return of my husband, and feeling myself perfectly able to support my children, I would now respectfully request your permission for them to return home again, at the same time rendering to you my sincerest thanks for the timely aid afforded to my family./ I remain with feelings of the highest respect / Your obedient servant / Ann Fehrenbach." An attached note confirms the discharge of both children: "Mrs. Ann Fehrenbach/ Oct 30 1845/ applying for her two sons Nicholas and Rich. Fehrenbach to be delivered up to her/ Oct 30 1845 application granted."

The story of the Fehrenbachs is almost self-explanatory from this Charleston Orphan House record. In the thirteen years of their existence in their adopted city, life had not turned out well. With a growing family, the father was unable to find steady employment as a watchmaker, even though the eldest son was apprenticed in the same occupation, doubtless to an established competitor. Their poverty was real, and the husband deserted the family in search of some means of income by going west to New Orleans, a city with a significant German immigrant population. He returned a year later, somewhat restored, but not exactly economically stabilized. The wife survived by availing herself of the city's benevolence in pleading to have two of her sons indentured to its orphanage, where they would receive something of an education and the promise of release as productive members of the community. The two boys were there only briefly, and after the husband's return, were released back to the family. The mother's efforts to gain entry for her children into the Orphan House speak of her strong resistance to accepting charity, of her immigrant background that instilled in her certain lessons of life, of her untiring efforts to keep her and her children's heads above the waters of want and destitution, of her relying on family and her faith to see her through hard times. Her last request to the civic institution to return her children to her shows her still capable of hope that the family's situation might be salvaged and that better times lay ahead. Anna Maria seems to have had faith in her husband Nicholas's plans for the future.

But whatever blessings might have been anticipated in Nicholas's return from New Orleans, shortly thereafter the decision was made to fold the tent in Charleston. Sometime after 1845, Nicholas moved his family to Sheboygan, Wisconsin, a small town north of Milwaukee on the shore of Lake Michigan—distant shores indeed. Why? Opportunity of some sort must have beckoned, sufficient to warrant what would have been an arduous trip from the South Carolina Lowcountry: probably westward, possibly back to New Orleans, then up the Mississippi, then east from some point to Lake Michigan. In 1846, the town of Sheboygan was a village compared to Charleston, with only about four hundred residents, and as one brief sketch put it, "no churches, newspapers or passable roads." But Wisconsin was a magnet for German immigrants, and Milwaukee, fifty miles to the south, would soon develop into a "German Athens" in the Midwest, and Wisconsin, of all the states, would harbor the largest number of German immigrants in the latter part of the nineteenth century. Perhaps this large tide of Germans to the less settled environment in Wisconsin was what swept Nicholas Fehrenbach along: he purchased property in the Village of Sheboygan already in 1848, and the 1850 Census lists the entire family, comprised of Nicholas, 44, Watchmaker, with personal property worth $1,000; Anna, 44; Edward, 19, sailor [inaccurately reporting birth in the U.S.]; Nicholas, 17; Premos, 15; Richard, 12; Caroline, 8 [there is no mention of Hermann Heinrich nor of Adeline Catherina Mariana]. How successful the watchmaker was in Sheboygan is questionable: the couple had yet one more child, Wilhelm C., born in Sheboygan in March 1851. But during the ensuing decade the family broke apart. The 1860 Census shows Nicholas, sen. alone in Sheboygan, and almost tragically, he is listed as a "convict". Whether he was incarcerated and the nature of his crime is not known. In 1857 he gave power of attorney to an Edward Gaertner to sell part of the property he had purchased in 1848, and in 1873 he sold another property in Sheboygan for one dollar. There is no record of his death and burial either in Sheboygan or Charleston. It seems most likely that he died a pauper in Wisconsin, having abandoned, or been abandoned by, his family many years earlier.

1860 WI census

1860 Census page indicating Nicholas Fehrenbach, sen. as a convict.

Sometime after the birth of Wilhelm, Anna Maria gave up the struggle and returned to Charleston with her family in tow. In 1856, Nicholas, jun. was married to a young widow, Antoinette Mehrtens, née Frank, at St. Matthew's in Charleston: witnesses were his uncle, Frederick Eduard Schroeder, and Jean Magnus Fredsberg. He is listed in the St. Matthew's records as "Restauranteur dahier" (local restaurant owner). By 1860 he operated the Teetotaler Restaurant adjacent to Institute Hall where the Ordinance of Secession was signed in December of 1860.[38] He and his wife had three children, Ida Juliana [b. 1857],

---

[38]   Robert N.S. Whitelaw and Alice F. Levkoff's photographic history of Charleston, *Charleston Come Hell or High Water: A History in Photographs* (Columbia, SC: R.L. Bryan Co., 1975) includes a picture of Nicolaus Fehrenbach jun.'s restaurant in the block of Meeting Street north of Chalmers St. In his *Charleston! Charleston!,* Fraser writes: "On December 17 more than 160 delegates elected from across South Carolina convened in Columbia to decide whether the state would secede. The twenty-three representatives from Charleston comprised the largest single delegation and like the others, they were primarily a wealthy, middle-aged, native-born, slaveholding elite of planters and lawyers. Following an outbreak of smallpox in Columbia, the convention reassembled in Charleston, where on December 20 in St. Andrew's Hall the delegates unanimously adopted the Ordinance of Secession from the Union. In the evening they signed it at Institute Hall. The news 'spread through the city like wild-fire,' the *Mercury* reported. 'The church bells rang. . . . artillery salutes were soon . . . thundering . . . union flags were . . . thrown to the breeze . . . volunteers . . . donned their uniforms . . .' An Englishman in Charleston described two young women of Charleston's upper class as 'ardent secessionists' who, when asked what would happen if the federal government encouraged slave revolts, answered: 'If the slaves rose, we should

Clarence Nicholas [b. 1859], and Edward Nicolaus [b. 1860], and after almost a decade, another daughter Linda [b. 1869]. The two sons died before the age of two and the daughter Ida is likely the Ida Fehrenbach who was married in Wisconsin in 1877. The youngest daughter Linda would marry a New Yorker by the name of Weston L. White, and her widowed mother would live with her and die in her household in Hartford, CT in 1903. Ida also lived in the White household according to the 1900 Census, obviously widowed.

The Fehrenbach jun. family in Charleston achieved some status in the German immigrant community. It was in the Fehrenbach home that the famous Heinrich Wieting breathed his last in 1868: it was not by coincidence that the ship captain who brought so many Germans to Charleston should be hospitalized in the home of an important member of the ethnic community and who was, as well, a fellow *Geestendorfer*. The 1870 Census shows the household of Nicholas, aged 36, owner of a barroom, Johanna A, aged 38, keeping house, Ida, aged 12, Linda, aged 6 [actually an infant about one year old!], William [the brother born in Wisconsin], aged 19, a clerk in a store, and Anna, aged 67, "at home". Three others are listed, none of whom are the age of a brother or a child, two of whom are listed as domestic servants, one black, the other a native of Bremen. They are residents of Ward 1 and neighbors of the Danish Consul, C. Wunderlich. Nicholas was sufficiently established that he could buy pew No.49 [Nos. 1-84 were sold either as a whole or half] in the new St. Matthew's Church on King Street in 1872, and the church records indicate that his mother, Mrs. M. Fehrenbach, gave a brass baptismal bowl. (Butt 1940)

Nicholas jun. survived his friend Wieting's death by twenty-three years, dying in Charleston in 1891, at age 58. His occupation at that time was given as *Planter*. Some seven years his senior, his widow outlived him by twelve years and is buried in Bethany Cemetery in Charleston, her remains returned to Charleston from Connecticut. There is something more to learn about the *restauranteur* Nicholas Fehrenbach, jun.—but in a later chapter.

The senior Fehrenbachs' experience articulates the humbling tale of an immigrant family that was able to achieve a degree of success only in the second generation. The elder couple would not have been among those sending enthusiastic letters back home, encouraging others to come and enjoy the good life in Charleston. Their American existence was a struggle from beginning to end—their story representative of one that was doubtless repeated more often than not.

---

kill them like so many snakes.' Eighty-two brown aristocrats dispatched a message to the mayor of Charleston: 'We are by birth citizens of South Carolina, in our veins is the blood of the white race in some half, in others much more, our attachments are with you.'" (Fraser 1991, 244).

—HERMANN KNEE AND FAMILY—

Other members of the family had more luck, or managed to make their mark by different means. In 1834 Johann Rosenbohm's sister Catharina had married Hermann Knie [once in Charleston, the name was usually spelled as Knee], a native of the small Lower Saxony town of Böcken. They immigrated to Charleston shortly thereafter, and their children were born in Charleston: Johann in 1836, Julia, in 1841, Hermann Carsten in 1844, Nicolaus Heinrich in 1846, Friederich Eduard in 1847, and finally, Clarence Andreas in 1851. Two of the boys died in infancy so that by 1850 the Census shows the household consisting of Hermann, 47, Catherina, 34, with children John, 14, Julia, 9, and Hermann, 7. Friederich had been born, but for whatever reason is not listed. Additionally, Catharina's father Caspar, 75, her sister Adelheid Bequest, 40, and the latter's daughter Adeline Bequest, 16, plus the man she would marry, Frederick Schroeder, 27, were members of this large household. Hermann is listed as "Shop Keeper" with real estate valued at $3,000. The extended family was living in the house on Church Street that originally had been purchased by Catharina's brother Johann and which he had vacated when he left Charleston in 1839. As mentioned above, Johann's widowed father Caspar had taken up residence there when he came to Charleston in 1841, and when the house was put up for auction in 1845, Johann's brother-in-law Hermann Knee had bought it.

Hermann Knee somehow managed the transition to his adopted community better than his brother-in-law Nicholas Fehrenbach. There are seventeen transactions under his name recorded in the Register of Mesne Conveyance in Charleston between the years 1845 and 1878, indicating that there was little grass growing under his feet from the time he arrived until he died. He was a known entity in the German community, having been accepted into the German Friendly Society already in December of 1836. He was a contemporary of the dynamic John Andreas Wagener and was involved with him as a founding member of the German Evangelical St. Matthew's Church in 1840. The Fehrenbach story indicates that he was a stabilizing force for the entire family, for example, providing the means for his sister-in-law Anna Maria to support her family while her husband was seeking his undetermined fortune elsewhere. He was a vital member of the Lutheran church community and was a key supporter of the German settlement in Walhalla, South Carolina, which Wagener and the St. Matthew's congregation organized for settlement by the increasing numbers of German immigrants to Charleston. Knee was, in fact, one of four committee members sent in 1849 to examine the land of Colonel Joseph Grisham in Pickens District that the German Colonization Society had negotiated to purchase. He was sufficiently sold on the idea of Walhalla that he was one of the first to purchase land in the town and establish a business there. In 1856 he was elected as a warden for the town after its incorporation by the South Carolina Legislature the previous year.

The senior Knees spent the war years in Walhalla, while their two elder sons were in Confederate service. After the war, both Hermann and his son Hermann Carsten were registered on the voter list in Oconee and Pickens Counties in 1866 and 1868, and Hermann was sufficiently prominent in the town's business community to be elected again one of six wardens in 1867. Hermann sen. died sometime before the end of the decade: a June 1871 entry in the Minutes of the German Friendly Society lists "Mrs. Knee" as one of fourteen "widows of former members" receiving a $60.00 pension from the Society. Her death was reported in Melchers's *Deutsche Zeitung* June 29, 1885. Benefitting from advantageous connections to other immigrant leaders, Herman and Catharina Knee were able to make a life for themselves that would have justified their earlier decision to emigrate: their immigration to Charleston and their faith in their ability to ground a community in upstate South Carolina—their courage as pioneers—can legitimately be described as a success story.

—FREDERICK EDUARD AND ADELINE SCHROEDER—

As indicated earlier, the 1850 Census showed Hermann Knee's sixteen-year-old niece [by marriage], Adeline Bequest, living in the Knee household, together with her mother, Adelheid Bequest—Catharina Knee and Johann Rosenbohm's sister—and Adeline's fiancé, Frederick Schroeder. In February 1852, Adeline and Frederick were married at St. Matthew's. Five children were born to them in the decade between 1853 and 1863, with only one, their son Julius—born in the first year of the Civil War—surviving to adulthood. Frederick was a native of the village of Ovelgönne bei Brake, about three miles northwest of Worpswede, not far from Geestendorf where Adeline was born. In some way he was acquainted with the Bequest widow and daughter prior to their emigration, and it is likely that he followed Adeline and her mother to Charleston where they had the family connection.

The story of the Schroeders as immigrants in Charleston is unremarkable, yet rather poignant. He was a merchant and operated a cigar store. As a family, the parents produced and lost four of their five children, all during the turbulent decade leading up to the Civil War when Charleston was a hotbed of political unrest. The circumstances they faced would not have been what they had anticipated in coming to America. "For the first time since the early years of the century, the city was again attracting Irish and German immigrants, but some Charlestonians distrusted these working-class immigrants who, they believed, were 'a worthless, unprincipled class . . . enemies to our peculiar institution [slavery] . . . and ever ready to form combinations against . . . the peace of the commonwealth.' Many white working-class women competed with black women for jobs as maids, and white male workers repeatedly complained that the city government failed to enforce laws prohibiting slaves hiring themselves out . . . . The competition between recent immigrants and blacks for work sometimes became vicious" (Fraser 1991, 227). As the owner of a cigar store, Frederick Schroeder would not have been in competition with a free black, but his choice of this occupation is a good example of the immigrant finding a niche position in a uniquely constrained labor market.

It was not only the choice of a line of work, but also the challenges of the social and cultural context that would challenge the immigrant. In 1846, the U.S. declared war on Mexico, and the ensuing arguments about permitting or banning slavery in the territories acquired during the war swept the matter of slavery from under the rug into the political arena. Then in 1849, thirty-six black inmates escaped from the Charleston workhouse:

> Most were immediately recaptured and tried the following day, and the ringleaders and two others were sentenced to death by hanging. But several escapees remained at large and hysteria swept the city. A mob gathered before Calvary Church, a nearly completed Afro-American church on Beaufain St. that white Episcopalians in the city were assisting in building. Some among the mob called it the 'nigger church' and they wanted to destroy it. Urging on 'the rabble of the city' were prominent citizens who sought, one observer noted, 'to arouse the fears of a community which had not forgotten the events of 1822.' They worried that as a meeting place for both free blacks and slaves, Calvary Church might come to threaten the 'public peace and order' (Fraser 1991, 228).[39]

While living in the Knee household in 1850, the soon-to-be-married couple would surely have been witness to the ceremonial funeral in Charleston of South Carolina's most famous John C. Calhoun: "Charleston was draped in mourning on April 25-26, 1850, for the funeral of John C. Calhoun, perhaps the most elaborate ceremony of its kind the city ever witnessed. Federal and state troops assembled in Marion Square in front of the Citadel to lead the funeral car, modeled on Napoleon's, which was flanked by a guard of honor and accompanied by distinguished pallbearers like Jefferson Davis as it moved through the streets to City Hall. Here the body lay in state for a day until interred in St. Philip's Cemetery. Boundary Street was soon renamed Calhoun. Admirers in Charleston raised $27,000 to pay off Calhoun's debts, enabling his

---

[39]   This is the church that Jane Thompson's rector, the Rev. Paul Trapier, was instrumental in founding. His role in that venture is detailed in a later chapter. See p. 132.

lowcountry-born wife to keep their upcountry plantation" (Fraser 1991, 228). Calhoun had been the state's most vocal advocate of nullification, an issue and a cause that would re-ignite the coals of secession before the end of the decade. His funeral involved—either as spectator or participant—almost everybody who was anybody, including members of the older and the more-recently-formed German fraternal or civic organizations. Nonetheless, these aspects of the Charleston context would have been unsettling to any German immigrant trying to get a footing in the city, and only those in the ethnic community who were completely acculturated could participate enthusiastically in the ceremony without questioning what the civic crowd-scene really meant.

This was a time when Charleston seemed afloat in its mid-century glory. The elite classes were enjoying themselves immensely, with parties in grand houses and strolls along the Battery, while the northern extent of the peninsula, the Neck, recently incorporated, was occupied by the less fortunate. During the same period, however, "the publication of two books . . . profoundly influenced public opinion in both the North and the South: *Uncle Tom's Cabin* and *The Pro-Slavery Argument*. The former was the classic attack on slavery and the latter its classic defense. *The Pro-Slavery Argument* contained essays by prominent Southerners quoting Aristotle, the Bible, and purportedly scientific evidence proving that blacks were inherently inferior. The book was published in Charleston" (Fraser 1991, 232).

As if the political turmoil in the air were not sufficiently stressful, "in the summer of 1854 a hurricane lashed through the city, flooding the streets, and yellow-fever-carrying mosquitoes returned bringing a virulent epidemic. While the disease raged in the city during the late summer, the Charleston press advised that 'no real dangers exist' . . . but from mid-August to mid-November 627 persons died." (Fraser 1991, 233-34) The Schroeders might well have thought they would have experienced fewer traumas had they stayed in their Hanoverian homeland where hurricanes and yellow fever would not have threatened to destroy them or their young daughter.

After the mid-1850s, just when the Schroeder couple was beginning married life as immigrant residents, Charleston began to suffer an economic downturn: "The economic downturn coupled with the steady stream of immigrants, sailors, and vagrants who straggled into the city seeking work caused growing unemployment. By the mid-1850s approximately 40 percent of the white population of nearly 9,000 were recent Irish or German immigrants. From 1850 to 1856 the number of inmates in the city's Poor House rose from 691 to 1,363 and the ratio of foreign-born to native reached seven to one. Class divisions became as obvious as racial divisions. Economically most whites living in the city had more in common with blacks than with the white elite" (Fraser 1991, 235).

By the late 1850s, Charleston's leaders made a concerted effort to clean up the city's act, and indeed, a significant amount of money was spent in beautifying certain sections, although nothing seemed to cure the city of the yellow fever pestilence. In 1860, Frederick Law Olmstead claimed that Charleston had "the worst climate for unacculturated whites of any town in the United States." And by the time the war was imminent, Charleston had come to resemble a military garrison:

> With a population of 40,522 in 1859—it had declined about 2,500 since the beginning of the decade—the city of Charleston ranked twenty-second in the nation, although in manufacturing it ranked only eighty-fifth. The most populous of the South Atlantic ports and the major distribution center for the state, Charleston more closely resembled a modern police state than any other city in the nation. Frederick Law Olmstead observed that 'the cannon in position on the parade ground, the citadel . . . with its martial ceremonies, the frequent parades of militia . . . the numerous armed police, might lead one to imagine that the town was in a state of siege or revolution' (Fraser 1991, 241).

It was, of course, during these times that Captain Wieting was unloading literally *boatloads* of German immigrants onto the wharves in Charleston, the large numbers of newcomers causing tension with the native whites and their slave labor force. For the most part, however, the Schroeders and their German neighbors living in the unsettled and ever-changing Charleston scene, kept their heads down and minded their business. Frederick and Adeline would have witnessed the first action in the Civil War—the bombardment of Fort Sumter in the Charleston harbor—although that famous first shot would likely have been more worrisome for the immigrant than celebratory, as it was for the native-born. The couple had buried three children by 1860, and Adeline would have been pregnant with their fourth child during the critical months leading up the action in April of 1861. Julius Nicholas was born just two months later, but Adeline herself would die in 1864 before the war was over. The family belonged to the St. Matthew's congregation, and Frederick served early on as financial secretary to the Church. He was among the original pew holders [No. 107] when the newly built church's pews were sold to members of the congregation in 1872. The 1900 Census shows him heading a household with his son Julius [also a "cigar dealer"] and wife, and four grandchildren between the ages 5 and 10. That census record of 1900 indicates that Frederick Schroeder had immigrated to Charleston in 1849 and had lived in the city for fifty-one years. When he died a widower in 1901, he was living at the same address—111 Wentworth Street—where he had lived for some time with his mother-in-law and where she had died six years previously. The entire family is buried in Bethany Cemetery in a prominent plot close to the cemetery's entrance gate. A laurel crown sits atop a broken obelisk marking the grave of Adeline.

The Schroeder memorials at Bethany Cemetery, including gravestones for both parents and children, as well as Adeline's grandfather, Caspar Rosenbohm. Adeline's monument with the crown atop the broken obelisk suggests her heroic, but shortened life.

VI

Main Lines, Two Of Three: 1840-1860

For those immigrants who had already arrived, the twenty years prior to the outbreak of the Civil War, despite stressful political tensions, was a period of relative stability for settling in, certainly in contrast to the five years that loomed on the horizon. Johann Rosenbohm had given up on Charleston and moved to New York. His married sisters were having their children—and burying many of them—while their husbands tried to make an economic success of their decision to immigrate to this southern city. Jane Thompson already had four children by 1840. Charleston had experienced cholera epidemics, "great" fires, and a number of other scourges. The city had made strides in public education by founding the High School of Charleston in 1839, and St. Matthew's Lutheran Church was established by 1840 through the dedication and energy of individuals leading the community of German immigrants. Even before Captain Wieting would be delivering large numbers of additional German immigrants to Charleston, there was a steady stream of German and Irish settlers who would attempt to insert themselves into the slave-based economy and the free black labor force. Among those arriving to begin life anew in the early 1840s were two German families that would establish blood lines lasting into the present—the Webers and Struhses.

—THE WEBER LINE—

In contrast to the other lines, the Weber family is the only one that does not derive from ancestors native to what had become the North German Kingdom of Hanover. The records of births and confirmations of St. Matthew's

Lutheran Church show two families with the name of *Weber* as members of that congregation, one Johann Weber and his wife Friederike, née Geschwein, and a Peter Weber and his wife Susanne, née Wastier [or Vastier]. The records specify the birthplace for both men as "Billigheim, Rheinpfalz, Bayern", suggesting that the two were brothers. Although Bavaria in the south was a predominantly Catholic area, the brothers were both Protestants. But like everyone in the area, they would have been subject to the emigration stimuli of overpopulation, land partibility, and unemployment that characterized the *push* in the southern German states in the early decades of the nineteenth century.

The essential details of the life of Johann and his wife are delineated in the St. Matthew's records and in Charleston city directories. The church record indicates that Friederike Geschwein was from Wulsdorf, a small village within the jurisdiction of Geestemünde. She and Johann were married at St. Matthew's on March 21, 1844, shortly after their immigration to Charleston. Coming from two widely separated regions in Germany, it seems unlikely that they were acquainted prior to emigration, rather that they were singles who met only after arriving in Charleston. Since so many in the German community in Charleston were from the closely connected region in northwestern Hanover, Friederike may have been following a pre-established chain of acquaintances or relatives. Johann was undoubtedly following his brother Peter. Peter Weber and his wife had their first child in Charleston before Johann and Friederike became parents: the latter couple's daughter, Susanna Elisabeth, was born March 1, 1845 and baptized at St. Matthew's with Peter and Susanne Weber as godparents—another indication that the two men were siblings and that the godparents were already resident in the community. The daughter's name was surely chosen in honor of her aunt.

Johann/John Weber worked in Charleston as a boot/shoemaker. Margaret Motes's redaction of the immigrant population in the 1850 census shows the household of John Weber consisting of John, 38, Friederika, 26, and C. Muller Weber, 25, another shoemaker from Germany. (Motes 2005, 136-37) The 1860 census confirms a bootmaker John Webber, 49, and his wife, 35, with two children, John, 4, and Virginia, a 3-month-old infant—both parents born in Germany, the children in South Carolina. The evidence of a relatively small household in 1860 is supported by the church record that shows that the couple's daughter Susanna had died in July of 1846, just a little over 16 months old, and that a son, Johann Heinrich, born at the end of March 1846, had lived only five days.

The city directories for the years 1849-1855 show the family living at 119 King Street. Twenty years later, the 1874-75 directory lists the widow [Johann Weber had died in 1872]—Mrs. F. Weber—selling "fruits" and residing at 86 King Street; her son John is listed as a "clerk". Four years later, "Mrs.

Frederica Weber" is still dealing in "fruits", but has moved to a neighboring house at 89 King Street, and John, jun. is working as a clerk for J. H. Hesse and "boards" at his mother's address. In 1881, Frederica has expanded her business somewhat and is selling "varieties"; John is clerking for H. B. Schroder. The 1882 directory shows her still operating a "variety store", and John has become a clerk at Lehmkuhl & Ohlandt and still living at home.

The family's story sounds typically unremarkable: an eked-out existence, acculturation within Charleston's sometimes glorious, sometimes troubled, antebellum history, survival during the years of the Civil War, a widow and son [the fate of the daughter Virginia is unknown], muddling through the years of Reconstruction before disappearing from the scene in the fog of Charleston's postbellum period. Coincidentally, the Johann Webers had begun their Charleston life in the same year that Anna Maria Fehrenbach was deserted by her husband and pleaded for assistance from the Charleston Orphan House, and their first daughter was born into the St. Matthew's congregation in the same year the Knees acquired Johann Rosenbohm's house on Church Street. While Johann and Friederike Weber were doubtless acquainted with those other members of the German congregational community, they would hardly have imagined at the time that they would play a supporting role in this immigrant family's long history.

At this point, it is the story of Johann's brother Peter that is of greater interest. The St. Matthew's record for Peter shows six children born to him and his wife Susanne Wastier/Vastier. Susanne, unlike Johann's wife Friederike, was also from southern Germany, from Wachenheim, a town not very distant [within 5 miles] from that of her husband's Billigheim [Wachenheim lies north of the town of Landau, close to Bad Dürkheim; Billigheim lies south of Landau]. And unlike his brother and his wife, Peter and Susanne likely emigrated as a married couple: they were from neighboring villages in southern Germany, and there is no record of their marriage in the St. Matthew's records. Their first child, Anna Maria, was born October 14, 1843, suggesting that her parents would have been married by the end of 1842. In any case, Peter and Susanne Weber had six children baptized at St. Matthew's: Anna Maria, Martin [b. November 26, 1845], Elisabetha Susanna [b. April 16, 1848], Heinrich Wilhelm [b. May 20, 1850], Georg Karl [b. August 23, 1852], and August [b. September 8, 1855]. The record for this family is otherwise rather sparse: the city directory for 1849 lists a Peter Webber at 13 Queen Street. The directories for 1852 and 1855 show Peter Weber working as a tavern keeper at 33 Queen Street, residing there as well. The family is noticeably absent from subsequent directories, and the St. Matthew's records offer no further mentions.

If the Charleston record appears inordinately scant, Peter Weber's genealogical heritage is in the records of the *Evangelische Kirche Billigheim*

[Bavaria, Kr. Bergzabern]. The evidence there indicates that Peter was born to Johannes Weber and his wife, Elizabetha, née Paul on January 12, 1813. The parents were married in 1808, and Johannes died in 1815—two years after his son had been born. Johannes was the son of Adam Weber and his wife Magdalena, née Blum. The record shows Johannes's wife, Elizabetha Paul, as the daughter of Peter Paul and Elizabetha, née Niederhauser. These records establish the immigrant Peter Weber's paternal and maternal lines back to the middle of the eighteenth century in Bavaria.

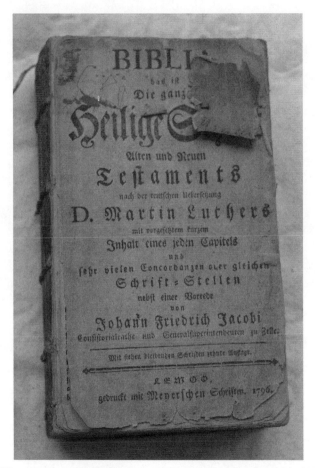

Bible published 1796 belonging to Adam Weber. In possession of his great-great-great-great-grandaughter, Martha Weber Miller.

Less information is known about Peter's wife, Susanne Vastier. Likewise a Protestant, her birth can be confirmed in the record of the *Evangelisch-Reformierte Kirche Wachenheim* [Bavaria, Kr. Dürkheim]: she was born March 5, 1828 to Jakob Wastier and wife Elizabetha, née Rattinger.

The record indicates that Jacob was a vintner and that both he and his wife were natives of the town/village.[40]

Of the six children born to the couple between 1843 and 1855, only two survived to adulthood. The daughter Anna Maria would marry another German immigrant, Charles Plath, a year after the Civil War ended, and her younger brother Charles (Georg Karl) would follow the Fehrenbach boys into the Charleston Orphan House. Peter Weber was dead by 1856 and his wife by 1859. One can only ponder how modestly they had survived economically by keeping a tavern, and how minimally successful they might have felt for getting two of their four children through infancy. Peter was nonetheless an active participant in the ethnic community: he belonged to a number of the German associations and served on committees in several of them.

With whatever capital it took to open a tavern, the immigrant couple must have decided that there was a market among the increasing numbers of their fellow European newcomers who would need to quench the stresses of immigration in such a public house. The Queen and Meeting Street address would have been a prime location—right in the middle of town. There was something entrepreneurial in Peter's decision to open a tavern: in 1850 there were only some 20-odd immigrants running taverns in Charleston; in contrast, his bootmaker brother Johann was one of about eighty shodding the feet of the city's inhabitants. (Motes 2005, 176-81) Neither's occupation, however, would lead to riches or social advancement.

Those immigrants prone to dull their suffering with drink—as was indeed the case with Nicholas Fehrenbach, sen.—would soon draw the attention of subscribers to the national Know-Nothing movement, a kind of nativist reaction to the increasing number of foreigners populating American cities. The movement disturbed the 1850s and was characterized by agitation for temperance, an intolerance of Catholics, and an ethic of extreme Puritanism. Bell argues, however, that the Know-Nothings had little success in Charleston: "In the city election of November 1855, their candidates for mayor and city council seats were soundly defeated by candidates of the South States Rights Party. Their failure to secure even a single alderman's seat on the city council signaled the virtual end of the American party in Charleston." He claims that Charleston's Germans were somewhat immune to what was happening within the larger American context: "Charleston's citizens were too tolerant of both

---

40   It should be noted that the orthographical change from *W* to *V*—a switch between the Wachenheim record and the St. Matthew's record—would be a logical and likely result from pronouncing the name in an English-speaking context, even though the Charleston scribe at St. Matthew's would more than likely have been of German origin: the immigrant would pronounce the *W* of her name as a *V*, and the [possibly] English-speaking scribe would use *V* to record the spoken consonant.

Catholics and foreigners to be swayed into the nativist camp. For the remainder of the decade, Charleston's Germans were not attacked in the press, either by name or implication. Charleston's Germans were more politically affiliated with other citizens of the city—and had stated that loyalty in writing. The city's German population had tacit permission, therefore, to be, and remain, German—as long as they first became Charlestonians" (Bell 1996, 225).

All the white noise of the era, however, took back seat to the evolving relationship between blacks and whites. The remnants of nullification still hung in the sultry air, brought to the forefront with the passing of John C. Calhoun and his 1850 funeral celebration in Charleston. The emerging abolitionist movement in the North elicited defensive reactions in the South, and the whole matter of slavery would lie just under the surface of everyday life until it erupted in 1860 with secession and the march to war. For the immigrant, these were times to keep one's head down and struggle in whatever occupational capacity one could best manage. Most European immigrants to cities such as Charleston would have left *land*—whether heritable or just occupied—behind and were now untied, unconnected, and insecure in their urban settings. Employment was paramount, for without it there was little recourse beyond the charity of the host citizenry, and that could indeed be exhausted. The very likelihood of unemployment because of the increasing numbers of German immigrants vying for livelihood with both enslaved and free blacks, as well as with other immigrant groups, led the leaders of St. Matthew's to create the German Colonization Society and to establish the Lutheran community in Walhalla, SC in 1850.

It is safe to say that Peter and Johann Weber never assumed any leadership role in the Charleston German community other than Peter's involvement in a number of ethnic associations: their names are not listed among the pew holders at St. Matthew's nor on the roll of the German Friendly Society. They did not move to Walhalla, but held out in the Lowcountry until their respective ends—the one, fortunate in a way to miss the imminent hostilities, the other, surviving through the war and halfway through the new order of Reconstruction. It was nonetheless the accomplishment of Peter and his wife, with the assistance of Johann and Friederike, that the Weber lineage was carried through their son, Georg Karl Weber, into succeeding generations so that it is still present in the Charleston community.

As noted earlier, Peter and Susanne's son Georg Karl/Charles landed in the Charleston orphanage soon after the untimely death of his parents. He was admitted on March 13, 1862 at the tender age of nine by his uncle, John Weber. The Orphan House records indicate that he was born October 23, 1852 in Charleston,[41] that on admission he was living on Trapman Street, and that he was Protestant. His entry into the orphanage occurred just one month short of the first anniversary of the Civil War's onset, and he spent the next five years there before he was released in November of 1867 when the war was over.

A close look at the Orphan House documents reveals details pertinent to Charles's story. The records include: (1) the application by Johann Weber to admit Charles to the Orphanage. In titled columns across a ledger-like page it reads:

- **Name of Applicant**: [handwritten] John Weber
- **Settled Place of abode**: [handwritten] 556 King St [this address is not consistent with the city directory listing in 1851, but is likely the more accurate]
- **Name of the Child**: [handwritten, in same hand] Charles Weber [underneath and in a different hand and different ink] nephew of the applicant
- **Age**: [in different hand and ink, but same as previous column, but in German, "9 Jaren 4 Monats boren 23 October 1852"
- **Sex**: [handwritten in hand of first and second column] male
- **Place of Nativity**: [handwritten, same] Charleston
- **Present place of residence in the city**: [handwritten, same] at Mrs J.H. Sassard [the "ss" is formed with a "scharfes s" [ß] indicating that the writer is of German heritage], Trapmann near Broad
- **If possessed of, or interested in any and what property:** [handwritten, same] abt $20.-
- **Religious Denomination**: [handwritten, same] Protestant

The application form stipulates that it was to be accompanied by recommendations from two or more inhabitants of Charleston and be countersigned by an Alderman of the ward in which the applicant resided. The application was duly signed by D. H. Amme, Th. Steiber, G. Chas Schwetzerd, and Henry Schwettmann—all members of the German immigrant community. Another handwritten document, an informal note, suggests that it was John Weber filling in the application form and only once falling into a German orthographical convention [writing Mrs. Sassard's name with the German ß],

---

[41]   The birthdate for Charles in the orphanage record matches the one for Georg Karl in the St. Matthew's record but for the difference in the months, the one claiming the birth month as August, the other, October. The church record is likely the more accurate. The August 1852 date, however, contradicts the date engraved on his headstone in Bethany Cemetery: that date is in error and was based on insufficient documentation when the headstone was placed on the lot much later by Charles's granddaughter.

while it was an official of the Orphan House entering the additional information regarding the relationship and birthdate in what is clearly a German hand. It is the latter's note that reads: "Application of John Weber for the admission of his nephew Charles Weber aged 9 years 4 mo.—27 Feb 1862, referred to [illegible]; March 13, 1862. Report favorable; ordered that the boy be received upon being bound according to law." The handwriting and ink on this document match that of the additional writer on the application form. (2) a handwritten statement by an official of the orphanage explaining the context of John Weber's application: "The lad Charles Weber is an orphan, for some time past supported by the applicant who is his uncle, but who from some cause has recently withheld his aid, and consequently the lad is thrown for support upon his sister, whose entire means consists of $6—a month, her wages. The sister is anxious that the lad be received into the house and the VC so recommends upon the usual terms." Initials follow as signature: "J. T.", a match for *James Tupper* who signed the indenture form for the Commissioners [here as "Vice Commissioner" (VC)]. (3) the *Indenture* itself, a printed form with blanks filled in, the first part of which transfers Charles into the care and supervision of the Commissioners of the Orphan House. This upper half of the form, dated March 13, 1862, states that Charles Weber, age nine years, "by and with the consent of John Weber, his uncle, hath placed and bound himself 'as an Apprentice for Education' to the Commissioners of the Orphan House . . . until he shall be of sufficient age to be bound an apprentice to such profession, trade or occupation, as may be suited to his genius and inclination, and from thence to dwell, continue and serve with such person to whom these Indentures shall be transferred . . . and which will be completed and ended on . . . 13 March 1874." The form bears the signatures of John Weber and several others, and includes an *X* [his mark] through the name "Charles Weber". The bottom half of the form is the indenture releasing Charles in 1867 [November 7th] to the custody of Charles Plath of Charleston. This is also signed, in this instance by "C. Webber" and Charles Plath. (4) a handwritten letter, dated Charleston, October 31, 1867, signed by Charles Plath and M. Plath [unedited]: "To/the Resp. Commissioners/of the/ Charleston Orphan House/Gentlemen/The humble undersigned, Sister and Brother in Law of the Orphan 'Charles Weber' (a Son of the deceased Parents Peter Weber & Wife) are desireous and humble praying, for releasing of the said Orphan 'Charles Weber' from the highly respected and Noble Institution, and the humble petitioner would take him to there own house, sending him for one year to the German School, for learning the German language, and after this time we will trye for a Apprenticeship of any resp. Mechanical Business. // In the hope, that the Resp. Commissioners may grant there humble petition, and we ever would remaining most thankfully with all our heart, as well as praying to our Lord God for his kindly Blessings to this Noble Institution/ We are remaining Gentlemen/ Yours/ Charles Plath,/M. Plath, born Weber." (5) a short handwritten document, dated November 7, 1867, recommending the release of Charles to his brother-in-law: "the Committee on [illegible] respectfully report that the applicant married the sister of Charles Weber: they have no children and the sister is anxious to have her brother. The applicant is a mechanic and seems to be an industrious man: he is well recommended. It is recommended that Charles Weber be delivered to his brother in law Charles Plath." There are two signatures, neither fully legible, and the notation "Adopted 7 Nov 1867".

These documents are fairly self-explanatory and objectively describe the course of Charles Weber's youth. Records at Charleston's Bethany Cemetery [purchased by St. Matthew's in 1856] indicate that Peter Weber died in January of 1856, less than a year after his son August was born [September 8, 1855] and that Susanne, his wife, died three years later on April 25, 1859. Although the records exist at Bethany, neither Peter nor Susanne is buried there. Their resting place was likely in the church's first cemetery—Hampstedt (Hampstead)—purchased in 1841 for German victims of yellow fever, but which no longer exists. When his mother died, Charles would have been only 6 ½ years old. The cause of the parents' deaths is not known, nor is it known what became of Charles's brothers Martin, Heinrich, and August: in all likelihood they died in infancy and were buried at Hampstead. There is only a single St. Matthew's record indicating that the infant daughter Elizabetha Suzanna died in 1848, aged 4 months. Importantly, however, the church records reveal that Charles's sister Anna Maria, his elder by nine years, married Karl Heinrich Plath on February 22, 1866. Karl Heinrich Plath was from Rostock, Mecklenburg, was some nine years Anna Maria's senior, and was employed in Charleston as a carpenter (*Zimmermann*). There is a record of a Carl Plath, aged 21, arriving in New York on the *Rhine* from Hamburg on May 30, 1853.

From all these records, it becomes clear that after his parents' death, Charles was taken in by his uncle Johann, but either because of the war or the financial strain on the bootmaker's household [Johann and Friederike had lost two children early on, but at this point had their 6-year-old son and a 2-year-old daughter] the uncle was forced to put him into the orphanage. As in the case of the Fehrenbach children, this was a customary course for parents or guardians at a time when, for many immigrants, life would have been a hand-to-mouth existence and when the orphanage was Charleston's pre-eminent charity, commissioned by the State early in the city's history to take care of the indigent and frequently orphaned populace. A child was entered because there was little other recourse, once there was well taken care of and educated, and was released only when arrangements could be made by family or the Commissioners themselves to insure that the individual would be educated or trained so that s/he would be gainfully employed and become an upstanding citizen of the community. About the time Charles was entered,

[a]fter extensive remodeling and additions, the Orphan House contained 130 dormitory rooms, large play, school, and dining rooms, and a hospital ward, all heated by steam. It was the largest building in the city, and by the end of the decade [1850-60] some 300 orphans were housed there. The towering cupola supported a statue of Charity and held the city's massive fire-alarm bell. The commissioners of the Orphan House expected the orphans to follow the moral code they demanded of their families and slaves. Between 1790 and the 1850s the commissioners rescued nearly 2,000 children from abuse and neglect, providing them with a good diet, a basic education, strict supervision, and safe areas for recreation. Over the years former inmates wrote that they appreciated the commissioners 'acting the part of fathers' and numerous former inmates became successful. The orphanage's reputation as an institution that reflected the citizens' generosity and social conscience became increasingly important to an elite that was being denounced for the cruelties of slavery (Fraser 1991, 237-38).

Charles would have remained in the orphanage until he was 21 had not his sister and brother-in-law petitioned to have him released into their care five years after he had been taken in. It was of course only two years after his mother had died that the Civil War had begun, and Charleston, while never an actual battleground in the war, was for two years under siege and bombardment and would become a scene of complete devastation for those remaining in the city. The war was well under way by the time Charles Weber entered the orphanage, and in many ways he was fortunate to have been a ward there for the duration of the hostilities. Through the effort and monetary means of George Trenholm, a pillar of commercial Charleston and a shipping magnate who would become the secretary of the Confederate Treasury, the entire orphanage was evacuated in 1863 and removed to what was considered a safer location in Orangeburg, northwest of the city. The orphans were returned after the war when Charleston's two-year bombardment was over.

Approximately three years after his release, the post-war 1870 census shows Charles at age 17 in the household of Charles Platt—the latter's or the census taker's anglicization of *Karl Plath*—aged 37, and wife Anny M., aged 26, and their 1-year-old daughter Anny. Young Charles is an apprentice at a sawmill where his brother-in-law is a miller. By this time, the Plaths had become members of St. Andrew's Lutheran Church a few blocks away from St. Matthew's. St. Andrew's records indicate that Charles was confirmed there on Easter Sunday, April 5, 1874. He would have been a late confirmand, given his age of 21, but he was already 15 when he came out of the orphanage and would thus have been delayed in receiving the customary instruction. Charles's future wife, Wilhelmena Struhs, had been confirmed at St. Andrew's six years earlier on Easter Sunday [12 April] 1868. It is probable that the two were acquainted with each other, as they say in Charleston, "from church".

By the time he was 21 in 1873, Charles understandably would have been anxious to make his way, independent of his sister and her family. He must have tried to go it alone at some point: the 1878-79 city directory lists a Charles Weber working as a clerk for H. Witt, residing at 133 Coming Street. But the next year's directory places him back in the Plath household, clerking for C. Platte [another variation on his brother-in-law's name], boarding at 23 Pitt Street—the Plath's address. He was thus still not fully independent of his sister and her husband, the latter continuing to provide both employment and a place to live.

But having survived his unsettled teen years, and facing an uncertain future, Charles married Wilhelmena Struhs on October 12, 1879. The marriage is noted in the St. Andrew's records, where Wilhelmena's name is incorrectly entered as *Streuss*. The marriage is also noted in Susan King's record of Charleston marriages. (King 2002) There the entry reads: "Weber, Charles aged 26 years married to Strauss, C.W. aged 25 years October 12, 1879 by Rev. W. S. Bowman[42] at 7 Minority Street. He is a native of Charleston and she of Walhalla, South Carolina. He a clerk." Despite the apparent confusion surrounding Charles's wife's name, it was this marriage that would ultimately link the Weber, Struhs, and Bequest lineages into a family unit.

The Plaths continued to figure importantly in the Weber story. They experienced Charleston's post-war decade of Reconstruction and the re-alignment of the threads of the social fabric. The 1880 census indicates that the couple had other children: the daughter named Anny who was listed in the 1870 census is now listed as Mary [10]; in addition there is a son Charles, 9, and another daughter Wilhelmina, 5. In 1880, Charles Plath was still practicing as a carpenter, though he would have faced tough competition in the rebuilding of devastated Charleston in view of a reconstructed labor force and new rulers. On November 13, 1880 Anna Maria died, and three years later [November 15, 1883], the widower Charles had his own 9-year-old daughter Wilhelmina admitted into the Charleston Orphan House. On entry, the names of both of Wilhelmina's parents are given, but the application for admission was signed by Wilhelmena Webber, "aunt". The child's address is given as 7 Wall Street, suggesting that she had been living with her newly married uncle Charles and his wife Wilhelmena—probably since the death of her mother. After almost a

---

[42] W. S. Bowman was one of the early pastors at St. Andrew's. The church at 43 Wentworth Street contains a large marble plaque to the right of the chancel that memorializes Bowman's ministry during the formative years of that church. One of Charles and Wilhelmena's sons, George Bowman Weber, carried the pastor's name.

generation, for the Webers it was as if things had come full circle: Wilhelmina was released from the orphanage five years later on October 11, 1888 and delivered to her uncle, Charles Weber—he who had earlier been released from the orphanage to her parents. She would remain in the Weber household until she was 18.

Between his wife's death and his daughter's entry into the orphanage, Wilhelmina's father Charles tried his hand at being a grocer. He apparently had stayed at the Pitt Street address after the death of his wife until 1881, when the city directory indicates that he had moved to 63 Rutledge Avenue at the corner of Nunan Street. In the 1883 and 1884 directories, he has upgraded his occupation to "merchant". The 1885 directory is the last in which he is listed. After that, the family virtually disappears from the Charleston record. With no record of Charles Plath's death, the anonymity suggests that he died a pauper and without family connections. Unofficially, however, the Plath name survived for years in a small black pocket notebook belonging to George Bowman Weber, Charles and Wilhelmena's son named for the St. Andrew's pastor who married them. At some point George B. Weber entered into his book the following four names and addresses: "Helen Plath (Mrs. Fred Traudt, 107-04 129th St. Richmond Hill, NY); Mrs. Charles Nelson (Margaret Plath) 63 S. Broadway, Nyack, NY (1939); H. B. Plath, Nyack, NY 10960; "Mena" Plath (Mrs. M. Esslinger), Hammond, Ind, 1425 Elm St." The black notebook was a kind of private diary, and after his death, the identity of these individuals was a mystery to George Weber's surviving daughter. But they are doubtless the names of his cousins, children of his aunt Anny and her husband Charles Plath: "Mena" is surely the Wilhelmina who was placed in the Orphan House and who was a sixteen-year-old in the Weber household when George Bowman Weber was born in 1890. The other names are not so obvious, and there are more of them than the extant records have accounted for: whether they are additional children of Anna Maria and Charles Plath or other relatives is not known. It is possible that there are currently Plath-Weber descendants located in cities other than Charleston.

The marriage of Charles Weber and Wilhelmena Struhs in 1879 brought a firmer footing to Charles's rather insecure youth. He was now 27 years old, needing to establish both himself and a family, and in many ways, getting a late start. In 1880, the census shows him working as a clerk in a mill, and Wilhelmena "keeping house". Their first child, Anna Charlotte Henrietta Weber, was born in July of that year. She would become the wife of John Frederick Bequest and effect the merger of the Weber, Struhs, and Bequest lines. The next year Charles was working for J. C. H. Claussen, one of Charleston's leading German businessmen, and residing at 7 Wall Street. In 1882 he was a "driver" for Claussen, and had moved to #9 Wall Street [the directory change in address is possibly just a numeration error]. The couple's second child, Charles

William Henry, was born on November 27, 1882. He would marry Marguerita Josephine Schumacher in 1913 and establish the Weber branch that lived for a while in Summerville, then subsequently in the Columbia/Newberry/Laurens, SC area, although one daughter remained in Charleston. In 1885, a second son, John August Louis, was born. In 1886 Charles was still a driver for Claussen but boarded [rented] at 60 Calhoun Street where the family remained until 1893. John August Louis married Marie Estelle Osterholtz Dyher in 1906 and founded the Savannah branch of the family, an extended line whose numerous progeny can be traced through four subsequent generations into the present. Charles and Wilhelmena's last child, George Bowman Weber, was born five years later on July 21, 1890.

Wilhelmena Struhs Weber and her son George Bowman Weber.

Given the difficulties of life during the latter decades of the nineteenth century, it is noteworthy that Charles and Wilhelmena's four children all survived into adulthood. The following citations from Fraser's *Charleston! Charleston!* suggest what they were up against:

- Charleston became a commercial backwater, and by 1900 its exports were only 2 percent of the national total. Goods that once had been hauled to Charleston for ocean transportation were going to other ports. Although the number of textile mills was increasingly dramatically, their yarn and cloth were carried out of state by rail rather than through Charleston, and the price of cotton kept falling. Nor could rice save Charleston as its price dropped due to the enormous amounts now being grown in the Mississippi Valley.

- The taxable value of Charleston real estate declined from $25 million in 1895 to $19 million in 1904 and the city's population relative to other American cities continued to decline: in 1870 it ranked twenty-sixth among urban centers, in 1890, fifty-third, and by 1910, ninety-first.

- [T]he persistently high rate of deaths in Charleston from 'diarrheal diseases,' which between 1865 and 1897 reached 5,274, second only to deaths from consumption, 6,972.

- Several small epidemics of typhoid fever between 1865 and 1897 caused 1,418 deaths; malarial fevers, diphtheria, and whooping cough exacted their tolls, and during 1891-92 about eighty persons died from a fast-spreading influenza.

- By the late 1890s . . . the first telephone poles in the city along Church St . . . . on January 24, 1899 . . . the first long-distance lines, linking Charleston and Augusta.

- [B]y 1900 WHITE ONLY and COLORED signs were being posted on restrooms, drinking fountains, doctors' waiting rooms, school, hotels, restaurants, parks, and playgrounds. An unwritten and unposted law banned Afro-Americans from the Battery and its benches . . . . In 1900 there were 4,229 'colored' and 4,211 whites between five and twenty years of age in Charleston schools. Yet there were 7,462 'colored' and only 302 whites over ten years of age who were illiterate (Fraser 1991, 327-36).

By the time Charles died in 1903, just 50+ years old, he had made for himself and his family what at the time might be called a successful, if rather ordinary, life. He had had to use his bootstraps in overcoming the odds of his youth, and his long tenure as a driver for the Claussen wholesale cracker, biscuit, and candy factory was steady work, but by no means enabling of wealth. It was just sufficient for the times. It does not appear that he ever owned his own home. At the time of his death, the family had moved again, this time to 20 Bogard Street, where they lived only for a few years. By 1905, his widow Wilhelmena had moved back to 60 Calhoun Street, where she lived with her daughter Henrietta [married in 1904 to John Bequest] who was clerking at F. M. Kirby & Co., and her three sons—Charles William, working at "Consd. Co.", Louis, working as a molder at Valk & Murdock, and George Bowman, just 15 years old. By 1907, the household was still at 60 Calhoun Street, Louis working as a molder at Riverside Iron Works, and Charles William driving for Marjenhoff Bakery. In 1908, Charles William was driving for Kornahrens Works, and young George had become a clerk at the Atlantic Coast Line Railroad—a job he would hold until he retired. Louis and his wife, and Henrietta, now Bequest, had previously established their own households: Louis was working in Savannah, and Henrietta had moved to the Bequest house around the corner on East Bay Street. Two years later [1910] Wilhelmena died, and in 1912, the city directory shows both Charles William, a clerk at the A&P Tea Co. and George, still in his position as clerk for the Atlantic Coast Line Railroad, residing at 335 East Bay Street. This address had for some time been the residence of the Bequests, and after the death of their mother, the two young bachelors had moved to live with their sister Henrietta and her husband John Frederick Bequest. But by this time, the Bequest household included three daughters Agnes, Ruth, and Helen, as well as John Frederick's widowed mother, Catherine Mehrtens. The *boarders* Charles William and George did not move out until they married—in 1913 and 1916 respectively—and established their own families. In the end, each of Charles and Wilhelmena's children would add descendants to the lineage established by Adam Weber and his wife in the south of Germany more than two centuries earlier to bring the Weber heritage into present generations.

—THE STRUHS LINE—

The same year Frederick Eduard Schroeder married Johann Rosenbohm's niece, Adeline Bequest, at St. Matthew's in Charleston, Wilhelmena Weber's parents were married there. Their daughter Wilhelmena, whom Charles Weber would later marry, would not be born in Charleston, but rather in upstate South Carolina—in Walhalla—the Lutheran conclave founded by the St. Matthew's congregation and populated predominantly by North German immigrants. These new arrivals stepped from their sailing ships onto Charleston wharves and shortly thereafter were convinced they might find better circumstances in the fertile northwest corner of the state where competition with the locals for employment would be less an issue. Wilhelmena's parents, Johann Wilhelm Friedrich Struhs and Anna Maria Dorothea Genthe, were in Charleston as immigrants by 1851, prior to their marriage at St. Matthew's in 1852. It turns out that they were the last German family members to immigrate prior to the Civil War, stopping in Charleston only relatively briefly before undertaking the move to Walhalla in 1853.

George Shealy's account of the upstate town's history suggests that the journey to Walhalla would have challenged the most fortified immigrant:

> No account has been located of the German pioneers' journey from Charleston to Pickens District. The only information available is an article in the August 22, 1900 *Keowee Courier*, taken from the *Charleston News and Courier*: 'Fifty years ago the Germans of Charleston who moved to Walhalla to take up their abode in the forest of the mountain lands . . . were obliged to go by private conveyance

for a great part of the distance. The railroads at that time carried them as far as Athens, Georgia, and from there their trip was made to Walhalla in covered wagons.' Such a trip would have involved a journey to Hamburg, S.C., where the line from Charleston stopped, and then obtaining conveyance across the Savannah to Augusta where they would have boarded a train for Athens. Wagons would have been obtained in Athens for the last leg of the journey (Shealy 1990, 53).

Johann and his wife were thus perhaps more pioneers than followers, although as natives of the same area from which so many in Charleston had come, they formed yet another link in the chain from northern Germany to Charleston.

The early part of the Struhses' South Carolina story reveals a lot about the German Lutheran community that was developing in Charleston in the mid-nineteenth century. In his article on immigrants and the Church, Reinhold Doerries writes: "What differentiated the so-called Germans from the French, the English, or even the Irish, was their apparent lack of cohesion. They were sharply divided by regional origin and culture; by such divergent dialects that English, in some cases, became their lingua franca; by church membership, and often by what can only be called rigid social or class differences" (Doerries 2004, 4). That assessment is valid when describing the general German immigrant community from the broadest perspective and only emphasizes the fact that the German community in Charleston was a distinctly differentiated group originating from a particular region, sharing a common linguistic heritage and religious orientation. As has been emphasized, the nineteenth-century German immigrants to Charleston were predominantly Protestant, both Lutheran and Reformed, from the northwest of Germany speaking *Platt*—subtly different dialects of Low German—and therefore a fairly cohesive group.

Doerries also points out that the church was one of the most significant social institutions in the developing multiethnic American society. In America it represented a welcoming receptiveness to the immigrant coming from the intolerant behavior of both Protestants and Catholics and offered a like-minded and linguistically-kindred haven for the newcomer in a strange land. By the 1860s, the largest Lutheran congregation in Charleston was that of St. Matthew's. Founded in 1840, its charter designation was *The German Evangelical Lutheran Church of Charleston, S.C.* Writing in 1924, S. T. Hallman summarized the evolution of the St. Matthew's congregation in his history of the Evangelical Lutheran Synod of South Carolina:

> [T]he first meeting held for the purpose of organizing this German Lutheran congregation was on November 26, 1840. A week later, December 3, an organization was effected with an

enrollment of 44, and Mr. J.A. Wagener was elected president of the congregation.

In 1841 Rev. F. Becker was engaged by the congregation to serve them for one year. During this year a lot on Hasell St. was purchased for $3,000 and a contract was made for the construction of a church building to cost $8,000. This building was completed in June, 1842, and dedicated June 22 of that year. On the same date Rev. F. Heemsoth was installed as pastor. He served the congregation until early in 1848. The first church building (years later) became the property of St. Johannes' Lutheran congregation.

Rev. Louis Mueller, D.D., became pastor April 1, 1848. He rounded out a full fifty years as pastor, death coming to him in April, 1898. Rev. W.A.C. Mueller, D.D., came to the congregation in January, 1892, as assistant to his father, serving in that capacity until his father's death, when he became full pastor. Dr. W.A.C. Mueller reckons that his father, while pastor of St. Matthew's, baptized 4,402 persons, confirmed 1,440, performed 1,503 marriages ceremonies, conducted funerals of 4,163 persons, and made 75,000 pastoral visits.

In 1856 the congregation established their own cemetery and called it Bethany Cemetery. This cemetery adjoins the city cemetery, Magnolia, and is the Lutheran burial ground for Charleston. Bethany Cemetery has an endowment of $40,000 for perpetual care.

The property on which the present church stands was purchased in January, 1867, and the cornerstone of the building was laid December 22, 1867. The church was dedicated Maundy Thursday, March 28, 1872. Upon this occasion some 3,000 people marched in procession from the Hasell St. church to the new building . . . . The building measures 64 feet by 157 feet deep, capped by a tower and spire that extend 297 feet above the sea. The ceiling of the auditorium is 72 feet above the floor.

In 1901 a clock and chimes of ten bells were placed in the tower at a cost of about $7,000.

A Sunday School and parish building was constructed in 1909 at a cost of about $20,000. The present property is conservatively valued at $125,000.

St. Matthew's congregation has the largest membership in the South Carolina Synod, numbering more than 800 confirmed members (Hallman 1924, 166-67).

That church's records, supplemented by those of three other churches—St. Johannes, St. Andrew's, and St. John's—substantiate the history of the entire German immigrant community during the process of acculturation.

The strong role the institutional church played in the everyday life of the immigrant was further strengthened by the development of a variety of associations. What Doerries calls "associationalism" (*Vereinswesen*) logically would have been an aspect of the Charleston Lutheran—for the most part North German—community. Doerries claims that "German-American church associations were part of an enormous associational network permeating almost every sector of American society in the second half of the nineteenth century . . . . Because most associations, besides their leisure-time functions, also served economic needs not provided by society at large, such as burial insurance, accident insurance, orphanages, old people's homes, and the like, workers often considered membership in these associations a necessity, and the church was hard pressed to create an associational network of its own" (Doerries 2004, 15). Good examples of the tendency to associate in groups, whether civic or religious, are the various church ladies' benevolent societies, fraternal lodges, and in Charleston specifically, the founding of the German Friendly Society already in 1766.

The local congregations that became the glue holding the immigrant community together had been established through a process of expansion from the earliest established congregations [mother churches] during colonial times to daughter groups which sought to enlarge the community of believers and establish a more permanent foothold in the developing society. St. John's Lutheran Church had been established in Charleston already in 1743. The ninth pastor to serve the St. John's congregation, and doubtless the most well-known, was John Bachman. He served from 1815 to 1874 and was a leading figure in antebellum Charleston. Born in Rhinebeck, NY in 1790, he was instrumental in establishing the Southern Seminary and Newberry College, as well as the South Carolina Synod. In 1830 he helped establish the Horticultural Society in Charleston. He was an outstanding naturalist and friend of John James Audubon. Together [as co-authors] they published *Viviparous Quadrapeds of North America* (3 vols., 1845-48). According to Hallman's *History*, John Bachman was responsible for training some ten ministers who went out from St. John's. He also "organized a negro congregation, to which the north gallery of the church was assigned for their exclusive use . . . . There were at one time 190 negro communicants. Dr. Bachman also organized for the negro children a Sunday School consisting of about 150 scholars, who were regularly instructed by thirty-two white teachers" (Hallman 1924, 124-25). The other Lutheran churches would foster less famous pastors and attracted the bulk of their members from the later German immigrant community. In 1853, St. Andrew's [originally designated *The Wentworth Street Lutheran Church*] was established out of the merger of Zion Evangelical Lutheran and a local Methodist church. In 1878, St. Johannes [German Evangelical Lutheran St. Johannes Church] was founded by a group of members belonging to the St. Matthew's congregation, who returned to occupy the original congregation's first sanctuary [built 1842] on the corner of Hasell and Anson Streets [the *new* St. Matthew's church on King Street had been built in 1871 and dedicated in 1872 to house the growing congregation].

Thus from early on it was the case that there existed a missionary zeal to establish new congregations. Local congregations' members contributed loyally to the mission idea, and there was additional help from established churches in Germany in the form of funds and pastors sent to the fledgling churches. It was this missionary zeal and a promise of a more hospitable climate [both weather and employment possibilities] that sent the Struhs couple to Walhalla.

Less than a decade after the end of the Civil War, G. D. Bernheim, a German Lutheran minister whose father was a converted Jew, traced the development of the various German settlements in the Carolinas, devoting an entire chapter to the founding of the congregation in Walhalla. Within the framework of the missionary mandate and the quest by some immigrants for a place to settle that was not constrained by factors that beset the immigrant population in Charleston, Bernheim wrote:

> . . . it was deemed advisable to locate a German colony somewhere in the interior of the State. Accordingly, about the year 1850, a land company was formed among the Germans residing in Charleston, through the energetic labors of Col. John A. Wagener, a public-spirited and enterprising German, and a large body of land was purchased in Pickens District, S.C. of Col. Gresham and others.
>
> The land was admirably located, being in the mountain regions of the Carolinas, exceedingly fertile and well adapted for the cultivation of all the necessary cereals, fruits and vegetables, with an abundant supply of excellent water, free from the heat of less elevated latitudes, and possessing a most salubrious climate, making this settlement a most desirable summer retreat for strangers from the low country . . . A town was soon laid out, and received the ancient German name, *Walhalla*, and the remaining land was divided into farms and sold to German settlers. So rapidly did the population in the new settlement increase, that Walhalla has become a place of importance, even to native American citizens. It has, of course, a Lutheran church, for nearly all the original settlers are of that faith. The church was erected in 1855, under the pastoral care of Rev. C.F. Bansemer; it was built with a spire 112 feet in height (Bernhein 1872, 544-45).

Hallman's account of the Walhalla community differs somewhat as to dates, but changes nothing substantively: "The town of Walhalla, lying at the foot of the Blue Ridge Mountains, was settled in 1849 by a colony of Germans from Charleston.

This colony was supplemented by other immigrants who came later . . . . With some help our Lutheran people in Walhalla got out the timbers, provided the material and built a house of worship highly creditable to themselves . . . . At the meeting of synod in January, 1862, it was reported that the church was completed and had been dedicated in May, 1861" (Hallman 1924, 186).

South Carolina state archives attest to the fact that Wilhelmena's father, Johann Wilhelm Friedrich Struhs, was naturalized in Walhalla in 1856. The record indicates that naturalization was a two-step process: the applicant first declared his intention to become a citizen, and then after a residency of three years, petitioned to have the citizenship verified. The Struhs records include the following documentation: "Before me, W.L. Keith, appeared John Wm. F. Struks, a native of Hanover, about 23, declares his intention to become a citizen of the U.S. renounces allegiance to Frederick Augustus . . . 1 Nov 1853, J.W.F. Struks" (Holcomb 1975, 227-30). This is the initial legal action undertaken by Johann Struhs. The fact that the applicant's name is spelled with a final *k* is a misreading of the handwritten *h* in the archival record. The repeated name at the end of the record [Holcomb's version of the archival original] represents the signature of the applicant. A second, more complete record indicates the finalization of the process: "The petition of J.W.F. Struhs, aged 27 years, a carpenter, born in Hanover, Germany, arrived in the U.S. in 1851, appeared before William L. Keith, 3 Nov 1853, renounces allegiance to Frederick Wm Augustus . . . J.W.F. Struks, Before J.N. Whitner. / We, the subscribers, have known the petitioner for 3 years, during which time he has resided in Pickens Dist . . . Martin C. Wendelken, H. Meyer, T. Hofer, 20 Oct 1856 / Certificate has J.W.F. Strauss" (Holcomb 1975, 230).

Several comments are in order here: (1) Following the pattern of other naturalizations abstracted from the archival record, the second record is the action taken after an interval of three years; (2) The recorder in 1856 writes the name correctly, i.e. *Struhs*, but the later abstractor errs twice in reading the name as *Struks*; (3) The record provides indisputable evidence that Johann Struhs emigrated to the U.S. in 1851; (4) The subscribers/signatories verify that Johann Struhs resided in Pickens District/Walhalla at least for the three years between 1853 and 1856; (5) Two of the subscribers—Wendelken and Hofer [*Höfer* in an earlier citation]—were themselves naturalized during the same period in the same district and were members of the circle of friends and acquaintances settling the area. Martin Wendelken was one of the first settlers in Walhalla: he had moved to Walhalla already in August of 1850 and was one of four household heads listed in the 1850 census of Pickens District. (Shealy 1990, 52) (6) The notation calling attention to the *certificate* bearing the name *Strauss* is of little significance, and appears, upon examination of the archival record itself, to again be no more than the erroneous reading of the handwriting from 1856. Regardless of the orthographical confusion in the record, there is no doubt that this is the individual who initiated the Struhs lineage in South Carolina.

Johann W. F. and Dorothea Struhs were actively involved in building both the Lutheran community and the actual church structure that stood for its presence in that idyllic apart of South Carolina. Records in the Oconee County [SC] Library [*German Colony Protocol*, translated by R. Schaefer] show that J. W. F. Struhs purchased Lot #76 in 1853, and that he still owed a small amount on the mortgage in 1858. The 1860 census shows the family still in Walhalla; J. W. Struhs's occupation is *Mechanic*. In the household were two children born to the couple: Mena, aged 8 [Wilhelmena, born in 1854, is incorrectly listed with a birth year of 1851], and her younger brother, Henry, aged 2 [John Henry, born 1859, is also incorrectly listed with a birth date of 1857]. The same census record indicated that both parents and children were born in South Carolina—a series of rather blatant errors whereby one can question either the thoroughness and/or accuracy of the census taker—Mr. D. P. Robins, Asst. Marshall at the 5 Mile Post Office in Pickens County, SC—or the truthfulness of the Struhs informant! The St. Matthew's record clearly states that Wilhelmena and John Henry were both born in Walhalla and that the parents were native Germans.

Family lore—to be sure, nothing in writing—has it that at the outbreak of the war in 1861 the family moved from Walhalla to Fayetteville, NC, where Johann was employed in building a number of homes in that community.[43] Although at the time of his marriage at St. Matthew's the newly arrived immigrant from Land Wursten gave his occupation as the proverbial *grocer*, he was known in the family as a carpenter by trade—consistent with his occupation in the census record as *mechanic*. The only other element of family lore is that he was killed in Fayetteville in an explosion—neither the nature nor the date of which has ever been determined.

There is no attestable record of when the widowed mother and children returned to Charleston—whether after the war or still during the hostilities. It would have been logical for her to seek the support of the larger German community back in the city where she and her husband had resided originally—if only briefly. The almost-post-Reconstruction Charleston city directory for 1875-76 shows Henry, aged 16, working as a clerk for D. Wellbrock and living on Beaufain Street, corner of Mazyck. It is thus certain that the family had returned to Charleston by this date—some four years prior to Wilhelmena's

---

[43] John Henry died in 1946, aged 86. His death certificate gives his birthplace in 1859 as Fayetteville, NC in contradiction to both the St. Matthew's record and the 1860 census record. The informant for the death record in 1946 was John Henry's wife, Annie Kornahrens Struhs: it seems that at some point John Henry had managed to conflate his birth in Walhalla with his early childhood (however brief) in Fayetteville. Annie gave John Henry's father's name as *William* Struhs.

marriage to Charles Weber in 1879. The first directory listing for the widowed mother is not until 1887, when she is shown to be residing as "wid Wm" with her son Henry, now 28, at 421 Meeting Street. When she died in 1900 of "cholera morbus" complicated by "cerebral congestion", she was living at 250 Ashley Avenue.

An Anna M. Gonthe, birth year 1832, arrived on July 6, 1852, in New York on the *Elisha* from Rotterdam. We can be fairly confident that this is the Anna Magdalena [Margarethe] Dorothea Genthe whom Johann Wilhelm Friedrich Struhs married in Charleston just weeks later in 1852. The St. Matthew's church record specifies that J. W. F. was from "Cappel, Dorum, Hannover" and Anna Dorothea, from "Alsum, Dorum, Hannover". Anna was the daughter of Friedrich Wilhelm Gente [d. 1855] and Tjede Magdalena Rebecka Adickes [b. 1790, d. 1851]. Cappel and Alsum are both small villages close to Dorum—in Land Wursten, the region in Hanover along the coast of the North Sea, north of Geestendorf. Johann Struhs probably was acquainted with his future wife already before he left Dorum: they were members of the same church community, and it was probably arranged that he come first to Charleston and that she would follow soon thereafter.

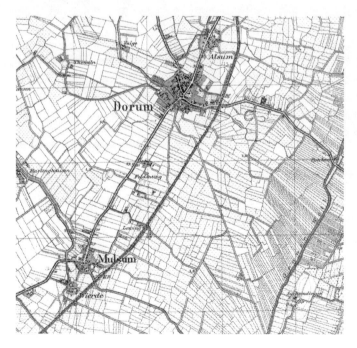

Area of Land Wursten showing the proximity of the towns/villages of Dorum and Alsum. From the American Geographical Society Library, University of Wisconsin-Milwaukee Libraries.

The early history of the several German families delineated earlier indicated that the Struhs lineage can be traced definitively back to Marten Struß, born in 1651 in the village of Flögeln. His grandson was the inhabitant of Cappel in Land Wursten from whom the immigrant Johann Wilhelm Friedrich descended. Anna Maria Dorothea Genthe's ancestry can be traced back to her great-great-grandfather, Johan Har Adickes, born 1720. (Behrens and Rothe 2008) Prior to their emigration, both belonged to long-in-place families that moved hardly beyond a neighboring village to find a spouse, that accepted the deaths of children in early infancy as God's usual will, that expected life to end early—if not in childbirth, then by disease or accident. They lived in households that were tied to the land or the sea that sustained them, where the household address was an unnumbered location identified by some characteristic of the landscape. That these two should decide to leave and come to America could only have been the result of multiple factors, many so personal that they are beyond conjecture. Nonetheless, their immigration to South Carolina can surely be viewed against that background of turbulence that marked the mid-nineteenth century in German lands. Even in this fairly remote northern coastal area, the winds of modernization would have blown, the unsettled political conditions would have put in doubt occupational futures and the options for financial security. The father of Johann Wilhelm Friedrich, born before the turn of the nineteenth century, would have weathered storms of change by the time his son would suggest that maybe his chances would be better elsewhere. The young Johann's mother would die shortly after his tenth birthday. What would hold him there against the lure of adventure and opportunity in post-colonial America? Besides, he would have reasoned, many of his fellow villagers in the north had already settled in the U.S.—most of them in Charleston. It would thus have seemed a logical step to follow that chain and join the ever-increasing and homogeneous religious community there. This pull felt by the young native of the agricultural/maritime northern section of Hanover was strengthened by the lure of the opportunity offered by the new, and doubtless widely advertised, upstate settlement in Walhalla. It was a dream to match the times, and young Struhs and his wife-to-be took up the challenge. They could not know how their lives would be intercepted by the war that would break out in the Charleston they had left, nor how they would have to deal with its results.

VII

THE IMMIGRANT AND
THE PECULIAR INSTITUTION

The salient aspect of Charleston's unique character as a southern city was its embodiment of the *peculiar* institution that dominated the social structure throughout the southern states. For all its contemporary usualness and historic footing in the South, slavery presented the immigrant community that had chosen Charleston for home with a unique set of circumstances that few other migrants had to face and which are not easily described in a condensed summary. The issues on the state and national stages, virtually all of which revolved around, or evolved into, the issue of slavery and a culture founded on it, have been examined from every aspect imaginable and are too numerous to comment on here. But some effort must be put into understanding the predicament of the immigrant community—and this family's members in particular—as it met, managed, and responded to slavery as manifested in Charleston during the decades prior to the Civil War. It is necessary to examine slavery's impact on the ethnic community in order to understand the immigrant experience in trying to become a useful member of a society that advocated human bondage and defended its morality with unadulterated conviction.

Slavery was the foundation on which almost everything was built. It was a given long before it was questioned and a way of life that few natives imagined could ever be changed. For the early colonial-era immigrants, it appears not to have been an issue prior to emigration and not something that couldn't be dealt with once they had settled in. But when the matter of slavery began to roil the surface of life after the 1830s, the complex issues involved in a culture based on it would have gnawed at the later immigrant and caused headaches and heartaches that no amount of equivocation could resolve. Already by the time Johann Rosenbohm was resident in Charleston, the politics of nullification clouded the air. How would the intrepid, even bold, young immigrant—no matter how savvy of, and/or reactionary to, the conditions at home in a volatile Europe—respond knowledgeably to the arguments of states' rights versus those of the newly fashioned nation, when, as Rogers puts it, "[n]ullification was the hand against the nation . . . . The purpose was to force each man to make a personal choice for the state or against it" (Rogers 1969, 162)? Barely off the boat, the immigrant was in no position to make such a choice nor understand why he should have to.

While slavery was endemic throughout the South, the case can be made that its character in Charleston and South Carolina was different from everywhere else. By the middle of the nineteenth century, South Carolina was a slave state in its entirety, and by 1860, before it seceded from the rest of the country, "the lack of immigration to South Carolina had produced a white population that was 96.6 percent South Carolina born. Hence, the state and its governing class were little influenced by outsiders from other states or abroad. In 1850 and 1860 respectively, 91.8 and 93.0 percent of the Palmetto State's legislators had been born in South Carolina. These percentages were by far the highest in the Lower South" (Barnwell 1982, 8). Numerically, the governing class operated in the context of a population in which they were a minority: As cited earlier, the equal number of whites and slaves [4000 each] that existed in Charleston in 1761 had evolved into a municipal population of 20, 012 whites, 19,552 slaves, and 3,441 free Negroes in 1850. (Rogers 1969, 141) Such was the reality that met the immigrant head-on, a kind of social and political wall against which there could be little resistance if one had any questions on the matter. In reality, the immigrant was in no position to question anything about the order of the society into which he had moved.

Looked at in closer detail—and possibly more from the perspective of the typical immigrant—"most rich Charlestonians were slaveholders, and almost all nonslaveholders were poor" (Johnson 1980, 73). The immigrant would more likely than not find him/herself in the economic category of the *poor*, eligible to be counted among the three-fourths of the city's population that did not own slaves. The relationship between wealth and slave ownership confirmed the ordinary immigrant's position at the bottom of the ladder: "Nine out of ten people who had less than $5,000 were slaveless. Of those who owned $5,000 or more, over three quarters were slaveholders. The mean wealth of slaveholders was $21,264, twelve times greater than that of nonslaveholders. Altogether, slaveholders owned 82 percent of all the wealth in the city." And if not already obvious, it was this distinction between slaveholders and nonslaveholders that "focused and reinforced the differences between Charleston's working class and the planters, merchants, and professionals who composed the city's economic elite. For example, 80 percent of the planters in Charleston and 53 percent of the lawyers reported owning $5,000 or more . . . . But only 3 percent of the carpenters, 2 percent of the clerks, and 0.2 percent of the laborers owned that much. Indeed, 79 percent of the carpenters, 93 percent of the clerks, and 95 percent of the laborers reported no wealth of any sort. The mean wealth of planters was almost $54,000; that of lawyers was over $14,000. Carpenters' mean wealth was $574, clerks' was $318, and laborers' was $80" (Johnson 1980, 73-74).

Aside from the great divide between the wealthy elite and the struggling underclasses, the immigrants would always constitute a minority within the overall social structure. While their numbers seem modest when measured against a total of native-born population that includes both black and white—10.8% in 1850, 15.55% in 1860—the foreign-born constituted no more than roughly a quarter of Charleston's white-only population in 1860. (Silver 1975, 10-11) In this minority status, the immigrant was playing on an uneven field, forced to accommodate a majority to which he was unequal in more ways than one. First, the traditions that surrounded slavery in the South and in Charleston were of long-standing, going back to the eighteenth century and derived from the skills of the black population that supported the region's economic base. Those skills were not easily dismissed by any upstart who might wish them to disappear in order to level the playing field. And while slave skills were honored and acknowledged as necessary to the majority community's well-being, that community had created a legacy of tension in exercising its control over the enslaved labor force. Within the four decades since the Vesey uprising in the early 1820s up to the fateful act of secession at the end of 1860, the Charleston governors, as was suggested earlier, had transformed their community into a police state and were overly sensitive to any hint of interference from the outside or from below. Throughout this period, the abolitionists at home and in the North served as the thorn in the side that festered to the point that, by the late 1850s, "most white southerners viewed themselves as prisoners in their own country" (Rosen 1992, 101), nervous, defensive, irritable, and unwilling to view any change in their historical course. Second, there was the reality of the labor force. While immigrants were blessed with both whiteness and freedom, those attributes were not always enough to overcome the fact that the enslaved black laborer enjoyed a monopoly within the urban work force up to the years immediately preceding the Civil War. Not only in Charleston, but in other southern cities such as Richmond, Mobile, and Nashville, "adult slaves represented a significant number of the urban workingmen, skilled and unskilled" (Berlin and Gutman 1983, 1181-82). If in Charleston the large influx of foreign-born would constitute almost half of the free work force by 1850, the immigrant would have to find his place where it was not already occupied by a native—black or white. Third, to the immigrants swept ashore by the transatlantic migration current and planting themselves in the South from the 1830s on, the political and cultural forces at work there would have been almost unfathomable—if they were understandable even to the ordinary native-born. The overwhelming complexity of the issues that were being argued must have left the uninitiated immigrant bewildered and torn if he attempted to justify his own position in the scheme of things, or if he had to make a decision as to which side he could/would/should support. A recent study of the politics and ideology in antebellum South Carolina [Sinha 2000] articulates the complex of issues bombarding the immigrant, issues that constituted a kind of white noise that those on the sidelines were forced to get used to. The principles of the proslavery arguments, the matter of the expansion of slavery into newly acquired territory, the instigation of southern nationalism, partisan and sectional rivalries, and the possibility and justification of secession were just some of the things adding to the stress of establishing a new life in a new country. The *noise* would have been hard to listen to, equally difficult to ignore:

> The explosive sectional controversy over the expansion of slavery into newly conquered territories, which tore at the heart of mid-nineteenth century America and paved the way for the Civil War, presented a golden opportunity for Carolinian planter politicians to impart to their section the political ideology of slavery, with its ideal of an independent southern nation. The territorial crisis of 1846-50 embodied not only the "ominous fulfillment" of American nationalism but also the coming of age of southern nationalism based on the defense of racial slavery. The slavery expansion issue brought into sharp relief the dichotomy between free and slave societies that had subsisted within the framework of the American republic for over half a century. Just as the northern vision of free soil and free labor reflected the deeply held beliefs of its society, the southern argument for slave soil was based on a vindication of slavery and the values of a slave society. This ideological polarization, spurred by the territorial controversy, would make the problem of slavery obtrude decisively into the national political arena.
>
> It is in this context that South Carolina's exceptionalism became pertinent and influential. Not bound by party allegiances or democratic practice, Carolinian planter politicians championed the cause of their class and section. Calhoun's notion of state sovereignty became the basis of the southern position on slavery in the territories and on the right to secession. Not just formal constitutional and political arguments, but the vindication of slavery as a superior way of ordering society and of a separate southern identity based on slavery would constitute the discourse of southern nationalism. During nullification, Carolinian politicos had developed

a systematic defense of slavery and the slaveholding minority in a democratic republic. The slavery expansion conflict fostered southern nationalism, which pointed to the inescapable conclusion that slavery was a higher good than the American republic.

The proslavery argument, which grew in scope and sophistication during these years, provided ideological coherence and unity to southern nationalism. A very basic and unequivocal commitment to slavery undergirded southernism. Talk of southern rights and honor was inextricably bound to the issue of slavery . . . . Southern leaders started contending with increasing frequency that the enslavement of African Americans had divine sanction and that slavery was the basis of all good society (Sinha 2000, 63-64).

Now against this background, what can be posited about the foreground in which the immigrant English and German family members acted and operated? Was the response the same for the Thompson family as, say, for the Webers? Probably not.

—THE ENGLISH EPISCOPALIAN

As a member of the established Episcopalian church community, the foreign, but English-born, Jane Thompson had matured by mid-century into a different status than the German immigrants who had already, or would later, become part of the family. As recounted previously, she left St. Michael's to join the fledgling congregation of St. Stephen's, where by 1838 three of her children had been baptized by the Rev. Paul Trapier. In the succeeding years, her continued involvement in that church is verified by one daughter's confirmation in 1856 and another's marriage in 1860. The records of those milestone events at St. Stephen's consistently deny the existence of Jane's husband James. Jane's marriage had been troubled early on, and it was definitively destroyed by James's involvement with another woman: although the Thompsons were never divorced, their relationship was acrimonious at best. By the time she would have celebrated her 50th birthday, she was a woman fighting for herself and her children by herself, trying to find firm footing during the troubled years leading up to the war.

In 1852, still legally husband and wife, James and Jane Thompson were involved in a foreclosure action on a property that ultimately became the family home and main property. It was the same property that Jane [in her name only] had acquired at auction ten years earlier [in September 1842] for $800.00. In the 1852 complaint/suit brought by George Walker, the court awarded [for $1,200] two lots known as "#115 and #116 of the Gadsden lands" on Laurens and Vernon Streets to the Thompsons. This property would constitute the bulk of Jane's estate later willed to her children. By 1860, the list of taxpayers in the City of Charleston shows her [under "Trust estate Jane M"] as having real estate property worth $25,000, and owning four slaves. The city directory for the same year nonetheless lists Mrs. J. M. Thompson running a private boarding house at 8 Laurens Street.

Thus the matriarch Jane Thompson could count herself among the one-fourth of Charlestonians who were slaveholders, and someone slightly above the mean in terms of slaveholder wealth. Her slaves at this time were essentially domestic servants, and her means of livelihood as the manager of a boarding house does not suggest that she considered herself among the elite wealthy. By no means had she climbed to the top of the social ladder, but she was distinctly not among the indigent, and as an Episcopalian, she was on the right side of things in the Charleston establishment. After some thirty years in Charleston, she would have outgrown her immigrant beginnings and taken on the prejudices of the southern native to whom she was ethnically and culturally closely related.

Someone prominent in her Episcopalian life—her former pastor, Paul Trapier—had become one of the leading clerics in Charleston. He had left St. Stephen's in 1840 to become rector of the city's principal Episcopal congregation, St. Michael's, but from the very beginning had not had an easy time with the establishment in the congregation. His pastorate there could be described as contentious, and not without notice in the larger community. His clerical and civic roles exemplified many of the tensions that characterized the period and would have been followed closely by most citizens and known in detail to every Episcopalian, including Jane Thompson. As a member of that Charleston *establishment* church community, Jane's own feelings and opinions about slavery as it evolved into the cause of South Carolina's secession and the years of the Civil War would likely not have been all that different than Paul Trapier's.

In *Charleston! Charleston!*, Walter Fraser comments on the stance of the religious leaders of the city with regard to slavery:

> No Southern city could boast of a more sophisticated, cosmopolitan, or scholarly clergy than antebellum Charleston, but they were ardent defenders of the status quo. Indeed, the Reverend John Bachman of St. John's Lutheran Church has been called the "chief religious spokesman for slavery." Many were good and kind men who in a paternalistic way were genuinely concerned for the spiritual life of blacks. The Reverend John Adger in a sermon at the Second Presbyterian Church clearly expressed the ideal of compassion and kindness toward the slave: 'Our mothers confide us, when infants, to their arms, and sometimes to the very milk of their breasts . . . a

race distinct from us, . . . yet they are not more truly ours than we are theirs; . . . children of our God and Father; dear to our Saviour; to the like to whom he died, and to the least of whom every act of Christian compassion and kindness we show he will consider as shown also to himself.' At the same time Bishop Gadsden, grandson of the Revolutionary leader and rector of St. Philip's Church from 1814 to 1852, frequently reminded blacks that they should 'fear God, obey the civil authority . . . . be subject unto their own masters and be contented in that state of life to which God hath called them . . . .' Likewise, Theodore Dehon, rector of St. Michael's Church, told his mixed congregation that St. Paul urged fugitive slaves to return to their masters (Fraser 1991, 204-05).

Paul Trapier fell honestly into the Gadsden/Dehon Episcopal tradition when it came to the issue of slavery. He had, in fact, married Bishop Dehon's daughter Sarah. Theodore Dehon's wife and Sarah's mother was the daughter of Nathaniel Russell, and Paul and Sarah lived with the widow Dehon in the now-famous Nathaniel Russell house on Meeting Street. Through his marriage, Trapier had cemented his position within the Charleston aristocracy, and his clerical and civic life doubtless always benefitted from that backdrop. By the time he was rector of St. Michael's, the scene had heated up considerably and he became less a defender of the status quo than an advocate of his own principles. To read his own recollection of his experiences as rector is to appreciate how difficult it was to run counter to the Charleston grain:

> In looking back upon it, I do think I was actuated in the main by a sincere desire to do good, and by a determination not to be deterred by the fear of man, by "the contempt of families", or by the desire to conciliate by sacrifice of principle, or the withholding of truth. But I am equally conscious of not having been discreet. I ran too rashly in the face of the prejudices of the congregation. I broke in too roughly upon their long-established usages. I laid too much stress upon trifles, and did not bring out as distinctly as I should have done in my preaching the great doctrine of grace. I had taken charge of a congregation made up in large part of old families, priding themselves upon ancestry and attached to the church rather because their fathers had been there than from enlightened acquaintance with its principles, and consequently bent upon going on as those before them had gone, whether there was reason for doing or not. It was enough for them that so far back as they could remember, or as their fathers had told them, such had been the usage in St. Michael's Church. To this they would adhere though it were in itself the merest

> trifle. My predecessors too had in two instances been Bishops, and who was I to disturb what they had let alone! With a people so wedded to things as they had been, I should have gone to work much more cautiously and slowly, not disturbing what I found there until I had won their confidence by a faithful ministry among them, unless in matters essential to integrity of faith or morals (Williams 1954, 26).

If in his early efforts to effect change in certain matters of doctrinal practice—what he could later refer to as "trifles"—Trapier managed frequently to ruffle the feathers of his congregation, his later, more public role as minister to what was to be established as a *colored* Episcopal congregation reveals how perfectly he was a personification of those characteristics that define the southern citizen's accommodation to a culture with slavery at its base. Here he would embody the paternalism of the elite whites toward a minority community that served them in every walk of life, here he would demonstrate the long-established role of the Episcopalian responsible for charity toward the underclasses, here he would walk the thin line between religious, denominational convictions and the racial tensions that pulled every which way in Charleston at mid-century.

In 1847 the South Carolina Episcopal diocese, at its Fifty-eighth Convention, resolved to establish a congregation of "black and colored persons", who, it was felt, "were already being crowded out of the white churches." Paul Trapier had resigned his rectorship at St. Michael's the previous November and was asked to serve as minister to the new church. Taking up this new assignment with formidable dedication, he advocated for this mission church by preaching throughout the city a sermon that was subsequently published [Charleston, 1848] as *A Plan for Giving the Gospel to our Servants*. Paul Trapier's sermon did indeed speak volumes about the religious community's belief in the sanctity of slavery, and it did not fall on deaf ears. Later that year, a small publication entitled *The Religious Instruction of the Black Population* appeared, [Trapier and Adger 1847] in which an anonymous author excerpted the main points of Trapier's sermon and then introduced *A Discussion on "the Religious Instruction of the Blacks" in the Charleston Mercury, between "Many Citizens" and the Rev. J.B. Adger* that had been "extracted from the *Southern Presbyterian Review*". That *discussion* was an effort to demonstrate the accord of Adger—the Presbyterian minister cited by Fraser above—with the main thrust of Trapier's argument and to refute the opinion of the individual who, in the name of "many citizens", had argued in the *Mercury* that instructing the slaves of Charleston was a bad idea, that establishing Calvary Church as proposed by the Episcopalians would lead to insurrection and total destruction of the social order.

The anonymous extractor writes that the Presbyterian Rev. Adger's sermon on the same subject had received "some notice" in the previous issue of the *Southern Presbyterian Review*, and it was indeed both Adger's and Trapier's sermons that had brought the Presbyterian minister into a public discussion/exchange with "Many Citizens" in the Charleston newspaper. Taking up the cause of Rev. Adger, the extractor writes: "In reviewing now his discussion with 'Many Citizens,' we would take occasion to state that previously to any public step, on his part, Mr. A. was for months engaged in consulting, confidentially, all the leading minds of the community, so far as he could get access to them; and in every case, with one or two exceptions, he received the strongest encouragement to proceed. The action of the Episcopal Convention . . . to, and of which Mr. A. was an eye and ear witness, appears strongly indicative of the favor with which all parties would regard the undertaking. Upon his list of subscribers were enrolled gentlemen of the highest character, and of every profession. The Presbytery of Charleston gave him their strongest sanction. The public mind appeared ripe for the movement. And we believe the public mind of Charleston is ready for every movement, respecting which it is satisfied, that it is really calculated to secure the moral and religious improvement of our slaves. It is true that on this subject a morbidness is exhibited in Charleston, which is to be found in no other city of the Southern States . . . And on account of the very morbidness of Charleston, we look for more judicious proceedings and sounder results from the religious instruction of slaves there, than can be expected, as we fear, in some other Southern cities where a laxer public sentiment prevails" (Trapier and Adger 1847, 6-7).

There then follow twenty-plus pages of theological justification for undertaking to instruct the thousands of the Charleston black population who could not be accommodated in the galleries of the city's establishment churches—primarily Episcopal, Methodist, and Baptist—and who thus were unable to receive any kind of "proper" religious instruction. The Episcopalians had demonstrated leadership in wanting to establish the missionary Calvary Church to serve a portion of the black population, and Rev. Adger, speaking for the Presbyterians and others, was publicly arguing in support of that mission. His theological arguments—altogether similar to Trapier's—abound with scriptural references and can be viewed as representing the wide-spread belief of the religious community that God sanctioned slavery, that the Christian master had the *obligation* to take the Gospel to the not-yet-uplifted slave, and that the entire social and political order stood to be immensely improved through the undertaking.

What is noteworthy in this tract is the zealous conviction with which it is argued that the Charleston Christian was following a scripture-based imperative to instruct those in bondage so that they might learn to be *Christian* slaves and thereby *better* slaves to their masters. The arguments are put forward not to convince the religious community, but rather to overturn the opinions of "Many Citizens" and his/their fear that the instruction and enlightenment of the black population that would occur with the newly founded Calvary Church would bring down the prevailing social order. The clerics Trapier and Adger were not preaching to the choir of Episcopalians, Presbyterians, Methodists, and Baptist church members—they were pronounced "ready" to affirm this "movement"—but to those in the civic community who doubted the efficacy of the undertaking. Here the clerics and the extractor promote a theological and doctrinal symbiosis between their *religious instruction* and the civic/social/political need for better-behaved, more Christian, more righteously motivated, more readily controlled, servants to the master race: "We tell the opposition that we have no doubt our scheme tends to elevate and improve the intellectual and moral character of the negro. Our object is to improve their minds and hearts.—Our belief is that self interest, as well as duty, calls on us all to help on this improvement. We want this mass of intellectual and moral death removed. We want this people made better, more intelligent, industrious, tractable, trusty, better men, better servants, better Christians" (Trapier and Adger 1847, 14-15). Thus argued, it would become clear to "Many Citizens" that the work of the religious community would bring great benefit to the commonweal and that, with God on its side and comfortable with slavery as the natural order in His world, the Church should, in fact, be thanked for leading the community in the right direction.

If this dispute between the religious and civic communities was smoothed over at the time, it did not go away entirely. The Episcopalians moved ahead, and through voluntary contributions a lot on the corner of Beaufain and Wilson Streets was purchased on which a brick church would be built. By early 1848, services were begun at the parsonage at St. Philip's, and in July of that year the congregation moved to Temperance Hall. In the early months alone, 276 slaves belonging to 121 owners "by all of whom consent has been given" were received into the congregation. Apparently sufficiently aware of potential racially-motivated resistance to the idea of an independent black congregation, precaution was taken to station someone from the City Guard nearby, although it was subsequently acknowledged that there were no incidents necessitating interference because of "the behaviour of the people." In the fall of 1848, the contract was let for the building of Calvary Church. But then in July of 1849 the public—what Trapier later recalled as "the rabble of the city, set on by some demagogues, and inciting the jealousy of the white mechanics against the Negroes"—reacted against the "liberation" of slaves, and services were discontinued at the Hall. Those against this effort to accommodate the slaves threatened to demolish the church and were deterred "only by the calling of a meeting of citizens, who appointed committees of some of the most influential men to examine into the whole subject of the instruction of slaves, and in particular into the scheme of Calvary Church." After a period of six months, the committees reported back, and approval was given to construct a church that would also provide "accommodations for 90 white members, by seats set apart and raised, and by a distinct entrance; keeping before the eyes of the congregation at all times, a sensible image of the subordination that is due to those to whom by the course of Providence, they are to look up to as their rulers." It was acknowledged that the planners had had no intention of weakening the "safeguards of public peace and order" and suggested that the modifications agreed upon should now be considered "deserving of attention, [. . .] a model for others engaged in the same laudable work." Calvary Church was consecrated in December of 1849: in the Sentence of Consecration, the Church is described as having been "erected and furnished (as a place) wherein the rich and the poor, the bond and the free, may meet together to worship their one Father, Redeemer, and Sanctifier, three persons but one God, to partake of His holy sacraments and ordinances, and to receive the teachings and exhortations of His holy word, His holy Church, and His duly commissioned ministry" (Thomas 1957, 201). In December 1849 the mission church's successes were reported to the Convention: "In 1849 there were 3 colored communicants, 10 white; in 1856 there were 51 colored and 18 white. In the period 1848 to 1856, 2,485 colored persons aged from 6 to 60 were admitted to the Sunday School; 78 were admitted to the Holy Communion . . ." (Williams 1954, 28).

The record of Paul Trapier's work at St. Stephen's, St. Michael's, and Calvary was published as "The Private Register of the Rev. Paul Trapier" in two issues of *The South Carolina Historical Magazine* in 1957. (Jervey 1957) That listing of all the instances of baptisms, confirmations, and marriages that Trapier performed demonstrates the degree to which the Episcopal church community in Charleston effectively served the slave and free black population and the extent to which it had integrated those individuals into its congregations through a sense of paternalistic responsibility and religious doctrine under the leadership of Paul Trapier. In his *Register*, no distinction is made between his own children's records at any of the three churches and those of slaves or free coloreds, except that the records for the white congregants carry no specification of status or race and no acknowledgment of anyone's "permission". He baptized, confirmed, and married his own slaves and servants just as he did for everyone else, and, it should be noted, many of the slave and servant ceremonies took place at the home of his mother-in-law, Mrs. Dehon—undoubtedly by his arrangement if circumstances required. For the residents of the city, Trapier's devotion to the cause of religious instruction and incorporation into the church body of the black population raised the eyebrows of those who feared too much integration, but at the same time, was representative of the attitude of many who perceived the necessity of a ministry "unto the least of these" in defense of a culture that depended on class and race.

Trapier resigned his charge at Calvary in 1857 after ill health had necessitated his taking a leave of absence the year prior. He was subsequently appointed on the committee of the diocese to prepare a catechism for persons of color. That was published in 1855 as *The Catechism Made Plain.* (Williams 1954, 65) For all his efforts to bring the gospel to the people of the peculiar institution, Trapier can be seen as a man of his times with a southern attitude that could not overcome the prejudices of his station and calling. After the Calvary experience he would remain a dutiful servant of the Church, although his life in his later years was one of increasing disappointment. Throughout the war he functioned in various clerical assignments as staunch supporter of the Confederacy and its defense of slavery and southern nationalism, but the inherent sickness of the times that could not be healed and his uncompromising standards brought him to a kind of tragic low-point—a descent that would have registered as synonymous with what many citizens of the Confederacy—both high and low—felt characteristic of their lives. His description of his predicament after the war makes it clear that he felt abandoned, disappointed, poverty-stricken, and somewhat awed by the depths into which he had fallen:

> Meanwhile our domestic embarrassments became more and more distressing. Confederate notes became valueless, and we could buy nothing. Happily in the apprehension of a raid from Gen. Potter some commissary stores were given out and we obtained a good supply of rice, and a small quantity of sugar and coffee. Our friends sent us from time to time sundry little comforts. But our capital was mostly gone; $16,000 sunk in Confederate securities, and about $14,000 rendered unavailable by the abstraction of coupon Bonds of Railroads in the Bank Safe captured by Sherman. Still our servants remained with us, till about the middle of July, when my daughter Sarah's maid Ellen went off. On the 20th of that month my old family-servant Diana, who had been born, as had her parents, and ancestors for generation, in my family, deserted us. And on the afternoon of the same day our man-servant William, whose father and forefathers had belonged to my Mother's family and who had been with me since he was a little boy followed her example. In a few days our washerwoman went—then her mother our cook with her husband, all hired servants, and we were left without any one to do menial service. Such is our condition at this time. My daughter prepares the food which my sons and nephew (Russell Dehon) cook. The boys attend to the feeding of the cow and hogs, and the mule let us by my nephew Edward H. Barnwell. My younger daughters

clean knives, and sweep the house. Our hired white woman (Elisa Steele) milks the cow, and attends to the chambers. My wife darns and mends, etc., and I gather vegetables, and help in drawing water, and we all help each other. My daughters have been doing a good part of the washing, ironing, and clearstarching. Thus we are brought down lower than we ever thought we should be. With more than half of my capital certainly gone, and the remainder unproductive for years, perhaps gone too—my salaries as Professor and Missionary both stopped—I have literally no money, nor any means of making any, unless by sending wood by a hired man into Camden from land which Mr. Sutherland kindly lets me cut it from to be hauled in my wagon by a mule lent to me by my nephew, and there are fifteen in family for me to provide for (Williams 1954, 31).

With a broader brush than he could use for his personal situation, he would also reflect on the current, rather deplorable state of the world in general:

Politically what changes! In Europe, Napoleon I hurled from the pinnacle of power to the death of Prometheus on a rock in mid-ocean, and his country after three revolutions again under one of this name, the temporal power of the Pope narrowed down to the environs of Rome and maintained even there by only the bayonets of France, while the lineal descendant of the elder branch of the Stuarts of England, and the legitimate sovereign of England, rules over the greater part of Italy, and threatens even the little left to his Holiness. Greece independent of the Turkish power, yet existing at the pleasure of the "barbarians" of Northern Europe, and under the kingship of a German. England almost republicanized by the Reform Bill and yet again under the control of her wonderful aristocracy; extending her colonies the world over, and founding future empires on the other side of the earth. China opened to intercourse with the rest of mankind and to the influence of Christianity, and even Japan partially unsealed. The gold-fields of California and Australia attracting streams of population, and stimulating enterprise beyond precedent. And, lastly, slavery drowned in an ocean of the best blood of the South, and my beloved country abased by the abhorred Puritan (Williams 1954, 33-34).

As suggested earlier, the lesson of what the Rev. Paul Trapier experienced as a leader in the South Carolina Episcopal Church would have resonated with the members of all the congregations he had served—black and white—and his religious convictions, moral stance, and civic ideals would have echoed the sentiments of many an Episcopalian in Charleston. As a leading cleric in a city that exemplified the complexities and dualities in the culture of slavery up to, and including, the years of the Civil War, he led by example, and those citizens and members of the established white Church who followed his leadership bought into the same racial prejudices, religious convictions, and regional patriotism demonstrated by Trapier. By the time the war was over, the disappointment, bitterness, anger, and sense of betrayal of many in the community would match that of the abject Episcopal clergyman.

In the absence of any documentation to the contrary, one may assume that the Anglican English immigrant Jane Thompson would have empathized with the positions taken, the conditions suffered, and the events experienced by her one-time rector and church-community mentor to the degree that she would have felt them congruent with her own. While she of course led a life that was distinctly not in the same orbit as Trapier's, the typical Charleston Episcopalian operated within a homogeneity of native cultural and religious influences that other immigrants did not. On examination, it will become clear that the context of the German immigrants in the family in Charleston with regard to slavery was not as monolithic as it was for the English-born and longer-established Episcopal residents. But whatever those differences, they would not prevent the convergence of the Anglican and Lutheran traditions within the same family in the latter years of the century.

—THE GERMAN LUTHERAN

The few historians who have written on the German immigrants to Charleston suggest that the newcomers approved of slavery and were enthusiastic supporters of secession and the war effort in the Confederacy. Andrea Mehrländer writes: "The Germans of Charleston approved and supported the institution of slavery and swore absolute loyalty to their adopted home." She cites the fact that although by 1860 the number of slaveholders in the city had declined, 8.9% of the Germans in the city owned a total of 325 slaves, and that "in the case of secession, this clearly meant a decision in favor of leaving the Union" (Mehrländer 2010, 66). Michael Bell sees "acceptance of the practice" in the fact that while "fewer of Charleston's German heads of household than Richmond's owned slaves (about 5 percent in 1860) they owned more of them (an average of 4.75 each)" (Bell 1999, 16).

Such statistics, however, are rather sweeping generalizations and warrant further investigation. Other historians have in fact cautioned that "immigrant workers in the urban South cannot simply be incorporated into the extant understanding of the nature of Southern society, the evolution of slavery, or the character of antebellum politics. Instead they demand reconsideration of all" (Berlin and Gutman 1983, 1200). Jeffrey Strickland writes that "[w]hite southerners fought the Civil War to preserve slavery. The German Charlestonians' response to the Civil War was mixed, and most of the Germans who fought for the Confederate Army were not committed to a slave society" (Strickland 2008, 61). In evaluating the attitude and stance of the typical German immigrant in Charleston with regard to the institution of slavery that the host community presented during the three decades leading up to the Civil War, one cannot dismiss the basic quandary of the immigrant, forced, as it were, to navigate between the overweening racial prejudice in a society that sanctified bondage, and the same immigrant's personal quest for independence that required and was dependent on individual freedom. In their study of the inherent tension between natives and immigrants, between free workingmen and slaves, Berlin and Gutman capture the essence of that dilemma: "But, if free workers were pulled in all directions, their allegiance to the slave regime was never firm. Men and women who had fled the landlord-dominated societies of Western Europe were hardly predisposed to sympathize with the planter class. Slavery remained the linchpin of the southern order, and the relationship of free workers to that institution continued to be ambiguous at best. Many were too newly arrived to understand it, and some found good reason to oppose it" (Berlin and Gutman 1983, 1197).

As was proposed earlier, the situation in Charleston presented to the nineteenth-century German immigrant a context different than almost anywhere else. Mehrländer's recent study of the Germans of Charleston, Richmond and New Orleans during the Civil War period already suggests that immigrants in these three southern cities exhibited different behaviors, and that the different metropolitan areas had only in common their location in the South. While much of the difference stemmed from the geographical location, economy, and character of the host city, just as much stemmed from the nature of the ethnic communities that settled in the respective locations. Those factors certainly impacted the Germans in Charleston and qualified their behavior.

As was iterated earlier, the immigrants who arrived in Charleston in the 1830s and 1840s found an already-established and acculturated German community that welcomed them less as fellow countrymen—there was no *country* common to them all—than as newcomers of a somewhat lesser sort. When the earlier ones had come, slavery was a part of the culture that had not been questioned and that since had been accepted as a matter of course in the process of acculturation. These were the founders of the German Friendly Society—men such as Michael Kalteisen from Württemberg, Jacob Sass from Hesse, John Siegling from Erfurt—an immigrant group that Rogers describes as "efficient, tidy, and educated" (Rogers 1969, 146). The *Neudeutschen*, in contrast, entered a society that was on edge, that felt threatened by an enslaved population that was difficult to control, that was accosted by political issues such as nullification, states' rights, political-party squabbles more and more oriented to regional differences, and before long, by a developing and increasingly viral abolitionist movement that hemmed in and interfered with the status quo. The new Germans let themselves in, settled throughout the city so that they did not form a distinct ethnic enclave, and set about to quietly find their place in their newly adopted home. By mid-century, the 1,817 Germans in Charleston represented 39 percent of Charleston's foreign-born and 9.1 percent of the free white population. The free whites themselves, 20, 012 in number, were 46.6 percent of the city's total population. The 19,532 slaves represented 45.4 percent of the total, and free blacks, 8.0 percent. (Mehrländer 2011, 397)

As this relatively insignificant minority group of Lutheran Germans from the Kingdom of Hanover and the neighboring Duchy of Oldenburg had arrived in increasing numbers, either on their own or through the encouragement and facilitation of Captain Wieting, they began to coalesce into a recognizable ethnic group, and it seems not to have taken too long before they—by virtue of their agreeable habits—won acceptance by the city's native-born as well as by their esteemed and now-acculturated compatriots who had preceded them. As discussed earlier, a number of leaders emerged from among them to become acknowledged representatives of the larger group—leaders and culture brokers who tried to effectively manage the rank and file among the immigrants, as well as the immigrant *image* within the Charleston community. Among them was the much beloved John Andreas Wagener, whose whirlwind of civic leadership resulted in the founding of St. Matthew's *German* Lutheran Church, a company of *German* Firefighters, the city's *German* newspaper, and an ethnically cohesive settlement in upstate South Carolina that provided a "safety valve" [Bell] for the new arrivals. His enduring leadership would carry him into the post-war era to become the city's mayor in the election of 1871. Wagener's fellow culture-broker, the editor of Charleston's *Deutsche Zeitung*, was Franz Adolph Melchers [1826-1899]. He had taken over Wagener's *Der Teutone*, and through this later official organ of the city's German immigrant community, "became the conduit through which the new arrivals were schooled in the 'proper' Charlestonian opinions about secession and slavery" (Bell 1999, 17). These two, with the addition of Captain Wieting, constituted what was earlier referred to as a "triumvirate" of mentorship to the city's Germans. For a substantial number of immigrants, it was the case that Wieting had brought them to Charleston where they subsequently benefitted from the financial and social infrastructure that Wagener had helped to create, all the while being tutored by the newspaper editor Franz Melchers, as he "translated Charleston and America to the new immigrants, interpreting the city's institutions in the immigrants' own language." Thus, as Bell asserted, "Wieting, Wagener, and Melchers . . . held considerable influence over each aspect of the immigrants' journey—all the way from the wharves of Bremerhaven to a settled and comfortable life in Charleston" (Bell 1994, 254).

Some family members did indeed find a place within the spheres influenced by the leadership triumvirate. Peter Weber belonged to the Charleston *Unabhängige Turnverein*, the *Democratische Frei Männer Verein*, the German Fusilier Society, the German Ingraham Association, the Savings and Building Association, and Walhalla Lodge—every one of which had connections with either Wagener or Melchers, or both. Adelheid Bequest and her daughter Adeline were members of the *Deutsche Frauen Verein*. Hermann Knee was a director of the German Colonization Society (*Deutsche Ansiedlungs-Gesellschaft*), the group that undertook to establish the town of Walhalla, founded under the direction of Wagener in 1848. Knee's nephew [by marriage], Nicholas Fehrenbach, jun., succeeded to the Wagener legacy as a member of La Candeur Lodge [founded by Wagener in 1857], and his cousin's husband, Frederick Eduard Schroeder, was an orderly sergeant in the Palmetto Riflemen and served on several committees at St. Matthew's German Lutheran Church.

The picture of such a concerted leadership and a homogeneous group of followers being able to fall into a "settled and comfortable" life is, however, somewhat debatable. While such generalizations may apply to a broad perspective, not all individuals will fit the mold into which the general community is frequently poured. Against the backdrop just described, within institutions founded for their benefit and welfare, with instructions from their own higher-ups, and daily reminders that they were guests in town, individual German immigrants to Charleston still had to deal with the cards they found in their own hands, half of which were imprinted with the word *slavery*, the other half with the word *freedom*.

In most cases, as mentioned earlier, the Charleston German community is portrayed as unconditionally loyal to the South. Mehrländer sees clear distinctions among the three cities she studied, and Charleston's Germans are portrayed as possibly the most loyal to southern causes of them all. She emphasizes the fact that during the years leading up to secession and the subsequent war, Charleston's Germans rallied to the cause by fielding numerous militia companies. It was a fact that by 1860 "Charleston's German minority not only had the oldest German militia unit in the United States—the Charleston German Fusiliers of 1775—but also could support six active militia companies of which five were formed between 1842 and 1859, including the only ethnic German cavalry militia of the South." She clarifies that "because ethnic militias did not belong to the regular militia, but rather to the voluntary militia of a state, and were founded on the private initiative of individual persons, their founding alone was a statement of the desire to participate in the military and political culture of the adopted country." To the degree that the community cohered, recognized itself and was recognized by others, acknowledged and listened to its mentors, the personages who comprised these militia units, according to Mehrländer, held considerable sway. The ethnic community's social life "was almost completely in the hands of . . . twenty-four militia officers who, through a complex network of clubs, nepotistic connections, and their business contacts as merchants, had created a watertight structure of mutual interests that allowed them to reach nearly every aspect of community life. The German officers of the antebellum militias of Charleston were democratically oriented, loyal adoptive citizens of South Carolina, and more than one-third of them belonged to the group of slaveholders. Because of their publicly declared acceptance of the Southern way of life, there existed a symbiosis based on mutual respect between the natives and the German immigrants" (Mehrländer 2010, 66-67). Mehrländer confirms what Bell had earlier proposed in his dissertation: "Charleston's late antebellum German community . . . appears to have been 'guided' in somewhat of a specific manner. What made Charleston's German-America so unique is that the community was so uniform in its appearance. And it was this uniformity that prevented embarrassing situations from breaking out between the native-born whites and the Germans. There were no German radical socialists in the city, personal liberty was guaranteed by the constitution, and the Germans bought-in to the political and social structures of the old south. Everything was as it should be" (Bell 1996, 261-62).

There is thus little reason to doubt that a symbiosis between the immigrant and native communities existed and that to external appearances the German minority presented a uniform front. Nonetheless, it is certain that there were cracks in this structure. For example: Bell's reference to the Walhalla settlement as a "safety valve" for those who did not entirely buy into Charleston's demands; the somewhat conflicting evidence that some Germans were slaveholders, while at the same time some not infrequently co-habited with blacks, and in some cases flaunted local custom by marrying them—behaviors that sometimes flew in the face of white citizens' customary attitude. These indicators speak to what must have been the equivocal nature of German immigrants' interactions with a culture that rested on slavery. To judge German immigrants' *loyalty* to a Southern way of life that argued against outside interference in defense of its system of slavery, and to see in the immigrants' social behavior a consensus with a Southern morality based on the inferiority of a laboring class serving a propertied elite to which they would never belong, is to ignore a number of factors that would counter the solidarity that some commentators find *distinctive*. No matter how loud the message coming from the *Deutsche Zeitung*, no matter how congenial the brotherhood in any of the numerous *Vereine*, the immigrant knew in his heart that he was guest in this community and that his conduct was under constant scrutiny. With or without instruction, Charleston's Germans appeared to be so well behaved because they were so anxious to please. They consistently demonstrated the propriety that would keep them in the good graces of their hosts. The *Neudeutschen* had not only to prove themselves to the *Altdeutschen*, but also to the wealthy planter society in which they would look for a *modus vivendi*. Better to do the right thing than to cause any trouble. When the corporate society appeared in trouble, it would be advisable to lend support—outward support at least. When in Charleston, it would be politic to do as Charlestonians did, and to adopt the ways of those who held the reins. As long as one stayed on the side of the most-of-the-time-comprehensible majority, there were advantages to lying low and getting on with the business at hand—that is, becoming a productive member of the local community and carving out a sustainable existence for oneself and one's family. That they vied for acceptance by the community at large led them to accept many of the ways of that community, for open dissent would carry risk, and any attempt to swim against the current would invoke unnecessary hardship when things were already hard enough.

Understanding this fundamental nature of the German immigrant's experience in Charleston goes a long way in explaining the ethnic conscience as frequently a troubled one. It explains how many of them in Charleston—while they seemed to the outside world to behave differently than German immigrants elsewhere—might have shared the sentiments of those Germans who settled in the hill country of Texas and who were loathe to subscribe to the idea of slavery, or those in the Midwestern and Middle-Atlantic states who were strong supporters of what was clearly a wide-spread and vocal antislavery campaign. The abolitionist Frederick Douglas's 1859 pronouncement that "a German has only to be a German to be utterly opposed to slavery. In feeling, as well as in conviction and principle, they are antislavery" (Levine 1998, 56), was wishful thinking: he was ignoring the fact that his estimation of the *Germans* was often contradicted by the actions of many German-Americans, that it was hardly ever evident in the politics of most of the German-American press, not often manifested in the subcultures within German ethnic communities, or obvious in the responses of many to the conflicts that played out on the national stage, such as "Bleeding Kansas" and Harpers Ferry. "The substantial diversity of opinion manifested with the German-American population," writes Bruce Levine, "makes clear that, as Frederick Douglas knew, one actually needed to be more than simply 'a German' to be 'utterly opposed to slavery.'" It was primarily the "radical democrats" who had impressed Douglas and who, as Levine writes, were the strongest antislavery German-Americans—those who "traced their ideological ancestry back to the European Enlightenment by way of the eighteenth and nineteenth-century Age of Revolution." Such liberally radical democrats "opposed all forms of political privilege and inequality, championing instead the recognition and protection of universal human rights. They aspired to a more stable and humane society governed by and in the interests of all actual producers, a society whose carefully monitored and regulated economy would safeguard . . . the 'social freedom and independent existence' of each and a just and amicable coexistence among all" (Levine 1998, 59). Their aspirations were the result of what had been brewing in Europe for much of modern times and which emanated from those conditions that compelled so many to emigrate—conditions that were "specific to Germany", as well as "ideological influences that were international in origin and circulation".

It was the case, however, that there were not many *radical* democrats who escaped the European "Age of Revolution" to settle in Charleston. Hardly any of the Germans in that city would have assumed anything like a *radical* stance on any issue. If any one of them had harbored or demonstrated *radical* or ostensibly *enlightened* thoughts regarding the South's peculiar institution, s/he would have sensed the distinct vulnerability of the lone voice in the wilderness. In Charleston the pressure of the culture would keep the ethnic community in line, and it was the sought-after approbation of the larger community that kept the symbiotic relationship healthy and immune to disruption.

Within this particular immigrant family, the English-born Jane Thompson owned slaves that she inherited: at least four of them were considered part of her "trust estate". In her urban household, these domestic servants were not agricultural workers under the control of someone belonging to the planter/plantation elite. But however they came to her, she had not freed them. She had contested within the judicial system in order to keep them, and considered them her due property. She likely held them as maternalistically as her Episcopal rector had paternalistically mentored those in his household and in his parishes. It is not known whether Jane kept her slaves until they were officially emancipated by Lincoln's proclamation in 1863 or under what circumstances they left her guardianship/ownership.

Among the German family members, Nicholas Fehrenbach, jun. is known to have been a slaveholder. The 1860 census slave schedule shows him in possession of five slaves—in reality, a 58-year-old mulatto woman and a 45-year-old black male [possibly a couple] and three mulatto children, aged 8 [female], 6 [male], and 3 [female]. At this point in time, these slaves under the ownership of a Charleston businessman would likewise have morphed into domestic servants, a class whose bondage seemed somewhat less severe than those who belonged to the plantation labor force. Nicholas jun. was of true immigrant stock, but had become a true German-Charlestonian in every sense of the hyphenated label. He was at various points in his life a bar and tavern operator, but by 1860 was classifiable as a "Restauranteur". As a well-known figure in the ethnic community, Fehrenbach *appears* to have had as few moral qualms about employing/owning domestic slaves as did any other Charlestonian who had means sufficient to do so. He did not inherit his slaves: they had been purchased. As the son in a German immigrant family, he had risen from his lowly status as a member of a struggling family that had had to place two of his younger brothers in the Charleston Orphan House. He had used his bootstraps to pull himself up into the ranks of independent businessmen and was acculturating himself in the city's ways. His success would likely have been attested by the fact that he too employed the existing labor pool—primarily slaves—in his home and/or in his business. Fehrenbach's uncle [by marriage], Hermann Knee, was also a slave owner—of a 45-year-old female, according to the 1860 census [slave schedule]. His ownership of a slave would have seemed entirely appropriate to his status in the Walhalla community and her labor a welcome contribution in the pioneering household. Lastly, Frederick Schroeder, as another Charleston businessman, had at one point five slaves in his possession—doubtless justified through his proprietorship of the cigar store/import business and his status within the commercial community.

That the Weber brothers, J. W. F. Struhs, Nicholas Fehrenbach, sen., Charles Plath, or numerous other Germans did not own slaves suggests that either their means were insufficient at the time or that they had an inherent distaste for holding bondsmen. In any case, whether slave owner or not, it seems that most of the family members were content to operate within their relatively small own backyards. They would count mainly among those who struggled to build and hold onto a life for their immediate family, to survive the odds that Charleston challenged them with. If they understood themselves to be part of a minority community which longed to be aligned with the majority society, some were passive followers, other only slightly more in the forefront—with only minimal distinction allowed by their individual circumstances.

The aspects of ambiguity palpable in the general German-American population seem to have roiled the surface of the Charleston German immigrant community less than in any other urban—or rural—setting. Bell was able to conclude that "the experience of German immigrants in antebellum Charleston was both successful and unique. The Germans were successfully able to form their own ethnic community within the bounds of Charlestonian society. The unique mix of dynamics which were present, both in Charleston and in the German immigrants themselves, caused Charleston's version of German-America to be different than those that developed in other American cities during the antebellum period. Charleston's Germans did not become truly 'German-Americans'—they became 'German-Charlestonians'" (Bell 1996, 265). But the hyphen between *German* and *Charlestonian* is important: it articulates the argument that the German immigrants there were not so of one mind that the peculiar institution supporting the host community was accepted unconditionally and without qualm. The German immigrant to the Lowcountry's jewel of a city was in a most peculiar predicament: the cards he had been dealt required demonstrated loyalty to a way of life that was foreign to the foreigner and which commanded allegiance without dissent to principles that countermanded those that lay deep within him. When the war became a reality, he would be tested further.

VIII

SECESSION AND THE WAR

So it was that the *peculiar institution* lay at the heart of the composite social, political, and cultural construct of everyday life for most antebellum Southerners, but especially for South Carolinians, and most particularly for Charlestonians—both native and immigrant. The reality of the relationship between whites and blacks was admittedly different in South Carolina compared to any other southern state, and there was every reason why that state was moved to lead the efforts toward disunion and why it was considered by the nation to be the hotbed of rebellion. For almost a decade South Carolina's leading citizens and its legislators had waved the banner and, unsatisfied with any mediating compromises, had moved inexorably toward independence and resumption of the state's "position among the nations of the world as a separate and independent State; with full power to levy war, conclude peace, contract alliances, establish commerce, and to do all other acts and things which independent States may of right do." As of December 20, 1860, the ordinance signed in Institute Hall on Meeting Street made it official: "We, the People of the State of South Carolina, in Convention assembled, do declare and ordain . . . that the union now subsisting between South Carolina and other States, under the name of 'The United States of America,' is hereby dissolved" (*Declaration* 1860, 10).

As was suggested earlier in regard to the matter of slavery in general, the immigrant's attitude doubtless would have been an equivocal one. Led, pushed and pulled, by contending but influential forces, the non-native antebellum Charleston immigrant would have labored under the stress of a personal tension that reflected the inheritance of different and less synonymous cultural factors. How easily could the immigrant accept the notion that what had been the beckoning, *United-through-revolution*-States—a *unified-by-trial* nation offering new hope, opportunity, freedom, and independence—should be dismissed, broken up, by a host community persistently arguing a separatist and unproven ideology? Even if the immigrant mind could comprehend the superficial arguments, to say nothing of the writing between the lines, it would have been almost impossible to swim against the current of a populace that had been whipped into a kind of secession frenzy that celebrated separation and condemned anyone who did not dance to the South Carolina tune. Ever since their individual arrivals during earlier years of the century, what might have seemed like white noise that had begun when the concept of nullification was first being discussed and disputed had, by the election of Lincoln in 1860, been tuned up to a deafening decibel level that no one seemed able to turn off. Indisputably *not* in control of what was happening, the immigrant might well have felt that the 1860 ordinance was a penultimate step that would surely bring darker times. While most South Carolinians had talked themselves into thinking that their defection from the Union would somehow be peacefully accommodated, most European immigrants would have thought it folly not to expect serious repercussions. They would have been sympathetic to the sentiment expressed by the elderly South Carolina statesman, Judge James Petrigru, who declared "South Carolina . . . too small for a republic, and too large for a lunatic-asylum" (Goodheart 2011, 12). Over the months that followed, they would be condemned to sit by and watch the changes that would happen to their new world.

The courses of the individual families were of course running parallel to the cultural forces that were in play on the municipal, regional, and national stages during the years leading up the Civil War. One might ponder over the personal contexts in which the immigrant family members would have experienced the political upheaval leading to secession and the subsequent military engagement between a confederacy of rebellious states and a Federal government defending the constituency of the Union. How did they manage the war years, how much of their immigrant selves came into play during the time that, quite literally, changed everything and after which nothing would ever be the same? Where were they in their immigrant lives when their adopted State decided to sever its relationship with the Federal government? How did they react to what became the new *law of the land*, what did they individually think about being residents of a *rebellious* State, exactly what did they experience when the war began or what did they go through during Charleston's prolonged bombardment—"an instrument of terror to carry out the wanton destruction of private property and the persecution of a civilian population" (Phelps 2002, 10)? Many questions with few definitive answers, only conjectures really: the response was doubtless different for each individual family, depending on whether one was of German or English origin.

Johann Rosenbohm, of course, had abandoned the Charleston scene already in 1839, apparently deciding that a life in New York held more promise than one in Charleston, a city abuzz with the nullification issue and seemingly almost always at odds with national policy. His sisters' families, however, had remained in Charleston to deal with the situation as best they could. Anna Maria, with seven children and an out-of-work husband, was not having an easy time of it already by the mid-forties. She thought herself abandoned by her husband—he despondent, unemployed, and broke—and had resorted to put two of her children in the Charleston Orphan House. She survived economically [barely] by operating a small dry-goods store subsidized by her brother-in-law, Hermann Knee, and sub-letting a portion of her rented quarters. But even after her husband returned and the sons were taken out of the orphanage, the family's situation did not improve. The Fehrenbachs then followed Johann Rosenbohm's example and went north—in their case to the new (1848) state of Wisconsin. But life in Wisconsin turned out to be no more a bed of roses than existence in Charleston had been. The family broke apart in the 1850s, everyone but Nicholas, sen. returning to Charleston. By the time the Civil War had been forced by South Carolina's secession and the assault on Fort Sumter had occurred, Nicholas Fehrenbach had run afoul of the law and had become a convict. He remained alone in Wisconsin until well after the war, while the rest of the family returned to Charleston to face the consequences of secession and, once the war began, endure the hostilities in the city to which they had originally come.

Catharina, married to Hermann Knee, had enjoyed a more stable existence than Anna Maria. Hermann was successful as a grocer and respected in the German community. He was fortunate to belong to the circle of Johann Andreas Wagener, and his friendship with Wagener gave him an instrumental role in the Walhalla undertaking. After the colony's founding in 1850, the Knees left Charleston to be among the founding families, and Hermann became a successful businessman in the upstate community. As established residents in Walhalla, the couple and their children were not among the crowds celebrating the ordinance's signing nor among those watching the fireworks at Fort Sumter a few months later.

Johann Rosenbohm's third sister, Adelheid Bequest, experienced the march to secession, managed to survive the assault on Charleston, held on tenaciously during the unsettledness of the Reconstruction years, and died only in 1895 at the ripe age of 86. During her years in Charleston, she lived close to, or with, her daughter Adeline married to Frederick Schroeder. As for the Schroeders, they had lost three children by 1860 but had a son born shortly after the firing on Fort Sumter. Frederick was 39 in 1862 and thus escaped the net that trawled for enlistees for the Confederacy. Adeline died in 1864 before the war was over, and her mother likely played an important part in raising the toddler Adeline left behind. The widower Frederick continued to build up his business, be involved in the German ethnic community, and witness—somewhat on the sidelines, but still resident in a bombarded city—the results of South Carolina's secession through the years of the war and its aftermath.

In the years immediately leading up to the war, the Peter Weber family was in the picture only through the couple's son Charles and daughter Anna Maria: both parents were gone by 1859. Their son was first in the care of his uncle and then in the Charleston Orphan House as of early 1862. Charles would be evacuated from Charleston along with the other children to safer quarters in Orangeburg for most of the war. He was within the protection of the orphanage when the fighting ceased and was not released to his sister and brother-in-law until 1867. Charles's sister Anna Maria was a mature 16-year-old when her mother died in 1859, and since she did not marry Charles Plath until after the war, she somehow weathered Charleston's turmoil all by herself, while her immigrant husband-to-be fought in the war as a Confederate soldier. Johann Weber was too old to be called into service for the Confederacy, but he and his wife and their surviving children would have experienced the Charleston home-front scene during the hostilities, whipsawed back and forth along with the reports of battle successes and battle losses, suffering, but withstanding, the shelling of the city for almost two years.

By the time secession and the war were imminent, the Struhs couple had undergone the train and covered-wagon trip to Walhalla where J. W. F. established citizenship and where he and Dorothea were heavily involved in building that community. They were thus absent from the brouhaha in Charleston when the Ordinance of Secession was signed, as well as the excitement surrounding the firing on Fort Sumter. But as the story goes, the family subsequently left the Walhalla settlement. The reason for the family's departure from Walhalla—whether in search of something better or because Johann Wilhelm Friedrich was recruited or volunteered into Confederate service—remains something of a mystery. As does his subsequent death in an explosion—whether the result of a civilian accident or a war-related incident. Equally undocumented is the sequence of events after his death that his widow and children experienced during the remainder of the war years and the beginnings of Reconstruction.

Beyond these descriptions of the personal circumstances of each of the families, yet more questions beg for answers. Did the family Germans who were slaveholders believe, like John Andreas Wagener, that "the Negro must be ruled by force" and, if necessary, "with the help of the whip" (Mehrländer 2010, 74), and therefore subscribe openly to the oligarchs' program to separate the State from the Union in order to maintain their *right* to own slaves? Did the Germans sense the heavy hand of the newly formed Confederate government when, through the Banishment Act of August 1861, it forced them to declare their loyalty to the Confederacy in order to remain in their new country—the *country* that overnight had rejected the one to which they had immigrated?

What did they all feel when hostilities seemed to be on their very doorstep? The 1862 Battle of Secessionville on James Island was only ten miles away; by July of 1863, Union troops had taken Morris Island, and Rear Admiral John B. A. Dahlgren had demolished Fort Sumter; in August General Quincy A. Gillmore, "reinforced by 3,000 fresh troops, had begun installation of the famous 'Swamp Angel,' a powerful eight-inch cannon capable of hurling 200-pound shells into the heart of Charleston itself" (Hoole 1945, 540-41). How strong was the sense of loyalty to a political and cultural entity that had been cultivated by the native majority and forced on the less acculturated newcomers? Did one question it, or go with the flow?

As if in answer to at least one question, Mehrländer suggests that *patriotism* was particularly strong among German women:

> [I]nspired by the activities of the ladies of New Orleans to finance a cannon boat through donations, a similar project was started in Charleston in the spring of 1862 with the significant support of the *Charleston Courier*. One Miss Gelzer donated five dollars, and thus began South Carolina's legendary Ladies' Gunboat Fund; a wave of donations poured in from women throughout the state, resulting in the financing of the gunboat *Palmetto State*. The list of donors, which is extant only for 1862 and discretely names no sums, names eleven German women from Walhalla, including the wife of the publisher of the *Deutsche Zeitung*, Franz Melchers, who was there at the time. In Walhalla . . . the German ladies were removed from the critical eye of the Charleston society and were thus under no public pressure to contribute patriotic donations. They did so in spite of this, because they all had at least one male family member in the ranks of the Confederate army (Mehrländer 2010, 69-70).

She indicates that the German ladies came from the Ostendorff, Bahntge, Wendelken, Ahrens, Mehrtens, Michaelis, Riecke, and Schroeder families. Mrs. Knee was apparently not involved, but the mention of the *Schroeder* name suggests that perhaps it was Adeline Schroeder who participated in this endeavor, visiting in Walhalla at the time to escape temporarily the tensions in Charleston. Mehrländer's last sentence, however, speaks volumes and really does not address the question about the strength or nature of *patriotism* or *loyalty* to a Confederacy carrying out military actions that took sons and husbands from families to face the very real prospect of death. Nor does it reveal what the typical immigrant went through in facing the realities of the war. While many of the wealthier native-born families became refugees, leaving their plantations to wander throughout the state in search of safer places, that was not an option for most of the immigrants who lacked relatives located elsewhere or the financial wherewithal to pick up and leave where they had just settled. Walhalla seemed the only option to escape the *hotbed of rebellion*—but only if one had the right connections.

What about the everyday life and business of those who spent the war years in Charleston? Did anyone in the immigrant family participate in the black market, encourage and benefit from the blockade-running that sustained every-day and mercantile life in a city and country under siege? As a matter of fact, records reveal that Frederick Schroeder was one of the Charleston merchants who were invested in the William Bee blockade-running Importing and Exporting Company—the first of a total of five trading companies that were incorporated in South Carolina in 1862-63 for the purpose of running the blockade. (Mehrländer 2011, 220) Mehrländer treats the Bee Company and its investors extensively, particularly the German ones. Several statements from her analysis provide a backdrop for Schroeder's involvement:

- Of the 245 Bee shareholders the twenty-six German businesses amounted to more than 10% and were thus overrepresented in relation to their population percentage in Charleston. They had purchased shares valued at $79,000: More than 42% of the participating German businesses were groceries; over 19% dealt in dry goods or sold spirits.
- The German businessmen were of course conscious of the risks of running the blockade. They trusted William Bee, because his company . . . had Germans at the decisive contact points.
- Investing funds in blockade-running was a two-sided affair for the participants: the ships chartered by Bee delivered urgently needed weapons and ammunition for the Confederate Army. In return cotton, which had collected in great quantities in the port of Charleston and was to bring profit in Europe, was exported. Until the end of the war this aspect of blockade-running was publicly considered highly patriotic.
- The Germans . . . were certainly interested in financial profits and had not bought the shares solely for patriotic reasons . . . . For these men there was never a question that they would have a future in the South after the war. Charleston had become their home; they had invested every cent in the new existence and refused to let a war destroy their achievements. To the contrary, they wanted to increase their property and, at the same time, do something for the Confederacy.
- There are fortune figures for 1859-60 for twenty-two of the twenty-six German companies that had invested in the I & E Co. According to these figures they possessed private and business fortunes amounting

to $481, 510 as well as eighty-nine slaves and were thus quite wealthy before the outbreak of the war. Much of this was invested in property and bound the men locally to Charleston or to the state of South Carolina. The profit in shares ... earned by blockade-running increased their prewar total fortunes by 147.6% to $711,000. (Mehrländer 2011, 219-33)

The evidence presented by Mehrländer suggests again a somewhat equivocal answer to the original question as to whether anyone in the family supported and/or profited from the Confederate blockade-running enterprise, and did they do so as a demonstration of patriotism or purely for self-gain? The initial investment by Frederick Schroeder [in partnership with A. Schroeder in a company known as *Schroeder Brothers, Importer of Havana Cigars*; the partner *brother* was doubtless his wife Adeline] with Bee was one share, valued at $1,000. The total taxed fortune of his company in 1859-60 was $20,000; his minimal stock profit through the I & E Co. was $9,000; in 1870, R.G. Dun & Co. listed his company's financial volume at $2,000—$5,000 with a rating of 3 (Fair), and in 1880, a volume of $10,000—$25,000 with a rating of 2.5 (Good). While Schroeder was thus a relatively small player in this game, he was nonetheless a successful businessman, belonged at the time to what would have been considered the wealthier class, and had every reason to want to increase his financial base which he as an immigrant had invested in an adoptive city and state that were now threatened. The evidence presented earlier that he held a number of slaves/domestics may indeed have affected his sense of loyalty or patriotism to a government bent on defending that kind of property, although it seems more likely that as an immigrant businessman Schroeder became a slaveholder in his new country because it was the easiest way to access the labor force and patently the way of life in the city in which he had settled, regardless of whether the idea of chattel ownership caused him any moral qualms or not. It is safe to assume that Schroeder took the risk in investing in Bee's company more for financial gain than out of demonstrative support for the new government that he was beholden to. Havana cigars would have been considered luxury goods, and importing them through the blockade would hardly have been viewed as supportive of the Confederate war effort.

Frederick Schroeder's involvement with Bee's I & E Company demonstrates that members of the German immigrant community had little choice but to carry on their personal and business lives during the war in Charleston, despite the city's vulnerability. Like his brother-in-law Hermann Knee and his wife's cousin, Nicholas Fehrenbach, jun., Frederick Schroeder had become a respected member of the German Lutheran community, a community determined to survive and prosper through the remaining years of the century. When toward the end of the century, the German ethnic community celebrated for an entire week the 50th wedding anniversary of J. C. H. Claussen and his wife Dorothea, Frederick Schroeder would be a prominent enough representative to compose and contribute a poem in Low German as part of the program [see footnote 16 above]. Typical of the many other now-settled immigrants of North German origin, he would have successfully maneuvered a half century of Charleston life, including the state's severing itself from the Union and the resulting and bitterly fought Civil War, to become a participating and acculturated Charleston citizen as the city moved into the twentieth century.

To be sure, the experience of the English Thompson family was not like that of the North German immigrants. Their backgrounds were different: the former had been there longer and their economic relationship to the city was on a different footing. There is no evidence that any of the Thompsons were engaged in blockade-running investments, other than perhaps as purchasers of some small goods that made their way onto the local market by that means. Nor were they investors in business concerns that reaped returns from the war effort. We might suppose, nonetheless, that Jane Thompson, as a slaveholder and member of the Episcopal church community to which so many of the old guard belonged, had tuned in to the leadership of ministers such as Paul Trapier and would have advocated for secession and welcomed the formation of the Confederacy.

During the period leading up to the war, the Thompsons were engaged in their own battles. As noted earlier, the marriage was troubled by the time Jane joined the St. Stephen's congregation—when James's name was not included as father to any of the four children baptized there, obviously by Jane's insistance rather than because James was not a member of the congregation. By the mid-fifties James Thompson was adulterously involved with Mary J. Ellis, with whom he lived until his death in 1872. One of the Thompson daughters was married in 1856, but the others did not marry until later, so that on the eve of secession in 1860 and the beginning of the war in early 1861, Jane still had four of her children under her roof, the eldest, 27, the youngest, 15. Sometime in the late 50s, the Thompsons' eldest son, Joseph E. S., went—or was sent—to New York for schooling. He was awarded a certificate from the "Executive Committee on Evening Schools of the Board of Education" in December of 1859. He married there and did not return to Charleston until 1870 or shortly thereafter. His story will be told in the following chapter.

As a slave owner, Jane held human property as well as real estate, and by the time the war began she probably no longer strongly identified with her immigrant origins. She might even have been found among the throngs who celebrated the secession *victory* and been counted among those who welcomed the war as a means to push back against the interference of the abolitionists and the dominance of the North. Her involvement in local politics, however, was likely curtailed by her involvement on more personal fronts.

The Thompson marital discord broke into the open before South Carolina undertook its own divorce. Jane brought suit against her husband in 1858 in a case that was heard before the Court of Appeals in its January 1859 term. Describing the suit as "a bill for alimony", the judge acknowledged that there had been a previous proceeding of a similar nature some ten years earlier that had been dismissed, but which "as will be seen hereafter . . . will have no practical effect in this case." The Court record is worth reading in full: it articulates much about the moral code of the period before the war [not that it changed dramatically afterwards!] and provides insight into the personal struggles of a family operating against the backdrop of everything that was afoot on the local, state, and national stages. The judge would summarize as follows:

> Again, after a long estrangement and separation, which had continued for several years, on 31st March, 1852, the defendant returned to his wife and family, and cohabited with her for a time—not exceeding a week. He then suddenly withdrew himself from her society, and has continued to live separate from her ever since . . . . [T]he plaintiff . . . bases her claim to a decree for alimony upon facts that have occurred subsequently to the 31st March, A.D. 1852, when the reunion and short lived reconciliation took place.
>
> The charges of the bill are that the defendant was of intemperate habits, and frequently beat and abused his wife, the complainant, stating a case amounting to *saevitia,* adulterous intercourse with another woman, and abandonment and desertion, without contributing anything to her support and the support of his children, which she bore to him, and this without justifiable cause.
>
> In regard to the first charge, there was not a tittle of proof to prove the *saevitia*; entirely unsupported by testimony, it falls to the ground; nothing more need to be said on that subject.
>
> As to the adultery, there was a great deal of testimony, and much of it was contradictory. The two principal witnesses brought forward to support the allegation, Emily Shepherd and Ann Gaskin, are women of such worthless and abandoned character, and such bad repute, as to render their testimony utterly worthless of belief. I cannot, with safety, predicate my judgment upon anything they have said. Striking out their evidence upon the question of adultery, I do not perceive that the proof is sufficient to support the charge . . . . Having thus disposed of the two first charges of the bill, I must now proceed to consider that which remains. I am to decide this claim for alimony upon the abandonment and desertion of the husband and the equity of the wife to a settlement of her own estate, upon which

the marital rights have not yet attached . . . . The marriage tie is of so indissoluble a nature, as not to be broken asunder for slight and trivial causes; for incompatibility of temper, uncongenial tastes and manners, or insulting language. To some minds these things are hard to bear, but parties placed in these unhappy circumstances, must submit and make the most of this condition. At least the law requires this sacrifice.

The causes which have led to the separation of this unfortunate pair, I incline to think, have not been fully revealed in the evidence. There is a mystery about it—some secret causes of disgust and alienation which have not been made public. But so far as the circumstances have been brought out, they leave the defendant without the shadow of justification. The history of the plaintiff, as brought to the view of the Court, does not exhibit her as a pattern of conjugal propriety—very far from it. But her life and manners present as high, a higher standard of propriety than his.

The defendant, after several years of separation from his wife and family, without contributing anything to their support and maintenance, on the last day of March, 1852, suddenly and unexpectedly returned to the house on the corner of Laurens street, where the family was then residing, and where the plaintiff kept a boarding house. He came to stay, he said, and that he was going to act as a husband and father should act. There is no doubt that a full reconciliation then took place. But, strange to say, without any quarrel, or any complaint on his part, so far as is known, within a week he again abandoned his wife and family, and has lived apart from them ever since. During all this time he has withheld from them all pecuniary aid in the means of living, and for the education of the children, acting towards the latter in the most unnatural manner. He *did* allow them the use of the house on the corner of Laurens street. And here, I am constrained to say, that Mrs. Thompson, thus deserted, with a large family, consisting for the most part of girls, did, by extraordinary energy and prudence, support herself and her children in a creditable manner, give her daughters a genteel education, and so raised them, as to manners, character and accomplishments, that two of them have formed respectable matrimonial connections. For a person placed in her situation, this was doing much and reflects the highest credit upon her.

I consider the overtures made by Thompson in May, 1852, about the time or shortly after the furniture was removed, as illusory. He wished her to go to him, and live with him in a house he had rented in Wolfe street. He did this under legal advice, and doubtless, supposed that in the case of a suit for alimony, it would have strong bearing in his favor. But why did he wish her to give up the rooms and comfortable house in Laurens street, where she had been so long living, and where she could carry on her business as the keeper of a boarding house, and go to the house in Wolfe street, where she could not have these advantages and comforts? The ostensible reason offered for the desired change is plausible. It was alleged to be that the latter house was nearer to the Rail Road shops, where he followed his business and trade. The insincerity of this assigning this reason is shown in the fact that very soon after the separation, one of his hands was severely burned, and in consequence maimed, and he was unable to work. During all this horrible sufferings from this burn, and when utterly helpless, he would not return to his family, but preferred to receive, rather, the charitable attention of strangers; to this day he has not labored in the workshops of the Rail Road Company, and it is doubtful if he ever will again be able to work at his trade; yet, he assigns the distance of Laurens street from the workshops, and the punctuality, &c. in the house of labor required there, as the reason of his unwillingness to reside with his wife in Laurens street. The plaintiff wisely refused to commit herself to that movement for as she said, if I go to live with him in Wolfe street, and he falls out with me, then I shall not have a place in which to lay my head. My mind is not without a suspicion that this overture was a *ruse* by which to get the family out of the house in Laurens street.

Under all the circumstances, my judgment is, that the plaintiff is entitled to a decree for alimony; what the amount shall be, I will hereafter declare.

The next part of the case which I will consider, is the application for a settlement upon the wife of the property which she has recently acquired as heir at law, and distributee of her sister, Mrs. Murray.[44] This will depend upon principles somewhat different from that in which alimony is allowed . . . .

---

[44] Elizabeth Murray had died in April 1855. Part of her estate would have involved her inheritance from her parents. It also likely involved several slaves that Elizabeth had inherited and doubtless kept. There are records (see *The Private Register of the Rev. Paul Trapier*, 1958) that Paul Trapier baptized Nat and Lydia, "slaves of Mr. Jas. Murray", at St. Michael's in 1842, as well as children of Harry and Lydia, "slaves of Mr. James Murray". Trapier also married Robert, a slave of Mrs. Bonneau, and Elizabeth, "slave of Mrs. James Murray", on October 25, 1949, "at her mistress' house, before many witnesses with consent of owners." See also Footnote 30 above.

In this case we have seen under what circumstances the defendant has separated himself from his wife. His circumstances are easy and competent; his rental is respectable. And so far from making provision for his deserted wife, he has cast her off, though the whole of his estate was derived from his marriage with her, or has sprung directly out of what she brought him in marriage. He has nothing, and all her real and personal estate, which she owned at the time of the marriage, has been so managed, that the title has vested in him absolutely, to her entire exclusion.

On this state of facts, my judgment is, that all the property, real and personal, which the plaintiff has acquired from the estate of her deceased sister, Mrs. Murray, be settled on the said Mrs. Thompson, the plaintiff, for her own separate use and benefit during her life, and after her death, to her children who may be living at her death, the issue of deceased children taking in the division the deceased parent's share . . . .

It is further ordered and decreed, that by way of alimony, the defendant, the said James Thompson, do permit the plaintiff and her family to live in, and occupy, without rent, and free from hindrance and molestation, the house and lot on the corner of Laurens street, where she now resides, until the further order of this Court.

It is further ordered and decreed, that the defendant pay the costs of this suit (*Reports of cases . . . 1859*, 10).

That was, however, not the end of it. It is easy to understand why Jane felt that she had not received from the Court everything she deserved. It is also easy to understand how much the cards of the time were stacked against her—or any woman in a similar predicament. The Court seems to conclude that it is acting magnanimously in its judgment for the plaintiff in deciding that the defendant is to let her continue to live in the residence rent free. There is no mention of the fact that the house on Laurens Street was a property that she had acquired at auction in 1842 in her own name. As a *feme covert* it automatically became the property of the husband—that house and everything else that was hers through inheritance from her first husband or from her father. Forever, it seemed, she had suffered losses by virtue of the men in her life, first through her father's machinations, now with her husband legally managing everything that was hers. At least the Court agreed to accord her her rightful inheritance after Elizabeth's death, and, because of James's marital behavior, to prevent it from falling into his hands.

The complainant Jane subsequently appealed her case on the grounds that: (1) "Because the Chancellor, having decided that the complainant is entitled to alimony, it follows that she should have some provision for her support adequate to her necessities; whereas, it is submitted that the decree has fallen far short of what should be awarded to her. That the abandonment of complainant by the defendant has been aggravated by his lewd and indecent mode of life, and as the property has been acquired entirely through the wife and her means, it is submitted that the whole, or at least the greater portion of the income should be assigned to her"; (2) "Because it is respectfully submitted that the Chancellor erred in his conclusion that the adulterous connection of the defendant has not been established by the testimony." In response to the appeal, the Court issued the following opinion [excerpted]:

> The plaintiff, wife, appeals as to the extent of this allowance, complaining substantially that the decree makes to her a very inadequate allowance, when the extent of the husband's income and the circumstances of aggravation in his conduct, particularly his adultery with Mary Ellis, are properly considered.
>
> We have a general impression that the allowance is inadequate under the circumstances of the case, but we cannot venture to prescribe any additional fixed sum until we know more precisely the extent of the income of the husband and wife respectively; and we desire the aid of further evidence and a report from the Master on these particulars.
>
> The amount of alimony depends largely on the extravagance of the husband's misconduct. Unquestionably his misconduct in this case has been great and without any excuse apparent in the evidence. He has left his wife without pecuniary contribution on his part, to settle two of his daughters in respectable marriages, and to procure remunerative occupations for some of his sons. He vilipends in this answer his wife as rendering a separation from her necessary, by reason of her drunkenness, and offers no testimony in support of the vile charge. He refuses to recognize any claim of his daughters on him, whether presented by written request by one who was sick for flannel to protect her person, or by another to shake hands with him in the street.
>
> But the great matter of aggravation is the alleged adultery of defendant with Mary Ellis . . . . It is very distasteful to proceed through the details, but we must to some extent justify our conclusion.
>
> The defendant in his answer does not deny the adultery. His answer is casuistically evasive. He does deny that he lived in "*open*" adultery with Mary Ellis, and that "he *recognized or treated*" her as his kept mistress, or that there was "any familiarity or sociability" between them which would have rendered the visits to his separate establishment by his wife and children unseemly; but all this amounts merely to an expression of sentiment on his part that he was not so

flaunting his adultery in the eyes of the community and his family as to make visits of respectable females to him compromise their character. In substance he denies notoriety of the illicit intercourse, and by negative pregnant, admits the existence of the intercourse. Again, he admits that an unmarried white female, still retained in his employment, was delivered on his premises of a bastard, (and another bastard seems to have been subsequently produced by her under similar circumstances,) and he says "it is impossible for him to say, and he does not know who is the father of the said child." It may well have been impossible for him to say who was the father of the child, if he suspected others to have intercourse with his paramour, but it was surely possible for him to say, if he had no illicit intercourse with Mary Ellis, that whoever might be, he was certainly not the father of her offspring.[45] And why was she not produced by him to contradict the adultery, if her testimony could have been effective?

The positive testimony satisfies us of the fact of adultery. Mrs. McLaughlin, an unimpeached witness, deposes as to facts inconsistent with any other conclusion. Besides that, the testimony of the defendant's witnesses, especially of his nephew, Thomas Thompson, concerning instances of familiarity in the master's lying on the bed of his servant and fondling her brats—indeed, without pursuing needlessly disgusting details, every portion of the testimony on the point, without a particle of contradiction, compels the conclusion that the defendant is living in degrading concubinage with his menial servant . . . . [B]ut where a husband deserts and abandons his wife and lawful children, and lives in the same city in concubinage with a servant, begetting bastards on her body, he had little claim to the indulgence of any tribunal which proceeds for the enforcement of law and morals.

This whole matter as to the extent of alimony depends on the circumstances of each particular case; and we have not the means of information in this cause to determine the precise amount which should be allowed. Counsel differ widely in their estimates of the incomes of husband and wife; and they differ as to the sources from which the estate of the husband has been derived, whether from his labor or accretion from his wife's estate at the date of the contract of marriage . . . . In some of these particulars we lack information. Besides it seems to us clear that the plaintiff, by way of what is

---

[45] A 2-year-old child of Mary Ellis, Mary Ann Ellis, died October 20, 1861, and is buried in Magnolia Cemetery.

called temporary alimony, or by any other name, is entitled to reimbursement for her expenses in a successful litigation.

It is ordered and decreed that it be referred to Master Tupper to inquire and report as to the extent of the incomes respectively of the parties to this cause, as to the sources of their derivation, and as to the expenses of the plaintiff in this litigation; and that he recommend to the Court what is a suitable allowance to the plaintiff for alimony under all the circumstances of the case. In the meantime the plaintiff must be protected in the enjoyment of the use or rent of the Laurens street house, which has been allowed to her by the Chancellor.

It is further ordered that the circuit decree be reformed according to this opinion.

There is no record of the reformed decree and no further evidence to examine to determine whether Jane Thompson ever received monetary satisfaction from her estranged husband. Her chances of a positive monetary settlement were not great. However long it might have taken Master Tupper to decide on the exact amount of her alimony, Jane would soon have to face the war years as if she were a widow. In 1860 she still had five slaves, a 24-year-old female and her offspring, ages 2, 6, 8, and 10—probably not the original slaves she had inherited, and possibly a family she inherited from her sister Elizabeth. As the victim of a somewhat scandalous marriage breakup, however, her survival as a single woman with a family to support in besieged Charleston would test the mettle of the best Episcopalian.

Even if one—of English or German background—had been of one mind with the secessionists, felt unconditionally threatened by the Yankee abolitionists, convinced that slavery was sanctioned by God and the natural way of things on earth, and of staunch conviction that separation from the Union meant the preservation of freedom to maintain the *status quo* under the aegis of a new government, the war as it came to Charleston might have changed one's mind. After the excitement of taking Fort Sumter and initiating the hostilities, Charlestonians had little choice but to accept what came their way. "Troops came and went. Men from other Southern states who had never traveled more than a few miles from home now took up residence in military camps in and about the city. Fortifications were built all over the area; on James Island, on the Charleston neck, and on the islands around the city" (Rosen 1994, 78). Almost immediately the Union blockaded the port city with warships, a move that quickly affected Charleston's economy. The response in time was to run the blockade, and Charleston was transformed into a center of privateering. "The blockade did, however, make life unpleasant for Southerners generally and Charlestonians in particular. Early in the war a merchant wrote that the 'blockade is still carried on and every article of consumption particularly in the way of groceries . . . [is] getting very high'" (Rosen 1994, 81). The German grocers would have questioned what they had done to deserve this state of affairs, while undoubtedly looking to blockade-running as a desirable effort on their behalf. But it was not long before Federal forces had occupied Port Royal, no more than fifty miles south of Charleston, and General Lee was in town by November of 1861 for the purpose of getting defenses readied along the Georgia and South Carolina coasts. Despite Lee's efforts—he himself was not sure they would be effective—the mood in Charleston was not a happy one. "'Everything looks very dark and gloomy,' Jacob Schirmer confided to his diary in November, 1861. 'Our enemies appear to be increasing their forces all around us.' The next month, Schirmer was even more depressed. 'There has not been any year of our life that has passed, that has been fraught with so many events which will ever be remembered and which should indelibly imprint on our minds the instability and uncertainty of all our hopes and expectations.' The acerbic Emma Holmes wrote, 'The fiercest wrath and bitterest indignation are directed towards Charleston, by 'our dearly beloved brethren of the north.' They say 'the rebellion commenced where Charleston *is*, and shall *end*, where Charleston *was*'.' Other Charlestonians worried about the city they loved. In May, 1862, Harriet Middleton wrote to her cousin Susan, 'Do you not hope that Charleston may be saved. I don't mind our house but I can't bear to give up the old streets and buildings, and the churches. I feel such a strong personal love of the old place.' Harriet Middleton, however, left town for the safety of Flat Rock, North Carolina" (Rosen 1994, 85). Middleton's sentiments were undoubtedly felt by many of the old families who had inherited Charleston's charm and Southern ways. The immigrant resident could hardly afford to feel quite so sentimental, literally or figuratively, about the old streets and buildings. They would have been worried about the roofs over their heads, if, in fact, they even owned them.

Less than a year [December 11, 1861] after the Ordinance of Secession had been signed, one of Charleston's worst fires swept through the city: "The fires spread from Hasell Street at East Bay to the market, to Meeting Street and eventually to the Ashley River along Tradd Street. It destroyed the Circular Congregational Church, the Art Association, and whole sections of Meeting Street and Queen Street. Ironically, it destroyed both St. Andrews Hall on Broad Street, where secession had been debated and enacted, and Institute Hall on Meeting Street, where the Ordinance of Secession had been signed . . . . Five hundred forty acres had burned, and 575 homes had been destroyed" (Rosen 1994, 86). The same Judge James L. Petrigru who had thought it folly for the state to separate from the Union ["too small . . . a nation and too large . . . an insane asylum"] and whose home on Broad Street fell victim to the flames, wrote to his daughter that ". . . the whole space in S.W. direction from the foot of Hasell street on the Cooper River side to the Ashley River at a point between Tradd and Gibbs street is one smoking ruin . . . . It is far easier to bear what comes from the hand of God than that which proceeds from the folly or wickedness of man" Rosen 1994, 86).

At the time of the great fire, Frederick Schroeder had his cigar importing business at 62 Meeting Street in Ward 1. Whether the Schroeders lived on the premises is not known, although the city's own 1861 census does not indicate them living at another location. But Ward 1 encompassed the area "bounded by north side of Queen, south by Ashley River, east by Cooper River, and west side of Meeting", so that the property at 62 Meeting would likely have been destroyed. The Schroeders were, however, only occupants: according to the census, the property belonged to the Estate of John Hunter. Years later the Schroder [the name no longer orthographically umlauted] Bros. import business was located at 219 Meeting Street "opposite the Charleston Hotel", suggesting that the 1861 fire had indeed interrupted the Schroeder family's personal and business life in the first year of the war.

Charleston wards in 1883. The ward boundaries were changed in 1882, so that Frederick Schroeder's business at #62 Meeting Street in Ward 1 in 1861 was located north of Broad Street in what is designated here as Ward 3. From the American Geographical Society Library, University of Wisconsin-Milwaukee Libraries.

Jane Thompson was possibly less directly affected—physically at least. She was living on Laurens Street, north of where the fire started, and in the opposite direction of where it had spread. Her trust property on King and South Bay would also have escaped the flames. James Thompson was living with his mistress in a wooden house he owned on the corner of Bogard and Sires Street—also far north of where the fire was located. Nicholas Fehrenbach, jun., however, ran the Teetotaler Restaurant at No. 76 Meeting Street, adjacent to Institute Hall. According to the census, he also owned the property directly to the south, Nr. 74 Meeting [occupied by Frances G. Ballot], but Fehrenbach and his family occupied No. 76. Both dwelling places were destroyed along with Institute Hall. Hermann Knee is listed as the property owner of No. 14 on the north side of Stoll's Alley, as well as a wooden structure at No. 36, and a brick structure at No. 38 Church Street. Whether any of them were touched by the fire is unknown. At the time, however, none of the structures were occupied by the Knees, who were in Walhalla.

The conflagration and its disruption, however, was only an interlude and did not stop the war. By early 1862, Union forces had advanced and were on James Island, perilously close to the city. William Grayson wrote: "People are moving in crowds from the city. Carts are passing at all hours filled with furniture . . . . The talk in the streets is when do you go; where are you going. Every one take care of himself and the enemy take the hindmost, seems to be the prevailing maxim. My younger folks are gone; some to Newberry; some to Anderson. My wife and I remain. I am adverse to play the vagabond at seventy-four. Besides if Charleston falls what part of the country can be safe from the marauding parties of the enemy [?]"

The Battle of Secessionville was fought on James Island in June of 1862. It was an early victory for the South, but dangerously consequential for Charleston. It only postponed the subsequent attempt to capture Charleston that began in April, 1863.

Charleston was not of any great strategic importance; Lincoln was not optimistic; but as the place where "rebellion first lighted the flame of civil war," the city had great symbolic value at a time when the Union needed a symbolic victory. Admiral DuPont's chief of staff wrote, "The desire was general to punish that city by all the rigors of war." Gideon Welles, the secretary of the navy, wrote, "A desperate stand will be made by Charleston, and their defenses are formidable. Delay has given them time and warning, and they have improved them. They know also that there is no city so culpable, or against which there is such intense animosity." The *New York Tribune* had written even earlier, "Doom hangs over wicked Charleston. If there is any city deserving of holocaustic infamy, it is Charleston. From the Confederate point of view, of course, Charleston was the ultimate symbol of the right of the Southern people to be free. It was the very place where Southern nationhood was first begun—politically and militarily. It had to be defended at all costs (Rosen 1994, 98-99).

It is questionable whether any of Charleston's inhabitants dwelling in the city at this time would have subscribed to the "Confederate point of view"—an ethereal concept for a politician involved in military defense, but hardly the mind-set of someone with feet on the ground and worried about where the next explosion would occur. Southern *nationhood* could go to hell along with the enemy soldiers firing the guns. First the Union Army attacked Morris Island, "really a sandbar, but in terms of lives . . . an extremely valuable piece of real estate in the summer of 1863" (Rosen 1994, 106). This would ultimately result in the Battle of Battery/Fort Wagner where the black soldiers of the Massachusetts 54th and their commander Robert Gould Shaw—the heroes of the movie *Glory*—died in great numbers. Battery Wagner was a victory for the Confederates, but was followed by the seven day bombardment by Union guns of Fort Sumter, beginning on August 17, 1863. After reporting that Sumter had been reduced to "a shapeless and harmless mass of ruins"—even though it was not taken—the Union General Gillmore, under orders from President Lincoln, turned his guns slightly to the northwest and began the bombardment of Charleston.

**The Charleston peninsula as target, under bombardment
by Union forces from all sides. From the American Geographical Society Library,
University of Wisconsin-Milwaukee Libraries.**

By this time,

> Life in the city was totally disrupted. Entire sections of town were vacant. Schools closed, as did most churches. The social class and caste distinctions which had marked antebellum Charleston began to blur long before the end of the war. By 1863 the makeup of the city's population had changed dramatically. Confederate soldiers from out of town—most of them uncouth and uneducated by Charleston society standards—were everywhere . . . . Slaves began to disappear, and it was difficult and expensive to procure a maid or housekeeper. Many Charleston ladies who were used to having slaves found themselves without. Women who had never before washed the first article of clothing or mopped a floor now learned about housekeeping . . . Many of the old civilities were gone. People's homes were damaged and could not be repaired . . . . The lower part of the city was bombed and shelled and the victim of mortar attacks on and off until its surrender a year and half later . . . . Fires abounded as the regular firefighters were now in the service of Confederacy . . . . Most of those who could do so left Charleston for Columbia or the upcountry. Others removed themselves north of Calhoun St., where the shells generally could not reach. Downtown Charleston became a ghost town . . . . The city was decimated, though there were few military casualties among civilians; the number killed is disputed. Reverend Porter placed it at eighty. "By 1864, the town presented the most extraordinary appearance," wrote Mrs. Ravenel. "The whole life and business of the place were crowded into the few squares above Calhoun St., and along the Ashley, where the hospitals and the prisoners were and the shells did not reach . . . . No one can tell what those wartime babies and their mothers endured. Some were born under fire; some by the roadside;—it was awfully biblical! To pass from this bustling, crowded scene to the lower part of the town was . . . like going from life to death (Rosen 1994, 121).

For 567 days Federal forces would almost continuously fire exploding shells on the city. "In February, 1865, Charleston was the 'mere desolate wreck' Sherman had described. Susan Middleton reported that the 'houses in the lower part of town are constantly broken open and plundered.' The lower half of the city was now totally uninhabited. 'To one walking through,' one Charlestonian later recalled, 'it seemed more like a city of the dead than anything else' . . . . Some Charlestonians felt betrayed by those who had led them to this unhappy pass . . . . Jacob Schirmer wrote, 'We are cut off from all communication . . . . Total ruin is staring us in the face'" (Rosen 1994, 137). The Confederate Army finally abandoned Charleston in February 1865, and Sherman, after he had captured Atlanta and Savannah, surprised everyone by leaving the ruins of Charleston to smolder and heading for Columbia.

As suggested earlier, other than the few in the family who had removed themselves or who were removed by the authorities, the rest of the composite immigrant family suffered life in Charleston during this period. After the 1861 fire, a number had been forced to move farther north in the city: the Schroeders relocated farther up Meeting Street; Nicholas Fehrenbach, jun., when he lost the property adjacent to Institute Hall, owned five other properties on Coming Street and had likely removed his family to one of them by the time the bombardment was imminent. When the Fehrenbach's young son Edward Nicholas died of scarlet fever in early 1862, the family was living at 314 King Street [upper King]. Jane Thompson and her husband were both fortunate to live where few shells reached, and her property on South Bay was apparently far enough south of St. Michael's steeple [the visible target according to which the Union batteries set their range] to escape destruction. Thus everyone survived to see the war end, to take stock of how far they had come or how far back they had been set, to lick their personal and commercial wounds, and to wonder about what they would have to do to engage the new circumstances that would define Charleston as it undertook to reconstruct itself from the ashes.

Those quoted descriptions of life in Charleston during the years of the war indicate how everyone came to lament the situation they found themselves in. But those perspectives of the home-front were mostly the viewpoints of citizens belonging to the upper class who were native-born and had the leisure to think that their thoughts, opinions, and views were worthy of being written down in their diaries and letters. For the immigrant family there was little incentive to encourage the recording of their responses. They had less to start with, and thus less to lose, not as far to fall, as it were, as those who were in society's top echelons. If they had managed to survive, there was little choice but to pick up the pieces and try to move on. By this time they would no longer think of themselves as guests in a host community who had best demonstrate good behavior—they had been through both the thick and the thin and justifiably had little sense of gratitude to those who had swept them along with this tide that had brought no reward and little more than existence itself. The remnant of life in Charleston after Appomattox would be nothing they had expected or wished for.

IX

SOLDIERS

At this juncture, an account is due of those in the family who were actually *in* the war, those immigrants or children of immigrants who experienced first-hand the division of their new-found country into two opposing armies bent on eliminating each other. From the very beginning it was clear that the South was woefully unprepared for what it thought it could accomplish, and its leader Jefferson Davis was no Abraham Lincoln. Before the first anniversary of Sumter, as historian James McPherson puts it, "the bloom had faded from southern enthusiasm for the war . . . . The south still had more soldiers than it had weapons to arm them, but that state of affairs promised to come to an abrupt and disastrous end in the spring—not because of a windfall of weapons, but because the one-year enlistment of nearly half the troops would expire. Few of them seemed ready to re-enlist" (McPherson 1988, 429). So on April 16, 1862 the Confederacy enacted conscription, making all able-bodied white male citizens between 18 and 35 liable for three years of service. A number of men in this immigrant family were caught in this net.

McPherson clarifies that there were several loopholes in the Conscription Act, and his account serves to explain some of the service records that will be examined shortly:

> A drafted man could hire a substitute from the pool of "persons not liable for duty"—men outside the specified age group or immigrant aliens. The practice of buying substitutes had deep roots in European as well as American history. Men called into militia service in previous wars, including the Revolution, had been allowed to send substitutes. Even the *levée en masse* of the French Revolution permitted substitution. This practice was based on an assumption that the talents of men who could afford substitutes might be of

more value on the homefront, organizing and producing the matériel of war, than in the army. But recognizing that substitution would not exempt all men necessary for behind-the-lines duty, Congress on April 21 passed a supplementary law specifying several exempt categories: Confederate and state civil officials, railroad and river workers, telegraph operators, clergymen, apothecaries, and teachers (McPherson 1988, 431).

The practice of hiring a substitute became somewhat controversial, and there were plenty of abuses. Since not everyone could afford to hire a substitute, it was not long before it was popular to claim that it was a "rich man's war but a poor man's fight." The Confederate Congress cancelled the privilege in December, 1863.

—THE FEHRENBACH BROTHERS—

Of the several family members who served in the war, it would be Nicholas Fehrenbach, jun. who alone would avail himself of the substitute privilege. Official and other records indicate that Fehrenbach entered "state service" at Charleston on November 6, 1861, and served in that capacity until December 31, 1861, that is, for a little more than a month and a half. When called into state service he was a founding member of Captain Cordes's Company of Cavalry, SC Militia, known as the "German Hussars", attached to the 1st Regiment, SC Rifles. Born in 1833, he was 28 years old and considered the head of the family, since his father had remained in Wisconsin when he and his siblings returned to Charleston sometime in the 1850s. By 1859 he was working as a confectioner at 312 King Street [upper King], and in 1860, as noted, owned and operated the Teetotaler Restaurant next to Institute Hall on Meeting Street. He had thus become a fairly successful businessman and, as a son of immigrant parents, had emerged into the security of success at a fairly young age.

Mehrländer has thoroughly researched and analyzed the members of the "German Hussars" militia unit and offers some interesting details:

- [S]ince Cordes' company was . . . the only mounted antebellum militia of German immigrants in the South, one might assume that its members were, on the basis of their social standing and fortunes, well-known representatives of the German community. The ethnic elites were much more likely to be found in various bureaucratic registers in 1860 than were the "large masses of poor foreigners."
- In May, 1859, the German Hussars included exactly eighty-nine men as their founding members . . . . Of these eighty-nine men only twenty-four owned real property . . . .

- The twenty-one slave holders among the founding members of the unit (23.6%) belonged to the elite of only 31% of all whites in the South who had slaves at all in 1860.
- At the outbreak of the war forty-three members . . . left the German Hussars . . . . Seven men were added, so that the unit rode out in 1861 with fifty-four men.
- Cordes' soldiers were older—an average of 31.8 years of age—than those of the other German companies in Charleston, which is logical in view of their economic standing. The average wealth of a German immigrant in North America in 1860 was estimated at $1,200. If one divides the total property of more than $158,000 among the fifty-four members, each member of the German Hussars owned property valued at an average of almost $3,000 and thus double the national average.
- Of the fifty-four men serving in the unit before the German Hussars were mustered into Confederate servicer, eleven offered substitutes at the time. However, substitutes, who were affordable at this early point in the war were, with the exception of Claussen, not offered by any of the propertied members. A "poor man's fight" can thus not be assumed here. (Mehrländer 2011, 171-72)

Mehrländer lists Fehrenbach with $7,400 in real estate, $2,000 in personal property, two slaves, and taxes paid in 1859 of $149.00. (Mehrländer 2011, 355) But if Nick Fehrenbach was not one of the propertied members to offer a substitute before the Hussars [later to be assimilated into Jeffford's Company D, 5th SC Cavalry] were mustered into Confederate Service, he nonetheless did so less than a year after he had enlisted at Charleston on February 17, 1862.[46] He would serve until the end of 1862, but then offered as his substitute

---

[46] Identifying particular military designations is difficult because of the continual mergers of companies and squadrons into differently designated units. What was identified as Captain Cordes's militia unit at its founding in 1859 ultimately became Company D of the 5th SC Cavalry Regiment. "This company was raised in Charleston District in June 1861, by Robert Josiah Jeffords . . . a Charleston merchant and former first lieutenant of the Charleston Light Dragoons. The company was assigned to the 1st (Martin's) SC Mounted Militia Regiment in September 1861, and was called up for active duty in response to the Federal occupation of Port Royal in early November 1861. Following the dissolution of Martin's Regiment in February 1862, Jefford's Co. was mustered into Confederate service as part of Jeffords' Squadron SC Cavalry, and later became Co. A, 6th (Jeffords') Battalion SC Cavalry, in April 1862" (http://www.sciway3.net/sc-rangers/5th_cav_cod.html). When N. Fehrenbach entered state service in November of 1861, he would have gone into the Jeffords Co. A and been part of the scouting action that took place in the vicinity of the Ashepoo and Combahee Rivers in Colleton County, south of Charleston and about 8 miles from Port Royal. The Jeffords Co.

his younger brother Hermann, who would have been just over 17 years old [born August 10, 1844]. After the January 1863 consolidation of the 14th and 17th Battalions South Carolina Cavalry and Captain Harlan's and Whilden's Independent Companies, South Carolina Cavalry, the records for Nicholas Fehrenbach consistently note his being "present" *by his substitute, H.H. Fehrenbach.* N. Fehrenbach is listed as "absent without leave since August 10, 1863." That is the date when Hermann re-enlisted in his own name when he turned 18. The participation of the Fehrenbach brothers seems not to have been the result of the April 1862 Conscription Act, although it may have encouraged the re-enlistment of Hermann once he came of age, since it was still in effect in August of 1863.

Why did the elder Fehrenbach brother send his younger sibling into harm's way? It could have been the case that the 17-year-old begged for a chance to be in the action. He had been born in Charleston, and at that point in his teens could have been caught up in the pro-secession political arguments and the initial enthusiasm for putting the North in its place. More likely, however, it was the fact that as the older brother and head of the family, Nicholas felt an obligation to keep his mother and siblings supported by remaining at home and carrying on his business—he could hardly leave them unprotected and to fend for themselves by some other means: there was not likely any other source of income. Besides, by the time he enlisted in February 1862 he had suffered the loss of his restaurant and his family's dwelling place in the fire that had burned much of the city the previous December: his personal and business life were in jeopardy and needed his attention. And there is evidence that Nicholas did not totally abandon the war effort: he was in fact engaged in blockade-running and served as a steward on the *Margaret and Jessie,* based in Wilmington, NC—the other Confederate coastal city heavily involved in running the Atlantic blockade (http://www.sciway3.net/sc-rangers/5th_cav_cod.html). After that ship was captured by Union forces in late 1863, Nicholas returned to Charleston to continue his career as *Restauranteur* well into the post-war years. It is hard to know whether his *service* in the militia/cavalry/blockade-running was inspired by a sense of loyalty to the Confederacy or simply a way of meeting his own social and/or business obligations.

The Company A to which Nicholas Fehrenbach had belonged operated in the Port Royal area throughout 1862, primarily in scouting actions and protecting what were thought to be strategic locations, but did not actually engage enemy forces. By January 1863, Company A had become Company D, and it is with the latter that Hermann Fehrenbach's service in the Confederate cavalry is associated. In April the Company was stationed in St. Andrew's

---

was in Cheeha, SC between February 17 and 28, and this would have been the station when Fehrenbach enlisted in Confederate service on February 17, 1862.

Parish and on the 27th, "pursuant to orders from Genl. Beauregard, this company with five others of the Regmt. began to march to Charleston, arriving at the Ashley River Bridge on the 29th at 10 A.M. & reported for duty to Brig. Gen. Ripley, Comdg. 1st Mil. Dist. S.C. thro' Lt. Col. R. Jeffords, Commanding the Regmt. Distance marched about fifty miles." When the company moved to Ballouville, SC for September and October of 1863, Hermann was one of the Privates whose reconnaissance mission behind enemy lines was accorded special credit "for the manner in which their several Scouts and reconnoisances [*sic*] were conducted & for their boldness & courage." Again in November and December 1863, similar praise: "In this month [of] Dec., Lt. Smith, Privates Barton, Seile, Muirhead and Fehrenbach made several trips to Warren's Island. These officers and men deserve much praise for the gallant and valuable services they have thus rendered our cause." (http://ehistory.osu.edu/uscw/features/regimental/south_carolina/confederate/5thsccav/CoD.cfm)

At his muster-in as his brother's substitute in February 1862, Hermann's horse was valued at $375, his equipment at $45. In the period July-August 1863 he was recorded as "absent; sick in hospital." For January and February 1864 he was "courier to Lt. J. Simons, Jr., Judge Advocate", and in April of 1864 the Regiment was in Greensboro, NC, on its way to Richmond. From April 30—August 31, 1864, his record shows him "absent; on horse detail, to report 9/15/64." He had been detached to the horse infirmary at Stoney Creek, VA, and he was captured there on December 1, 1864. He was sent to Point Lookout, MD, as a prisoner of war—an experience he likely never forgot. Point Lookout was a Federal prison site that may have been only slightly better than the notorious Confederate Andersonville prison. Reid Mitchell describes the conditions in both Union and Confederate prisons, several times mentioning the Point Lookout prison:

> Once confined, prisoners frequently did suffer from abusive treatment, although less as a result of systematic enemy policy than of individual acts of cruelty, overzealousness, or fear. For example, a North Carolina soldier at Point Lookout recorded instances of guards shooting prisoners for "peepin threw the cracks of the plankin" of the fence, for crowding around the gate, and for "jawing" a Yankee sergeant . . . .
>
> Ill treatment also included poor food. At Point Lookout the prisoners sometimes ate rats to supplement their diet. One Confederate, kept in a prison near Charleston, complained of being fed only one-half pint of soup and one-half pint of mush a day, and of being denied salt . . . . Francis Boyle, a prisoner at Point Lookout and Fort Delaware, advanced an explanation for the short rations there that expressed a common Southern opinion about the North. The insufficiency of

> food was due less to deliberate cruelty, in his opinion, than it was to Yankee greed and corruption. At Point Lookout the authorities denied the prisoners, first, coffee and sugar, then molasses; at the same time they reduced the meat ration and shrank the size of the bread loaves issued. Upon arrival at Fort Delaware, Boyle estimated the daily ration to be about six ounces of meat and four ounces of bread per man . . . (Mitchell 1988, 45-46).

Fehrenbach was fortunate that his stay at Point Lookout was not a long one. He was exchanged along with more than a thousand other soldiers on February 10, 1865. Possibly as a result of his stay at Point Lookout, he was admitted to the Jackson Hospital in Richmond, VA, on the 16th of February and granted a 60-day furlough on the 21st. He was likely back in Charleston by April when at Appomattox the war ended. Having survived his war experiences, he too became a Charleston "restauranteur" and operated a tavern until well into his later years. Hermann Fehrenbach was a member of an immigrant family, but by the time he was 21 he had offered himself wholeheartedly to the defense of the City of Charleston, the State of South Carolina, and his now-defeated country. His mother might well have thought her debt to the Charleston Orphan House had been repaid in full. Hermann died in 1905 in Jacksonville, FL.

—THE KNEE BROTHERS—

The 1860 Federal census shows the Knee family resident in Walhalla and comprised of 58-year-old Hermann, his wife Catharina, née Rosenbohm, 45, and sons John, 24, Hermann, 16, and Frederick, 12. Already by August of 1861 Catharina Knee would have to worry about her two eldest sons going off to war: John enrolled in Confederate service on August 28, 1861, and Hermann was in by the middle of that December. Service records indicate that John signed up at Camp Pickens and was in a Company commanded by Joseph J. Norton: it soon became Company C, one of ten companies of the First Regiment, South Carolina Rifles, known as Orr's Rifles. Those companies were organized in July of 1861 for three years or the [duration of] war, comprised mostly of recruitments from the upstate counties of Abbeville, Anderson, Marion and Pickens. According to a compilation by Victoria Proctor "the unit was first stationed on Sullivan's Island and called 'The Pound Cake Regiment' by the other troops because of its light duty. Then in April, 1862, it moved to Virginia with 1,000 men. Assigned to General Gregg's and McGowan's Brigade, it fought with the army from the Seven Days' Battles to Cold Harbor. Later the regiment endured the hardships of the Petersburg trenches and the Appomatox operations" (http://sciway3.net/proctor/marion/military/wbts/OrrReg.html).

This eldest Knee son apparently had sufficient musical talent to serve as a *musician* and was transferred in late 1861 "not from the company, but . . . to the roll of the band which is kept by the adjutant and on which he is to be paid." Some *musicians* served as drummers, fifers, or buglers—performing such critical military functions as providing and keeping the cadence during a march, or communicating musically coded orders above the din of battle—but they were usually chosen from the youngest among the group. John's age [25] and the unspecified nature of his assignment suggests that he was not one of the above, but performed his duty as an instrumentalist of some sort in what was the organized company or regimental band. Bell Wiley, in his *The Life of Johnny Reb*, notes that instrumental music served as an "important source of diversion" for the soldiers, providing "marching airs for drills" and occasionally giving concerts. He acknowledges that the musicianship was often somewhat questionable: "Difficulty of procuring instruments, scarcity of cultivated talent, and the stringencies of campaigning prevented the maintenance of high-class bands . . . there can be little doubt that the majority were of inferior rating. But even so, their contribution to happiness and morale was considerable." General Robert E. Lee is reported to have remarked, "I don't believe we can have an army without music" (Wiley 1971, 156-57). If a regiment or company had an organized group of musicians, they were likely a somewhat protected entity, not soldiers who performed only when they could lay down their weapons: their function in relieving the stresses of battle was considered too important to the unit to allow loss or decimation by being found among the *wounded*, *killed*, or *missing*. The band was necessary, whatever the occasion. Wiley writes that:

> [A]t . . . times bands of the opposing armies participated in unpremeditated joint concerts. At Murfreesboro, for instance, on the night before the great battle, a Federal band began just before tattoo to play "Yankee Doodle," "Hail Columbia" and other tunes popular in Northern camps. After a little while the Union musicians yielded to the Rebel band which played a group of Southern favorites. These voluntary exchanges had continued for some time when one of the bands struck up "Home, Sweet Home." Immediately the other band joined in, and in a few moments the tune was picked up by a multitude of voices of both camps. For the brief period that the countryside reverberated with the notes of Payne's cherished song the animosities of war were lost in nostalgic reveries, and the fading away of the final notes found tears on the cheeks of scores of veterans who on the morrow were to walk unflinchingly into the maelstrom of battle" (Wiley 1971, 317-18).

To whatever degree his assignment in the band provided protection from the hail of musket fire and/or hand-to-hand combat, the carpenter/musician John Knee survived in his lengthy service until the very end of the war. His records indicate that he was on the list of prisoners of war "belonging to the Army of Northern Virginia, who have been this day surrendered by General Robert E. Lee, C.S.A. commanding such army, to Lieut. Genl. U.S. Grant, commanding armies of the Unted States. Paroled at Appomatox Court House, April 9, 1865." Before that momentous day, he had been admitted to Jackson Hospital in Richmond on August 22, 1864 suffering from hepatitis, but was released less than a month later [September 14] to go back to his brigade [McGowan's]. His service records do not indicate that he was otherwise wounded. Little is known about his return after the war to civilian life. The 1880 census reveals that at some point he had married Lucinda, a woman from Tennessee eleven years his junior; no children are listed. He applied for a pension from the Confederacy in Sevier, TN, suggesting that the couple lived in her home state after their marriage—not all that far from his home in Walhalla.

John's younger brother Hermann apparently did not possess comparable musical ability, and his service to the Confederacy took a different course. He enlisted four months after his older brother, on December 17, 1861, in Captain Wagener's Company, Co. A German Artillery, SC Light Artillery [formerly Werner's Co. 1st Regiment Artillery]. This unit was incorporated into the 20th Regiment South Carolina Infantry, formed January 11, 1862. Records show that the unit he joined had been one of those engaged in the battle of Port Royal in November 1861. As detailed below, his unit would be involved subsequently in the defense of Charleston harbor in August and September 1863 and active during the bombardment of the city. Hermann Knee's records show his rank varying from Private, to 1st Sergeant, to 2nd Sergeant, to 5th Sergeant: the first notation of his promotion to sergeant is in February 1862.

An excerpt from a regimental summary reveals some of what Hermann Knee experienced:

> The 20th South Carolina was organized on January 11, 1862 in response to the call for an additional 12,000 troops from South Carolina. Ten companies were formed in the central part of the state and elected officers. The regiment departed for Charleston on January 13th. Unlike many units that were rushed to the front, this unit remained in camp drilling for several months. While many units fought themselves out in the middle years of the war, the 20th South Carolina lost more of their men in relatively obscure battles in the last year of the war . . . .
>
> On March 4, 1862 the unit moved to James Island near Secessionville and served on guard and picket duty. At an unknown

date they relocated on Sullivan's Island and four companies manned the siege guns on Battery Marshall . . . .

During the long period of fighting on Morris Island that summer, they would take their turn at picket duty, coming over by steamer after dark and returning the next morning. On July 14, they lost 4 killed and 8 wounded. On the night of August 30 while returning from Morris Island, the steamer was forced into the main shipping channel because of low water. The ship was mistaken for an enemy ironclad and came under heavy bombardment from the Confederate batteries. Many of the panic stricken men leaped off the steamer as the captain tried to beach it. Luckily, the water was shallow enough that most of the jumpers could touch bottom and waded to shore. The regiment lost 16 killed, either injured by the shells or drowned. Between the 31st and August 7, they lost 1 killed and 6 wounded and between the 15th and 23rd they lost another 2 killed and 11 wounded.

On May 25, 1864, the regiment departed for Richmond to join Kershaw's Brigade . . .(http://ehistory.osu.edu/uscw/features/regimental/south_carolina/confederate/KershawsBrigade/20thscv.cfm).

We cannot know exactly where Hermann Knee was at any point during the siege of Charleston harbor, i.e., to know whether he was on Sullivan's Island, or on Morris, at which battery, or to pin down the nature of the skirmishes in which he undoubtedly participated. His records show him as "present" from his enlistment to the last week in December 1863. But the November-December 1863 record states "absent; absent without leave since December 24, 1863", and the January-February 1864 record indicates that he was "last paid" October 31, 1863, with the additional notation: "Deserted December 25, 1863." His final service record reads: "Oath of Allegiance to US, subscribed and sworn to at Chattanooga, Tenn, March 14, 1864. Place of residence: Pickens Co, SC; Complexion: dark; hair, brown; Eyes, blue; height, 5 ft. 9 in."

The reason(s) for Hermann Knee's desertion and subsequent oath of allegiance to what had previously been the enemy's government cannot be known. In her seminal work on the topic of desertion by soldiers on both sides, Ella Lonn challenges her readers to accept her analysis of "what seems to record a nation's shame", and cautions that "there can be no cause so just or beloved that war in its behalf will not be attended by desertion among its defenders . . . The fires of patriotism burn more brightly at the outbreak of war than towards its close. Men at the beginning of the struggle are more oblivious of personal discomfort, less selfish than they become as the struggle progresses, and more willing to contribute in all ways to the expected victory" (Lonn 1928, 5-6).

Hermann Knee, jun. was the son of German immigrants, and it is not inconceivable that after two years of service—particularly at a point when the *cause* held anything but a bright future—he could well have felt that there was little point in his suffering further for the "burning American question of State rights". While he had not been conscripted, he was a sufficiently *foreign* enlistee to wonder just why and for what purpose he was a participant "at the gate of Hell" fighting for reasons he had barely lived long enough to identify with. Among the many factors that contributed to desertion in the Confederacy, Lonn writes of one that may have been particularly relevant for Knee: "Men sincerely believed that they had a kind of right to serve in certain localities—usually near their homes, and were averse to being transferred to other points. Numerous desertions followed the transfer of some troops to the Army of Virginia in 1863" (Lonn 1928, 16). Knee's record for the period September-October 1863, three months prior to his desertion, indicates "transferred from Co. A, 20 Reg SC V[olunteers], October 10, 1863." This would have been shortly after the end point of the fifty-eight-day battle over Charleston harbor, when "the war—along with public attention—moved on to the more dynamic campaigns in Virginia, Tennessee, and Georgia" (Phelps 2002, 27). At this point, Knee could have despaired of continuing on in the war farther removed from his home in South Carolina and his parents in Walhalla. Additionally, as Lonn explains, "speculation and extortion, which seem inseparable from any government in time of war, were rampant throughout the Confederacy in the months of 1863 and were resented as the cause of military disasters on the ground that the army was not adequately supplied, and that the fortified posts were not provided with requisite stores . . . . This wrong was generally held responsible for the derangement of prices and was loudly condemned by press, public officials and private citizens . . . . A war situation, certain to provoke bitterness if no one had been to blame, was held intolerable by the soldiers when they thought it due to the greed of the very men for whom they were fighting" (Lonn 1928, 17-18). While such conditions would have negatively affected any soldier, it would likely have hit harder the immigrant Lutheran son whose parents had raised him in a pioneer Protestant home based on a moral righteousness still not fully attuned to the Southern way. And for a final straw, "from 1863 the element of discouragement and hopelessness of the struggle was added to the natural weariness from the strain of the long, bitterly fought war. Some mail bags captured by the United States officers showed already in 1863 that letters of Southern soldiers breathed but one sentiment—weariness of the war. Soldiers saw, despite desperate and heroic efforts, defeat everywhere, saw their toils and sufferings unproductive against apparently inexhaustible numbers" (Lonn 1928, 18).

It is unnecessary to make more of Hermann Knee's Christmas 1863 desertion, or to search for more plausible explanations for why he left. There is no further record beyond his taking the oath of allegiance to the Union from which his home state had seceded. It is doubtful that he was aware of what had become of his older brother: they served in different areas and would have found it difficult to maintain contact. Too many different factors would have affected their respective experiences and attitudes. If John's musical ability kept him alive to experience parole through surrender to the Union armies at Appomattox, Hermann's desertion and parole by swearing allegiance to the Union kept him out of harm's way until the war was over. Thus at the young—but mature—age of 24, Hermann was able to appear along with his father on the Oconee and Pickens Counties, South Carolina 1868 Voter Registration list among the white, free citizens of Walhalla. Walhalla was still the home of the gods, certainly for those who had served and survived. The German-born Frau Knee, who would have despaired in 1861 at the thought of possibly losing two of her sons to the Confederate cause, could in 1864 be relieved that one at least had returned from Tennessee to his home. That made it easier when, after the final surrender a year later, her other son exchanged his Walhalla home for one across the border in Tennessee. She could be proud that both had served in their fashion, and both were alive.

—CHARLES PLATH—

They would probably never know each other as members of this extended immigrant family, but Hermann Knee and Charles Plath were both enlistees in Company A, German Artillery, SC Volunteers. Charles Plath enlisted on May 20, 1962, in all probability in response to the earlier Confederate conscription enacted on April 16th. He likely saw much the same action in the defense of Charleston harbor that Hermann Knee saw, whether or not they were on the same detail at any given time. Though both German [among the many in the unit], the one was younger, had been born in Charleston, and had parents living in Walhalla, the other, ten years his senior and an immigrant bachelor on his own. Plath remained in the unit after Knee's desertion, and when the regiment departed for Richmond in late May 1864, Charles Plath would have seen additional action en route. There are no service records for him after October 1864, but clearly he lasted through the following year until it was all over: in less than a year after the war had ended, he and Anna Maria Weber would start a new life in Charleston.

There is one noteworthy aspect to Plath's service records, however: on a special requisition from the headquarters in Mt. Pleasant, dated March 3, 1864, two flannel shirts were requested for Pvt. C. Plath "who is suffering from rheumatism". Given the difficulties the Confederacy was having in supplying its troops with clothing, weapons, and remuneration, this request for an individual aching soldier seems impressively caring. The previous

November-December he had been reported sick in camp, and whether it was for the same rheumatism or something else, the March request indicates that he had survived the camp illness—unlike many of his compatriots, more of whom would fall victim to the lethal conditions of a sick camp than to the bullets and shells fired by the enemy—to remain a valuable enough soldier to deserve special attention and warm clothing. Thus healed, he could participate in the final months of fighting in Virginia before heading back to Charleston.

—JOHANN WILHELM FRIEDRICH STRUHS—

Accounting for this individual's involvement in the war is fraught with difficulties. Cited earlier, the 1860 census verifies J. W. F.'s residence in Walhalla as a 33-year-old mechanic married to "Lena", aged 28, parents to daughter Mena, aged 8, and son John Henry, a 2-year-old toddler. With the conscription in 1862 of men between the ages of eighteen and thirty-five, it would have been difficult for him to escape the call if he had not already enlisted. There are, however, no Confederate records for anyone under the name *Struhs*. But that name has presented difficulties and experienced variant spellings often enough that it is likely that the service records under the name John H. Strouss [an orthographical rendition of the way *Struhs* would be heard] are the ones relevant here. That individual had enlisted already in August of 1861 in what was known as Captain Bachman's Company. According to the service record notation, "this company subsequently became Company B, Artillery Battalion, Hampton Legion South Carolina Volunteers. The artillery battalion became separate and independent companies some time prior to August 25, 1862, about which date the Legion was re-organized." If the recollections of W. H. Grimball can be trusted, the company's personnel were as involved in battle action as any. Grimball served for a time as commander of the unit and would remember the various transitions the unit underwent after the Hampton Legion was reorganized as follows:

> After this reorganization the company was separated from the Legion. The artillery battalion commanded by Major Lee was enlarged and he promoted. The company continued in this command until 22d June, 1862, when it was assigned to Pender's Brigade in the division then commanded by General A. P. Hill. On 28th July, 1862, the company was assigned to General Hood's Texas Brigade . . . . When General Hood was promoted to the command of a division, of which his brigade formed a part, this company, together with the South Carolina battery commanded by Captain Hugh R. Garden; the North Carolina battery commanded by Captain Reilly, and later

another North Carolina battery commanded by Captain Latham, constituted the artillery battalion of the division.

The company continued thus to serve until some time after the battle of Gettysburg, when troops from the Army of Northern Virginia were sent to other parts of the Confederacy.

This company was then sent to South Carolina and was stationed near Pocotaligo, S.C., on the Charleston and Savannah Railroad . . . .

The company participated in the campaigns of the Army of Northern Virginia up until . . . it was sent back to South Carolina, including besides skirmishes and minor affairs, the battles of Seven Pines, the seven days battles around Richmond, Second Manassas, Boonesboro Gap, Sharpsburg, Fredericksburg, operations around Suffolk, Va., and after returning to South Carolina, participated in the operations between Savannah and Charleston, including the affairs near Coosawhatchie, Talifinny, etc.

When the troops were withdrawn from South Carolina the company went with the troops of this department and were concentrated with them in North Carolina. At Fayetteville, N.C. the company was temporarily attached to General Wade Hampton's Cavalry command and with it participated in the affair at Fayetteville. It was also present with the army at Averysboro and Bentonville, S.C. (Brooks 1912, 280).

Strouss's records end after the period May-June 1864, and it was not until March of 1865 that both the "Fayetteville affair" and the battle at Averysboro/ Averasboro took place, the first involving the capture of the Confederate arsenal in Fayetteville that manufactured and repaired weapons for the Confederacy, the second, the first deliberate, tactical resistance to the infamous march of Federal forces through Georgia and the Carolinas. The coincidence, however, of J. H. Strouss in a company comprised mostly of Germans that fought in Fayetteville [and close-by Averasboro] in connection with the takeover of an arsenal and resistance against the advance of Sherman on his war-path might explain the little understood, but nonetheless preserved, family lore that the immigrant Struhs died in Fayetteville in an *explosion*. There is no official record of Strouss's death, but an unrecorded death during the Confederate struggle is more plausible than the absence of any other obituary. The family lore suggests that the entire family had moved from Walhalla to Fayetteville. There were many families that followed their soldiers from one place to the other, and it was not beyond a pioneering German woman's fortitude to travel with small children to accompany her husband's artillery battalion marching from South Carolina to a crossroads in North Carolina. Hanging onto an unknown future in a barely settled rural village could well have seemed the lesser part of valor than taking her two young children to accompany her husband—be near him—in the highly unsettled present. We only know that Dorothea Genthe Struhs was back in Charleston as a widow at the latest by 1874-75, probably earlier: she most likely returned to the destroyed city soon after the death of her husband. There she would reconstruct her life around her children during Reconstruction, and see her daughter Mena married to Charles Weber in 1879.

—MICHAEL LAWRENCE OR LAWRENCE MICHAEL MURRAY—

In her will filed in January 1877 two months before she died, Jane Thompson sounded a little angry and perhaps even a little sarcastic when she bequeathed to her second-born son by John Michael Murray, "Captain" Lawrence M. Murray the sum of twenty-two Dollars to buy a mourning ring, suggesting that he was sufficiently well-off that she needn't leave him anything else. Whatever their relationship in 1877, her eldest son had not remained for his entire youth in the Thompson household, although he was still a 13-year-old member of that family, along with four half-siblings, according to the 1840 census. By the 1850 census, however, he was using the name Lawrence Michael, was working as an "engineer", was married to Sarah, and had a 7-month-old son, L. M. [Lawrence Michael, Jr.?]. Sometime after 1850, Lawrence Michael moved his family to New York, and was still resident there in 1870—in King's County, i.e., Brooklyn, NY. It is unclear how closely Jane Thompson had kept in touch with her eldest child. Was she somewhat bitter because he had grown up and moved out of her household and lived with her sister? Had her marital troubles with James Thompson been the cause of her losing her son by John Murray? Who exactly had provided for his education as an engineer? How close was she to his wife and child? What took him to New York? Did she know that by 1870 he had a family of five children, one of whom was named Cunliff [the 7-month-old listed in the 1850 census, born in South Carolina]? And as an immigrant southern Episcopalian who suffered and survived the bombardment of Charleston, did she know that her son was fighting on the Union side during the siege of her city? Was that why in her will she referred to him as *Captain* Lawrence Murray? No answers to those questions, but the last two surely signal an ironic twist in the story of this southern family.

Lawrence Michael Murray, aka Michael Lawrence, was 36 when he enlisted as a Private on August 25, 1863 in Company A, 54th Regiment, NY Infantry. It seems likely that Lawrence was caught in the conscription of soldiers that Lincoln ordered in March 1863. James McPherson explains:

By the beginning of 1863 recruitment in the North arrived at the same impasse it had reached in the South a year earlier. The men likely to enlist for patriotic reasons or adventure or peer-group pressure were already in the army. War weariness and the grim realities of army life discouraged further volunteering. The booming war economy had shrunk the number of unemployed men to the vanishing point. The still tentative enlistment of black soldiers could scarcely begin to replace losses from disease and combat and desertion during the previous six months. Like the Confederacy in early 1862, the union army in 1863 faced a serious manpower loss through expiration of enlistments . . . .

The draft was a national process. Congress authorized a Provost Marshals Bureau in the War Department to enforce conscription. This Bureau sent to each congressional district a number of provost marshals whose first task was to enroll every male citizen and immigrant who had filed for citizenship aged twenty to forty-five. This became the basis for each district's quota in the four calls for new troops that Lincoln issued after passage of the conscription act in March, 1863. In the first draft (July 1863), provost marshals called up 20 percent of the enrollees, chosen by lot in each district (McPherson 1988, 600).

Interestingly enough, the 54th that Lawrence joined had originally been recruited principally in Brooklyn and New York City of German immigrants known as the "Barney Black Rifles". It was mustered into service for three years between September 5 and October 16, 1861. The regiment left the state in late 1861 and served in numerous brigades and divisions in the Army of the Potomac and the Army of Virginia. It then served "in the Department of the South, 1st Brigade, Gordon's Division, 10th Corps, on Folly Island, S.C., from August, 1863; in Schimmelpfenning's Division, 10th Corps, from January, 1864; on Morris Island in February, 1865; at Charleston, S.C., from March, 1865; and it was honorably discharged and mustered out, under Colonel Kozlay, April 14, 1866, at Charleston, S.C." (http://dmna.ny.gov/historic/reghist/civil/infantry/54thInf/54thInfMain.htm). The 54th, should it not be clear from that summary account, participated in the siege of Fort Wagner, the bombardment of Fort Sumter, and a battle on James Island in the summer of 1864. Michael Lawrence was thus likely fired on by the artillery unit in which both Hermann Knee and Charles Plath served—and vice versa—as Union forces repeatedly tried to take Battery Wagner. As one of Brigadier General Gordon's 3,400 troops, Michael Lawrence fortunately did not die at the hands of his enemies—fellow Charlestonians defending his mother's city. At his muster-out in Charleston on April 11, 1866, he was back in his hometown, and may have visited his mother

Jane. Would she have greeted him as a prodigal son, or bitten her tongue at the nerve of this *Yankee* fighting for the other side?

Whether or not he saw his mother in Charleston, Michael Lawrence went back to New York shortly after his service ended. His daughter Mary was born sometime in 1867 and his son Harvey was already 1 year old in 1870. Lawrence Michael Murray would return to Charleston after his mother died and claim his birthright, the property on King and South Bay, which he sold in 1880.

—BERNHARD HEINRICH BEQUEST—

Remarkably, another member of the family served the Confederacy before he actually became a resident of Charleston—not in any military unit, but rather as a blockade-runner. What follows here is a brief biographical sketch of the rather daring teen-age years of the author's great-grandfather. The passage furnishes a hitherto unknown account of Bernhard Bequest's pre-immigration years and provides a segue to the following chapter, which develops the history of the Charleston Bequest family that began once Bernhard settled in Charleston as a 21-year-old immigrant—a young man already in possession of a colorful past and, to all appearances, ready to take on the world. The details in this summary of his early life comprise the only extant account of his youth—found remarkably in a volume on Confederate military history published in the closing year of the last century [Ellison Capers, *Confederate Military History: a library of Confederate States history*, Vol. 5]. Bernhard Bequest's story is in a sense thrice remarkable: in the first instance, his adventuresome participation as a civilian in a war between factions to neither of which he belonged; secondly, a biography discovered and revealed only through current efforts to digitize historical source material; and thirdly, the bringing to light at this writing what no one in the family of the current—or preceding—generation ever knew about this individual's history. Bernhard Bequest may have shared his biography with his wife in the course of his married life, but if either his wife or his own son knew of his fabeled past, that knowledge was never passed on. Except possibly for military historians who may have waded through Capers's detailed account of South Carolina's troops and military personnel, the reader and Bernhard Bequest's currently living descendants are reading this for the first time.

According to the biographical account by Capers [authored in his rank as Brigadier-General in the Confederate Army], Bernhard Bequest, a native of Germany, took to the sea as early as age 14, around 1858. He came to Charleston on one of Captain Wieting's last crossings, arriving in Charleston "two weeks after the capture of Fort Sumter", that is, toward the end of April, 1861. According to Capers, "the Confederate flag was flying, and he promptly declared his allegiance to it." Whether that was actually the case will never be known. Wieting's ship, the *Gauss*, had departed Bremerhaven on 14 March and carried only eleven passengers—the few individuals [the eleven "intrepid" souls cited in Chapter III, p. 27] brave enough to depart for Charleston in the face of reports of the tinderbox conditions there ever since secession the previous December. There is no record of when the ship arrived: the list of Wieting's ships bringing immigrants to Charleston and New York cited earlier [see pp. 26] does not furnish arrival dates for eight of the thirty-four voyages, and there is no list of passengers as would normally have been found in the Charleston *Deutsche Zeitung*, since the paper was not published between 1861 and 1870. The young Bequest, of course, knew of the other family members already in Charleston. It seems likely that he would have attempted to join up with his aunt Adelheid and his first cousin Adeline and her husband Frederick Schroeder. But again, there is no record of any family reunion, and according to Capers, it was only a few months later in 1861 that Bernhard

> hid himself on the little blockade-running steamer, Ruby, and on revealing his presence after the boat was at sea, was put to work as coal-passer during the trip to Nassau. At that port he shipped on the blockade-runner Stonewall Jackson, Captain Black commanding, which on the first trip out was sighted and chased by the United States cruiser Tioga, and compelled to throw overboard part of her cargo and put back to Nassau. This unfortunate vessel at her next attempt to reach Charleston was fired upon and struck as she was crossing the bar, and run ashore, where she was burned with the cargo, young Bequest making his way thence to the city with the mail pouch. His next voyage was from Wilmington, and reaching Nassau he shipped on the Fanny, Captain Moore, with which he made four successful trips. Later he was on the Cyrene, but being taken sick at Nassau, he returned to his home in Germany in June, 1864, and remained until September, when he sailed to Nassau by way of New York, and made a trip into Wilmington on the Rosso Castle. Sailing again on the Watson, they reached the Wilmington bar in time to witness the terrific bombardment of Fort Fisher, upon the fall of which fort blockade-running came practically to an end. Returning to Nassau, he opened a small store and remained there until October, 1865, when he came to Charleston and engaged in business and planting at the town of Mount Pleasant, on the bay (Capers 1899, 455).

There is more in the Capers account that will be revealed in the Bequest story that follows. For the moment, the reader can be relieved that this exciting—if not dangerously risky—period in the life of a barely-20-year-old sailor did not end tragically. By the time the war was over, something just as challenging would await the young North German in the destroyed city of Charleston.

X

THE LAST TO COME

The last German immigrant in the family to come to Charleston arrived just barely after the smoke had cleared. The decline in immigration had started already in the late 1850s, and the civil war in the U.S. had stifled both the number of immigrants and decreased the percentage of those immigrants from German lands choosing the United States as a destination. There continued to be political crises in Europe between the French, the Austrians, and the Prussians, but the increase in immigration to the U.S. after the Civil War was primarily the result of the dam created by four years of war opening up and releasing those who had waited for the hostilities to come to an end.

A pent-up desire to leave home in Germany and the good sense not to attempt to immigrate into a war zone does not apply, however, to the case of Bernhard Heinrich Bequest. According to the Capers account, he had been in and out of Charleston ever since he first set foot on U.S. soil just after the initial firing on Fort Sumter. He spent several months in Nassau as a shop-owner after witnessing the bombardment and fall of Fort Fischer at Wilmington [January 1865], ultimately returning to Charleston from Nassau in October of 1865. His decision to forsake his business in Nassau and to settle in Charleston appears to have been the result of both a desire to settle into a more stable business environment, as well as the pull of the chain that had been started by Johann Rosenbohm. The *New York Times* archive contains a "letter from Nassau" that was published in the Charleston *Courier*, June 20, 1864, describing the business conditions in Nassau, some of which pertain rather obviously to the naval blockade of Confederate ports. It also suggests the concerns of someone engaged in business there, similar to the young Bernhard Bequest. The "letter" reads:

> To give you some idea of the business of the place, Major W. told me
> the other day that there were one thousand tons of bacon and pork

here belonging to the Government and awaiting shipment, much of this is spoiled, and much more destined to be in the warm Summer months approaching. There are eight or ten vessels now in port loading. Three of them have just arrived from England and more are expected. It is thought that there will be twenty-five or thirty vessels running between this place and Wilmington during the coming Summer. I fear that all of our cotton will be taken away without giving back much substantial benefit, and we will be left at the close of the war without a bale for credit. There are some facts with reference to the sending out of Confederate bonds, which it seems to me should be brought to the attention of the Government. They are sacrificed out here and in Europe at about eight pence on the dollar, and as that is better than paying twenty for one for exchange, a great amount of them are sent out, and in that way our obligations at the close of the war will not be to ourselves, but in great measure to these English, who are buying them now at a merely nominal sum. The business . . . is carried on to an enormous extent (http://www. nytimes.com/1864/06/20/news/business-at-nassau.html).

Bequest, for one, would opt for what looked like opportunity in Charleston rather than risk in Nassau. By the time he came to Charleston in late 1865, his first cousin Adeline Schroeder had died the previous year, but his aunt Adelheid was still there, as was Adeline's husband, together with other individuals in the extended family such as the Fehrenbachs. Although not all of these individuals were *close* relatives, they all belonged to the group that had originated in Geestendorf and its environs, a group that collectively might have enabled the entry of a young newcomer into a broken-down South and a city all but destitute. But the young Bequest understood that he would be joining relatives who had experienced the full force of the war and the turmoil that wracked Charleston and probably did not expect to receive much in the way of assistance from them. In many ways, Bequest's conscious decision to come when he did suggests that he recognized the challenges he faced and could perceive the disastrous conditions in Charleston as a foundation for opportunity. It was doubtless his youth and a kind of immigrant courage that led him to appreciate that the realities of the ended war had substantively changed the nature of his destination and the means of starting a new life in a host environment.

Bernhard Heinrich Bequest's story starts shortly after the French Revolution and is intriguing because it brings a third nationality into the family portrait. He did indeed descend from a German heritage, but it was a Frenchman who created this branch of the family and whose name ended up as a unique entry in the nineteenth-century Charleston city directories. Prior to Bernhard Heinrich's immigration, the only individual carrying the Bequest name in Charleston was his aunt Adelheid [once her daughter Adeline had married Frederick Schroeder], a widow who had been married to his uncle Bernhard [likely his namesake] in Geestendorf. The lone widow Bequest's unusual name seems not to have raised any question among the growing German ethnic community in Charleston, no one taking notice of the name's non-Germanic form or sound. The name's uniqueness among the family's German compatriots went unexplored for generations, and no one thought seriously about a French heritage mixed in with the German and English origins. This is how it came to be.

The Nohrdens were farmers in the by-now-familiar Hanoverian town of Geestendorf. They had been there since the seventeenth century and are represented by entries in the records of the same *Evangelisch-Reformierte Kirche Geestendorf* that recorded events in the life of the Rosenbohm family. On the basis of information in Erika and Klaus Friedrichs' two-volume work, *Das Familienbuch des Kirchspiels Geestendorf (heute Bremerhaven-Geestemünde) 1689 bis 1874*, the Bequest lineage can be traced backward to Allrich Nohrden, whose birth year was likely around 1675. Allrich's spouse is unknown, but his son Bohl was born around 1700 and died in 1774. Of Bohl's seven children by two wives, his fourth son Johann [b.1755] married Mette Seedorf in 1779. Their daughter Meina was born 29 June 1787. In her early twenties, Meina Nohrden met a French seaman by the name of Bequet Benoir Olivier and became pregnant. That union was the beginning of the Bequest story.

The record has already noted that under Napoleon and the three Coalition Wars the map of Europe was completely redrawn: on the German map, the number of German states was reduced from more than 300 to 39. By 1808, the thousand-year-old Holy Roman Empire had been effectively dissolved. Among all the changes in government and allegiances, North German lands [primarily the Kingdom of Hanover and the Hansa cities of Hamburg, Bremen, and Lübeck], together with the Kingdom of Holland and the Grand Duchy of Oldenburg, were annexed to France in 1810 and the territory was considered to be one of the *pays réunis*. At that point, the village of Geestendorf lay in occupied territory. When Napoleon tried to isolate Britain [whose king was a German to whom the Kingdom of Hanover belonged] through the imposition of a blockade, he sought to control the northern coast of Europe by sending additional troops and customs officials to major ports. The coastal town of Geestendorf would have received some attention in this regard, and the presence of French military officers, specifically naval officers, in the North German town/village that was in territory annexed to France would have been accepted reality within the historical context.

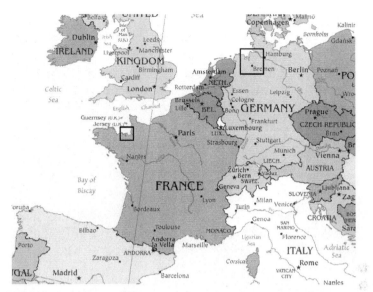

The Brittany coast in relation to the North German coastal area close to
Bremen. From the American Geographical Society Library,
University of Wisconsin-Milwaukee Libraries.

The Geestendorf Lutheran-Reformed church record has an entry dated 24
November [year undecipherable, but likely 1810] under the heading *Geborene
uneheliche* [Born Illegitimately], marking the baptism of Bartelemy, the child of
Corporal Rondal of the French navy, and Margarethe Bechsen [or *Peeksen*]. The
record details that Margarethe worked in Lehe, was born in Wulsdorf [Geestendorf,
Lehe, and Wulsdorf were contiguous villages], that the [illegitimate] child had
been born on the 18th of the month at 11 o'clock in the house of the tavern keeper
(*Gastwirth*) Georg Ludwig Fammy, and that the child was being baptized that day
in the same house. The witnesses are listed as Corporal Wolff, Corporal Bequi,
Henriette Fammy, wife of the tavernkeeper, and Meina Nohrden, daughter of
the farmer and smith (*Baukoethner und Schmidt*) Johann Nohrden. Imagine that
Margarethe and Meina were friends and that the male sponsors were friends
of Corporal Rondal and fellow naval officers. The group at the baptism likely
originated as a double date of two local German women fraternizing with two
French naval officers stationed in the area. These ecclesiastical records are
testimony of village life with the church at its center: this would have been the
normal pattern at the time, when individuals traveled little and children stayed in
the community in which they were born. Within a span of almost two hundred
years, the same pattern would be repeated in the Charleston community, where
immigrant families centered their lives within a church community, associated
closely with each other within their ethnic society, and where many families
became interrelated by marriage within a few generations.

Some seven months after Corporal Rondal's son had been born of his German mother, unmarried Meina Nohrden gave birth to twins on July 13, 1811. The church record indicates that a corporal in the French navy by the name of Bequet Benoit Olivier, born in "St. Benoit du Sonde im Department de Cisle milaine" had acknowledged that he was the father of the twin boys born to Meina at 6 p.m. two days prior in the house of her father, and that the children had been baptized that very day. The one son was named Johaim, the second, Betja-Benedic. The names of the witnesses to the baptism are undecipherable in the microfilmed copy of the original [available from the Salt Lake City Library of the Church of Jesus Christ of Latter-Day Saints]. Some aspects of this entry are critical and deserve comment:—the birthplace of the father is a mishearing by the German pastor of *St. Benoit des Ondes*, a village on the coast of Brittany, not far from St. Malo and St. Michel;—what appears in the handwritten record as *Department de Cisle milaine* is again a mishearing of what the corporal would have spoken as *Department d'Ille et Vilaine*, the official designation for that larger geographical region of France in which St. Benoit des Ondes is located;—the name *Johaim* is a French version of *Johann*;—Bequet Benoit Olivier is the same "Corporal Bequi" who stood witness earlier for the baptism of Corporal Rondal and Margaretha Bechsen [*Peeksen*]'s son: here we have his full name and know that the earlier recorder misheard *Bequet* as *Bequi*—the Frenchman speaking his name, the German pastor writing it as he heard it. In any case, this French corporal is the origin of the Bequest lineage whose story follows.

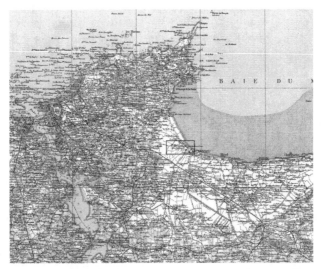

Brittany's St. Benoit des Ondes on the Bay of St. Michel, birthplace of Bequet Benoit Olivier/Bernhard Olivier Bequest. From the American Geographical Society Library, University of Wisconsin-Milwaukee Libraries.

Three months later, on October 24, 1811, Bequet Olivier and Meina Nohrden were married in her home. One can only theorize that the groom's military assignment in Germany seemed permanent enough for him to take this step, or that he already had intentions to stay in the area in spite of his military obligations, or that he and Meina had determined that their relationship was worthy of being legitimized. Part of the reality was the fact that the French Empire would collapse by 1813: despite wide-spread conscription, desertions were common, as well as self-mutilation and marriages—both of which exempted one from military service. In the case of Bequet and Meina, the corporal did not return to France, and in the years following, the family took its legitimate place in the community. Over time, the French naval officer became an integrated member of the North German, very Lutheran, community.

In 1815 the couple had a son Carsten, and Bequet is identified in the baptism record as an inn—or tavern-keeper (*Gastwirth*). Another son Bohl was born in 1816. Other family members' children were born and baptized, and the record shows Meina and/or Bequet often serving as witnesses. On February 11, 1820, Meina gave birth to another set of twins, a daughter Meina, who lived only one day, and a son Ludwig. In 1822, another son Heinrich was born, but lived only six days. Then on March 23, 1826, under the heading *Getaufte eheliche* (Christenings—legitimate), the entry records that the ferryman (*Fährmann*) *Bernhard Olivier Bequest* and his wife Meina, née Nohrden, had their daughter Mette [b 16 March] baptized. Witnesses were Meina's father, Johann, sen., and her brother, Johann, jun. This particular entry is noteworthy, and indicates that Bequet Benoit Olivier has germanicized his name, switching the order so that his Christian name becomes his surname, his former middle name [Benoit] becomes his Christian name *Bernhard*, and his original surname is placed in the middle. The addition of the *s* in the transformation of *Bequet* into *Bequest* is inexplicable according to any orthographical or phonological rules and seems rather arbitrary—if indeed it was an attempt to make the French into something more *German*. The *s* at least favored a German pronunciation, rather than the original, which would have been awkward to sound for the North German speakers of *Plattdeutsch*.

Throughout the record following this 1826 entry, the new name is used inconsistently. An entry that will assume importance somewhat later is the one for May 24, 1831: Nicolaus Fehrenbach, a watch salesman (*Uhrenhändler*) and wife Anna Maria, née Rosenbohm, had their son Eduard baptized. One of the witnesses was Adelheid Rosenbohm, Anna Maria's sister. The August 4, 1831 entry [burial of a stillborn daughter, born two days earlier] cites Bernhard reverting to his earlier name—Benoit Olivier Bequest. There is no explanation for the regression in using the earlier name format, other than to suggest that the change has not taken effect on a permanent basis.

Then on December 2, 1832, the entry records the marriage of the bachelor [*Junggesell*] Bernhard Bequest, son of local resident (*Einwohner hierselbst*) Benoit Olivier Bequest, to Margarethe Adelheid Rosenbohm, daughter of Caspar Rosenbohm, also a local resident (*des hiesigen Einwohners*). This young Bernhard who now surfaces in the record is the illegitimately born [1811] twin, Betja-Benedic—using the name under which he was confirmed in 1827. It turns out that the son's marriage was also a little after-the-fact: an entry for May 2, 1833, records the baptism of the couple's first son, born April 12, 1833, named Bernhard. The new father's name is given as Bernhard Bequest, his occupation is farmer (*Koethner*), the same as that of his maternal grandfather, Johann Nohrden. The child lived only for a year according to the entry of April 8, 1834, in which the two men using the same name are distinguished by specifying the young father as Bernhard Bequest, "the son of Bernhard Bequest married to Meina Nohrden." On January 12, 1835, a daughter Adeline was born to young Bernhard and his wife Adelheid. It is she who would later emigrate and marry Frederick Eduard Schroeder in Charleston. Another entry records the death of Adelheid Rosenbohm Bequest's mother Adelheid, née Buggeln, wife of Caspar Rosenbohm,[47] on January 5, 1836 at the age of 65.

Without belaboring the church record further, the young immigrant Bernhard Heinrich Bequest who arrived in Charleston in late 1865 was the son of the surviving twin born to Meina and Bequet in February of 1820. This Ludwig Olivier/Bequest and his wife Tette Hencken were parents to six children: Bernhard Heinrich [b. December 20, 1844], Johann Ludwig [b. February 27, 1847], Minna Henriette Cathrine [b. April 20, 1849], Carsten August [b. August 13, 1851], Dorothea Louise [b. September 26, 1854], and Therese Rebecka [b. December 20, 1857]. All three brothers would come to Charleston, with Bernhard Heinrich leading the way.

In October of 1865, Lincoln was already six months in his grave, and President Andrew Johnson was now in charge of the turmoil resulting from more than a decade of efforts to reconstruct the South. Bernhard Heinrich Bequest's decision to leave Nassau and come to Charleston at this time signaled his intention to both become a citizen of the United States—which at that point

---

[47] There is reason to think that the name is of Jewish origin. Caspar's birth around 1770 would have been within the era when countless Jews in Germany converted to Christianity, so that the Rosenbohms' inclusion in the Lutheran *evangelische-reformierte* church would not have been unusual. Deborah Hertz's book, *How Jews Became Germans: The History of Conversion and Assimilation in Berlin* (New Haven: Yale University Press, 2007), provides a fascinating account of the conflicted situation of Jewish families in Germany at this time. For any number of reasons, Jews assimilated themselves into the dominant protestant society, and their descendants continue that inheritance, however diluted it became in subsequent generations.

had not formally been re-united, and which had barely begun the process of healing—and to capitalize on its new beginnings. It is his postbellum story that reflects most clearly the changes that would affect the acculturation process of the city's German ethnic community and which would transform the German immigrant into a *white* Charlestonian.

Only some four months after his arrival in October of 1865, Bernhard Bequest married Gesine Rigbers on February 8, 1866 at St. Matthew's German Lutheran Church. Bernhard was a 22-year-old experienced sailor and businessman; Gesine was his senior at age 24. Whether they were already acquainted in Germany is not known, but in light of Bernhard's past escapades, it seems more likely that they met first in Charleston. Her family was from Horstkamp-Delmenhorst/ Oldenburg, a town not too distant from Geestendorf. After their marriage in 1866, with both husband and wife in their early twenties, the couple would have been intent on surmounting the challenges Charleston presented less than a year after the war. Doubtless Bernhard's early experiences as a blockade runner and businessman in the Bahamas would now stand him in good stead. True, there were the fellow Germans in the St. Matthew's congregation, and their marriage indeed took place within that center of fellow congregants and family members. But with Bernhard's previous experience, and as was suggested earlier, it is not likely that the couple expected or received much assistance from the community of immigrants who had preceded them. The post-war period was distinctly different from the earlier antebellum context: anyone settling in the broken-down city could hardly expect much from the broken inhabitants who would have had little to give, constrained as they were by their concerns for their own survival and rehabilitation. The post-Civil War City of Charleston was indeed a unique *host* community: Herbert Spencer's coinage of the Darwinian phrase "survival of the fittest" would have been an apt warning to any late-arriving immigrant to Charleston planning to begin anew with the remains of what was no more. In May of 1865 General Sherman had visited Charleston and had written: "Anyone who is not satisfied with war should go and see Charleston, and he will pray louder and deeper than ever that the country may in the long future be spared any more war." And in September, a reporter from the North had toured Charleston and described it as "a city of ruins, of desolation, of vacant homes, of widowed women . . . . of deserted warehouses, of weed-wild gardens, of miles of grass-grown streets." (Fraser 1991, 273 and 275)

By 1866, however, things had begun to look up somewhat, and Bernhard Heinrich's vision of resurgent opportunity might well have had some basis in reality:

> . . . economic stimulus came in 1866 when the City Council passed "an ordinance to aid in rebuilding the Burnt District and Waste places of the city of Charleston" by providing low-interest loans for citizens who agreed to build in brick . . . . George Williams cleared

away ruins and demolished older structures along Church, Pinckney, Anson, and East Bay streets and built fifteen large cotton warehouses at a cost of about $100,000. The city banks clustered along Broad St. near the intersection with East Bay were renovated, but much activity focused on King St., especially where the fire of 1861 had gutted buildings. The city's Episcopalians welcomed the return of the bells of St. Michael's, which had been sent to Columbia for safe-keeping. Upon surviving the fire there of 1865 they were sent to England for recasting in their original molds and then recrossed the Atlantic to be placed in St. Michael's steeple in 1866 (Fraser 1991, 282).

Bernhard was naturalized on November 9, 1868, almost exactly three years after his arrival. He and Gesine were married for only six years before she died in 1872 shortly after giving birth to a daughter, Theresa Louise. Theresa later became the wife of John Henry Gieschen, and their four daughters' descendants have brought the Bequest/Gieschen line into the present. When Theresa Bequest Gieschen died in 1907, she was a member of St. Andrew's Lutheran Church. At some point after 1882, the Bequests had moved from St. Matthew's to join that sister congregation. Bernhard Heinrich's surviving son's children, grandchildren and several great-grandchildren were all baptized at St. Andrew's.

After the death of Gesine, Bernhard Heinrich did not remain a widower for very long. The following year, he married Catherine Mehrtens on July 3, 1873. According to the St. Matthew's record, Catherine was 18 when she was married, and was from Südwede, a small village in the vicinity of Geestendorf. There is record of a Catherine Mehrtens, born about 1845, arriving in New York on July 31, 1865 on the *New York* out of Bremerhaven. If the ten year age discrepancy [frequently fibbed or inaccurately remembered!] between the ship's manifest and the church record can be allowed, it is likely this Catherine Mehrtens who became the second wife of Bernhard Heinrich Bequest.

It was probably entirely logical that Bernhard Heinrich should set about to establish himself as a grocer—that was what so many of the North German immigrants to Charleston had tried to do, that is, fit themselves into the occupational niche of merchant that the Charleston planter-dominated and slavery-dependent society had allowed newcomers to occupy. That had been the antebellum pattern, and now, with questionable conditions prevailing in the city itself, it would have been similarly prudent to merchandize something that everyone needed. Bernhard Bequest thus set himself up in the rural village of Mt. Pleasant, across the Cooper River to the east of the Charleston peninsula—a town that would later become a local resort for Charleston residents, reachable by ferry from the mainland—and began to purchase land.

The family's domicile in Mt. Pleasant is attested by several Charleston death records: one for an infant, Henry L. [doubtless *Heinrich Ludwig*] Bequest who died February 10, 1878, aged 17 months. The child's birth and death are recorded at St. Matthew's: born September 9, 1876, christened September 16, 1876, buried in Bethany Cemetery on February 11, 1878. The birthplace is given as Mt. Pleasant. Another child, Anna Meta Adeline [likely named for Bernhard's cousin, Adeline Schroeder] was born September 16, 1878, died, and was buried three days later at Bethany. Anthony Bequest's birth in Mt. Pleasant is likewise in the St. Matthew's record: he died as an infant [1 yr., 5 months, 17 days].

In Mt. Pleasant, Bernhard Bequest progressed from being a grocer to become a *planter*. The records at the Charleston Register of Mesne Conveyance show legal transactions for Bernhard Bequest in Mt. Pleasant from July 1867 through May of 1879, verifying him as a landowner involved with mortgages and leases of land for personal and commercial purposes, many of them of considerable value. One of his last transactions was the sale of Mt. Pleasant lots and other items to a fellow German, Otto F. Wieters. The transaction shows Bequest owning a grocery store known as the "Seven Mile Store on the Georgetown Road", as well as a grist mill and a sloop. He became a citizen of sufficient influence that he served the Mt. Pleasant community for eleven years as a town councilman, and for the four years between 1876 and 1879 he served as the town's *Intendant* or mayor. Throughout this extended period of residence in Mt. Pleasant, the family continued to be a part of the St. Matthew's congregation. It was not until 1882 that the family left the more rural Mt. Pleasant location and relocated to the city proper. The birthplace of the couple's one surviving child, John Frederick Bequest, born September 9, 1882, is given as "Charleston".

As mentioned earlier, all three sons of Ludwig and Tette Hencken Bequest immigrated to Charleston. Bernhard Heinrich's younger brother, Carsten August, had followed his elder brother to Charleston the very next year [November 1866] when he was only 15. He did not become naturalized, however, until 1893 when he was 41. The second younger brother, Johann Ludwig, was in Charleston by early 1872, although the exact date of his immigration is unknown. He and Bernhard were both married to Rigbers sisters, Bernhard to Gesine, and Johann to her younger sister, Catherine Margaretha [b. 1854]. The younger couple settled in Mt. Pleasant as well, and their children's births are recorded at St. Matthew's Church, as is Catherine's death in 1892. The widower Johann/ John then married Mary Emma Condon, a woman from Pennsylvania, in 1893. Another Rigbers sister, Anna Margarethe, was married to Eike Englemann, and the St. Matthew's records attest that Johann Ludwig was one of the sponsors at the Englemann son's baptism at St. Matthew's in 1872.

In their new Charleston environment, the Bequest brothers and their families were very much intertwined, each attempting to find and establish their place in the post-war society that was being reconstructed during the twelve years after the end of the war. They numbered among the courageous—or the foolhardy—who navigated the rough waters of a social framework that was turned inside out by emancipation and the new orders of Reconstruction. Much of how they fared can be gleaned from Charleston city directories during the three decades from 1870 to the end of the century.

Though resident in Mt. Pleasant, Bernhard was initially listed as a grocer on the corner of Calhoun and East Bay Streets, but by 1879 he had begun operating a lumber yard. He is frequently listed both as Benjamin [middle initial *A* or *H*] and Bernhard [middle initial *A* or *H*] at different locations, suggesting that he was working two enterprises under variant names. The middle initial confusion likely resulted from the information for the Directory being reported orally, the German *A* [ah] and *H* [ha] easily misheard/misunderstood. Bernhard's trying to establish himself as a lumber merchant was consistent with the fact that lumber milling had developed as a major industry in the Lowcountry: by 1883 there were at least a dozen sawmills operating in the city. (Fraser 1991, 309) By 1885 Bernhard had moved his wood yard to 335 East Bay Street where he had been resident since 1882. That move to #335 was a final one for Bernhard and his family: that was the house where his son John Frederick was raised and where, after Bernhard's death in 1899, John Frederick continued to live with his mother. John F. moved back to the house after his marriage and raised his children there. It was still the family home when Agnes Catherine Bequest and Ruth Wilhelmina Bequest met their respective future husbands, Alston Grobert Jones and John Louis DeAntonio—Alston living two houses to the north, and John, next door to the south.

In the 1876-77 directory, Carsten August is advertised as a dealer in "Dry Goods, Groceries, Provision & Liquor" in Abbeville SC. A decade after his arrival, he had gone to upstate South Carolina to establish himself there. There was a Lutheran community in Abbeville, and similar to the story of Johann Wilhelm Friedrich Struhs and his wife, August and his family may have been pulled to the area as part of the missionary movement to settle and establish Lutheran congregations that was dominant at the time. August remained in Abbeville for several years. By 1881 he was back in Charleston and opened a business, *Rohde and Bequest*, under his and his wife's name [she was Augusta Rohde]. A couple of years later he was operating a "hay, grain and feed, and grist mill" on Queen Street. By 1888 he was trying his hand at something new and owned a saloon and restaurant on King Street. August was naturalized in 1893, and seems to have been the most entrepreneurial of the three brothers: he was one of the corporators of *the Palmetto Soap Manufacturing Company*, chartered July 31, 1893, with capital stock valued at $25,000, and was also listed as one of two corporators of the *German-American Trust and Savings Bank*, chartered February 13, 1893 to do a general banking business with capital stock worth $40,000. (Reports and Resolutions 1893, II, 49, 58) By 1896, August had become the president of the German-American Trust and Savings Bank.

The youngest brother John worked early on as a "clerk" for the elder Bernhard, and later in various other capacities: as a driver for the Palmetto Brewery, a stableman for Claussen Brewing Co. [a business operation of J. C. H. Claussen—still a pillar of the German community, still of some influence to this immigrant family], as a policeman, and at the Morris Island Light House.

The city directory listings frequently include under the Bequest name that of Adeheid, identifying her as a widow. She lived for years at 64 Meeting Street, next door to her daughter Adeline and Frederick Schroeder, but by 1887 had moved to 111 Wentworth Street, the residence she shared with her son-in-law and where she died in 1895. The 1894 directory lists for the first time *Miss Teresa Bequest* as a housekeeper for E. McCrady,[48] and living at 335 East Bay. Recall that Theresa was Bernhard's daughter, born 1871, by his first marriage to Gesine Rigbers; she had become a step-child of Catherine Mehrtens and at this point was the elder of the two children in the Bequest household.

---

[48] This is undoubtedly the individual whose prominence justifies the following description in Fraser's *Charleston! Charleston!*: "During the 1880s local authors like Colonel Edward McCrady, began publishing articles in the local newspapers that nostalgically recalled the Old South as the best of times. McCrady was born into a well-to-do family in Charleston in 1838, educated at the College of Charleston, and admitted to the local bar in 1855. During the Civil War he rose to the rank of lieutenant colonel and was severely wounded at the Second Battle of Manassas. Following the war be built a highly regarded legal practice, won election to the state House of Representative from Charleston County, and in 1882 wrote and introduced legislation at the state level that upon adoption became known as the Eight Box Law, a complicated voting process designed to confuse voters, especially Afro-Americans. Well-connected by family, church, politics, and the military with South Carolina's 'master class,' McCrady devoted more and more time to justifying 'the Lost Cause' in speeches and writings, condemning the selfishness and aggressiveness of the North on the eve of the Civil War and justifying the South's secession. Like others of his generation, especially the ex-Confederate officer class who enjoyed a worshipful following, McCrady glorified the pre-Civil War South" (314). The reader may theorize what kind of employer he was, and wonder to what degree his ideas might have been shared with the young Miss Bequest, his domestic employee.

It is interesting to note further that the house at 30 Anson Street where Teresa Bequest worked was listed for sale in Charleston's newspaper, *The Post and Courier*, on May 17, 2009. Described as "the Edward McCrady House," the listing reads: "This beautiful Greek revival brick Charleston Single features spacious double piazzas overlooking the private garden and brick terrace. This historic home has been recently restored with all modern conveniences and offers gated off street parking. Priced at $1,499,000." There may still be Bequest ghosts in Ansonborough.

During this extended period, the efforts of the three Bequest brothers to establish themselves as wage earners or businessmen ran parallel to the growth of their respective families, albeit not without confronting the high infant—and adult—mortality rates that prevailed at the time. August and his wife Augusta Catherine, née Rohde, were second cousins from Geestendorf, both with Nohrden blood in their veins. Their first child, Heinrich Christian, was born 1877. A second son Bernhardt was born in September 1879 in Abbeville where the family had moved, but lived for only sixteen days. Another son, Johann Ludwig, was born early in 1881 when the family was back in Charleston. He died in 1908 at the age of 27. The couple's fourth child, August Blohme Bequest Jr., was born July 18, 1883, and enjoyed a long life in Charleston until his death in 1961. August Jr.'s middle name was undoubtedly something of an honorific chosen by his parents in recognition of the Hanoverian immigrant family who ran the Blohme Milling Company manufacturing flour, grist, and meal—doubtless friends and possibly a mentor of sorts to August Bequest, sen. The *Jr.* is engraved on the tombstone at Bethany Cemetery in Charleston despite the difference in the names of father and son. A daughter, Annie Agnes Catharina, was born July 16, 1887, but died at age 18 in 1905. Agnes Catherine Bequest Jones was named for this cousin [first, once removed]. By the end of the century, the August Bequest household numbered six.

John Ludwig had three children by his first marriage to Catherine Rigbers, but the absence of death records for all but one [John, b. Mt. Pleasant, d. June 20, 1890, aged 4 months] suggests that none survived infancy. His second marriage in 1893 to Mary Condon was without issue. There is no record of John's death; Mary died of influenza in 1919 and is buried in Charleston's Bethany Cemetery.

Bernhard and Catherine had four children die in infancy: John Frederick was their one surviving child. Bernhard Heinrich died before the century ended, on October 28, 1899. After thirty-four years of struggle during the hard times of Reconstruction and the fading of Charleston into the backwash of the South, there was not much to validate a career that had begun with daring adventure, a vision of opportunity, service to the public good, and dedicated effort as seaman, landowner and merchant. As executrix of his estate, his wife Catherine enumerated the substance of what he left behind:

- the engine, boiler, shafting, saws and all machinery appurtenant to the wood yard business at No. 288 East Bay, Charleston, S.C. ($225.00);
- six carts ($100.00);
- three sets of harness ($10.00);
- three horses ($100.00);
- one mule ($50.00);
- tools ($2.50);

- one wagon ($25.00);
- wheel-barrow ($.50);
- window shades ($.10);
- desk ($5.00);
- clock ($.50);
- two hundred and nine cords of wood at $2.00 a cord ($218.00);
- schooner "Leonora" ($50.00);
- stoves and office chair ($1.00);
- one watch ($20.00);
- household and kitchen furniture ($100.00);
- buggy and harness ($25.00);
- good accounts as per schedule annexed ($269.02);

Total: $1201.62

It was all auctioned off for the sum of $500.00. Bernhard willed a separate $85.00 to his son John Frederick.

If the details above seem to constitute the sum and substance of Bernhard Heinrich Bequest's private and public life, they deserve additional attention within the framework of Charleston's history between the end of the Civil War and the turn of the century. As suggested earlier, the postbellum founding of the Charleston Bequest family can be viewed as typically representative of changes that took place in the acculturation of the city's German ethnic community and the transformation of the German immigrant into a white Charlestonian in the latter part of the century.

The Capers account that told of young Bernhard Heinrich's blockade-running days closes with a few more details of the mature Bequest's biography: "Since 1885 he has conducted a successful business at Charleston, is a member of the German artillery, and has twice served as king of the German rifle club." Capers's words of faint praise suggest that Bequest was not only a successful businessman but also an upstanding citizen true to his cultural heritage. They should be read in the knowledge that it was as a former Brigadier-General in the Confederate Army that Capers was selecting individuals for inclusion in his volume of South Carolina military history whom he considered worthy of mention. Capers himself was a South Carolinian born in 1837, and after the war was Secretary of State for South Carolina. In 1867 he entered the Protestant Episcopal ministry, received his D.D. degree from the University of South Carolina in 1889, and was elected Bishop by the Convention of South Carolina in 1893. Whether or not his words articulate a certain bias, Capers's summation of Bernhard Bequest's thirty-four years of life in Charleston warrants closer analysis.

Capers began his write-up of Bernard H. Bequest seemingly in awe of Bequest's youth and daring, calling it a "romantic story" and noting that the German native had begun a "seafaring life" at the age of 14. The reality was not all that *romantic*, and it was not the case that Bernhard just took to the sea with the wind behind him, looking for adventure. He came from a family of seafarers in Geestendorf who had for generations lived and worked the North German coast either as sailors of one kind or another and/or as small farmers. His great-grandfather, a Frenchman, had been in the French navy and described as "navigator" (*Navigateur*); his grandfather had been at one time a ferryman (*Fährmann*), and a sailor (*Seemann*); and his father worked as a ship's carpenter (*Schiffszimmermann*), a boatman (*Jollenführer*), a skipper (*Schiffer*), and as a pilot (*Lotse*). For certain, the sea was in his blood, and when he began his "seafaring life" it was likely because his father Ludwig had died in 1859, aged 39. Bernhard Heinrich was the eldest of six children, and his mother Tette would have expected him to become the head of the family. After his father's death, opportunity for advancement in his native Geestendorf—which by this time had been been incorporated into the free port city of Bremerhaven as the major center for emigration from German lands—would have been overshadowed by the pull of opportunity in the United States, even if that country on the other side of the Atlantic seemed to be headed for fracture into two sections. That he should set out across the sea to arrive in Charleston in 1861 after hostilities had begun had undoubtedly to do with the fact that he could make the crossing with a fellow Geestendorfer, the well-known immigrant mentor, Captain Heinrich Wieting, whose ship *Gauss* departed Bremerhaven *before the firing on Fort Sumter*, and the fact that he had family in Charleston where Wieting's ship was headed. His young age had little to do with the fact that, if reports of conditions in the United States were to be believed, time was running short to seize the day and take his chance like others had done before him.

Capers wrote that young Bequest arrived "two weeks after the capture of Fort Sumter", when "the Confederate flag was flying", then quickly assured his readers that "he promptly declared his allegiance to it." If this rhetoric is not just wishful thinking on the part of the ex-Brigadier-General, it nevertheless seems somewhat heavy-handed to ascribe such patriotism to a 17-year-old who, after all, was not yet a citizen, not even, apparently, a committed immigrant. Bequest's actions, "several months later" when he took up blockade-running by stowing away on the *Ruby*, suggest that he was more interested in the potential of financial reward and the chance to use his sea legs than some ideological support for the resources-scarce, newly formed Confederacy. One of Bernhard Bequest's Charleston connections was another Geestendorfer, Nicholas Fehrenbach, jun. Nicholas was some ten years older than Bernhard, but they were of the same generation. Nicholas was a successful businessman when the war started, and a known entity in the Charleston German community. Recall that while he had engaged his younger brother as his substitute in Confederate service, he worked as a blockade-runner on the *Margaret and Jessie* out of Wilmington—prior to that ship's capture in late 1863. It is probable that Nick Fehrenbach exercised some influence on the younger Bernhard's decision to undertake blockade-running: the potential financial reward would have been good reason for the businessman-on-the-make to be thinking about it, and the risks would have seemed minimal to the young seafarer, who was also interested in the opportunity for quick financial gain. Bernhard, it turned out, held onto his blockade-running job longer than Nicholas. He did quite well for himself on the Charleston-Nassau run and garnered sufficient means to start a business in Nassau before deciding to come back to Charleston as an immigrant. When he moved to Charleston and Mt. Pleasant in late 1865, he likely arrived with more in his pocket than the typical immigrant.

There is no doubt that the blockade-runner knew what he was doing beyond the challenges of the operation. Just how much of a sense of loyalty he developed while working to supply the Confederacy is questionable, and the reality of the Confederacy's fall does not seem to have negatively impacted his decision to return and start anew in the U.S. as it was undergoing repair. The opportunity for financial gain seems to have outweighed any nationalistic sense of actively abetting the South's rebellion, and it is hard to imagine why a young German would have felt compelled to defend the Southern aristocracy resistant to the multiple pressures to change its ways. With potential riches at hand, there is little reason to attempt to justify the actions of the barely-beyond-his-teens sailor, or to ground his activity in a romanticized patriotism. He was working for himself, and whatever ship's captain he managed to sign on with. It was not incumbent upon him to become a committed Confederate then in order to become the white Southerner he later became.

It is really Bernhard Bequest's timing that draws our attention. If the Capers account is taken at face value, Bernhard Bequest's arrival in October 1865 would have tested the best of men. Six months earlier, the President of the United States had been assassinated, and the man who had surrendered Fort Sumter just before the young German had landed in Charleston for the first time, had raised the U.S. flag over Fort Sumter again—exactly four years to the day. The Confederacy was no more, and the provisional government that President Andrew Johnson had established for South Carolina had been in operation only for several months and was still attempting to chart the course it was supposed to take. South Carolina was under U.S. military command. Only a month before, in September, a convention had met in Columbia and had drawn up the state's new Constitution—adopting the "Black Codes"—and state offices in Charleston were closed and the government resettled in Columbia. Bernhard Bequest was going to try get his footing in Charleston as a grocer and a farmer on Mt. Pleasant at the same time South Carolina was going to be resurrected from its ashes. His beginnings after the war coincided with the implementation of Presidential Reconstruction, Andrew Johnson's questionable efforts to carry out what Lincoln had initiated with the Emancipation Proclamation. It might not have seemed the most propitious time to undertake a new beginning, but it was a new slate on which the word *opportunity* was written in caps.

Eric Foner, in explaining what he calls "the anatomy of Presidential Reconstruction", claims that the most critical issue of the time was the re-creation and management of the labor force under radically changed conditions:

> One problem took precedence as the new Southern legislatures assembled . . . . The ferment in the countryside and ideologies and prejudices inherited from slavery together convinced the white South that coerced labor was necessary to resume the production of plantation staples. With their personal authority over blacks destroyed, planters turned to the state to reestablish labor discipline. Laws regarding labor, property rights, taxation, the administration of justice, and education all formed part of a broad effort to employ state power to shape the new social relations that would succeed slavery.

None of this affected Bequest's efforts directly—at least not initially. But the temper of the times as centered on the labor question, together with the enactment of the "Black Codes" by the convention in Columbia, signaled the character of the room that Bernhard Bequest stepped into, including the elephant, as it were, that sat in the middle:

> Mississippi and South Carolina enacted the first and most severe Black Codes toward the end of 1865. Mississippi required all blacks to possess, each January, written evidence of employment for the coming year. Laborers leaving their jobs before the contract expired would forfeit wages already earned, and, as under slavery, be subject to arrest by any white citizen. A person offering work to a laborer under contract risked imprisonment or a fine of $500. To limit the freemen's economic opportunities, they were forbidden to rent land in urban areas. Vagrancy—a crime whose definition included the idle, disorderly, and those who "misspend what they earn"—could be punished by fines or involuntary plantation labor; other criminal offenses included "insulting" gestures or language, "malicious mischief," and preaching the Gospel without a license. South Carolina's Code required blacks to pay an annual tax from $10 to $100 if they wished to follow any occupation other than farmer or

servant (a severe blow to the free black community of Charleston
and to former slave artisans) (Foner 1990, 92-93).

While the spirit of these numerous efforts throughout the South to
suppress the rights of the emancipated black population was so mean and
in violation of the reigning ideology of free labor that they went unenforced
or were soon declared void, Foner concludes, nonetheless, that "the legal
system of Presidential Reconstruction had profound consequences, limiting
blacks' options, reinforcing whites' privileged access to economic resources,
shielding planters from the full implications of emancipation, and inhibiting
the development of a free market in land and labor" (Foner 1990, 97). South
Carolina's Black Codes were declared void already in January of 1866, just a
month before Bernhard Bequest and Gesine Rigbers began their married life.

It would be inappropriate here to try to reconstruct a history of
Reconstruction in Mt. Pleasant, in Charleston, or in South Carolina in order
to assess the effects that each of those contexts might have had on the Bequest
family as it moved through the post-war period. So much was in upheaval that
it is difficult to note even the most significant sign-posts along the historical
road that the Bequests and the other family members who had survived the war
would have to travel. Nonetheless, the following "historical travelogue" will
demonstrate how the course of Bequest family events [in **boldface**] intersected
with history [from Rogers and Taylor 1994, 101-110]:
:

—1865: November 13:   South Carolina ratified the Thirteenth Amendment which
had freed the slaves

—1866: **February 8:**   **Bernhard Heinrich Bequest and Gesine Margarethe
Rigbers marry**

December 19:   South Carolina rejected the Fourteenth Amendment

December 20:   Legislation passed to establish an immigration commissioner
to encourage immigration of European whites to offset the
black majority

—1867: November 19-
20:   The first election in which the freedmen fully participated
was held to elect state and local officials

—1868: January 14-
March 18:   A convention drew up the Constitution of 1868. The
convention was composed of seventy-six blacks and
forty-eight whites

June 2-3:   The first general election was held under the Constitution of
1868

July 9: Francis L. Cardozo became the state's first black secretary of state

July 9: South Carolina ratified the Fourteenth Amendment

November: Ulysses S. Grant was elected president. South Carolina cast six electoral votes for him

November 9: Bernhard Heinrich Bequest becomes a naturalized citizen

—1870: U.S. Census: [South Carolina] Whites: 289,667; blacks: 415,814; others: 125; Total: 705,606

February 1: Jonathan Jasper Wright became the first black elected to the South Carolina Supreme Court, serving until his resignation December 1, 1877

November 28: Alonzo J. Ransier became the first black South Carolinian to be elected to the office of lieutenant governor

December 12: Representative Joseph H. Rainey was the first black South Carolinian to be sworn in as a member of the U.S. Congress

—1871: October 17: President Ulysses S. Grant issued a proclamation suspending the writ of habeas corpus in nine South Carolina counties

December 24: Theresa Louise Bequest born

—1872: November: Ulysses S. Grant was reelected president. South Carolina cast seven electoral votes for him

—1873: **July 3: Bernhard Heinrich Bequest and Catherine Mehrtens marry**

October 7: Henry E. Hayne was the first black accepted as a student at the University of South Carolina

—1876: **April 19: Bernhard Heinrich Bequest elected Intendant of Mt. Pleasant, SC**

July 8: At least one white and four blacks were killed in a race riot in the industrial town of Hamburg, SC

September 9: Bernhard Heinrich Ludwig Bequest born

September 16-19: At least one white and about forty blacks were killed in race riots at Ellenton in Aiken County

October 17: President Grant issued a proclamation which placed federal troops at the call of Governor Chamberlain

November: The tempestuous and disputed gubernatorial election between the incumbent Chamberlain and Wade Hampton took place

Rutherford B. Hayes was elected president. South Carolina's seven electoral votes were disputed but eventually counted for Hayes

November 28: Federal troops occupied the State House

December 14: Wade Hampton, disputing Chamberlain's election, took the oath of office as governor

—1877: April 10: President Hayes ordered federal troops withdrawn from Columbia. Chamberlain conceded the gubernatorial dispute, leaving Hampton as governor

March 1: The General Assembly passed legislation to end public executions

March: The University of South Carolina was divided into two branches: whites attended in Columbia, blacks in Orangeburg

December 10: Wade Hampton was elected to the U.S. Senate

—1878: February 10: **Bernhard Heinrich Ludwig Bequest dies**

September 16: **Anna Meta Adeline Bequest born**

—1879: April: **Bernhard Heinrich Bequest's Intendancy of Mt. Pleasant ends**

—1880: U. S. Census: White: 391,105; Black: 604,332; Other: 140; Total: 995,577
[South Carolina]

—1881: April 19: **Anna Meta Adeline Bequest dies**

—1882: September 9: **John Frederick Bequest born**

By the time Bernhard and Catherine Bequest's one surviving child was born, the period known as Reconstruction—generally understood to have run from 1865 to 1877—was over. Bernhard's three years of public service that had begun toward the end of Reconstruction had lasted two years beyond, and the family was now residing in Charleston proper on East Bay Street. Bernhard by now was the *successful* businessman that Capers had described, and would live for twenty more years after ceding the mayor's office in Mt. Pleasant to his successor, Charles E. Carrere. The immigrant Bequest did indeed weather thirty-four years in the reconstructed city between his arrival and his death, but his life in Charleston would ultimately transform him into a different man at the end than he had been at the beginning.

Bernhard Bequest initially settled in Mt. Pleasant because conditions in the city of Charleston at war's end were so uninviting that it would have been foolish not to choose the less prostrate location close by. And if he intended to enter the merchant/grocer niche like so many other of his countrymen, he was quick to understand the advantages of acquiring land. Thus his farm interests and efforts to purchase land are in evidence already soon after his arrival: his initial contract on Mt. Pleasant land is recorded by July of 1867.

A sense of what life was like in the small island village at that time can be culled from a letter written by Henry Slade Tew to his daughter in February 1865. Tew was a storekeeper and the Intendant of Mt. Pleasant from 1868 to 1870. Three mayors served the town between Henry Tew and Bernhard Bequest, but the character of the town changed more slowly than mayoral incumbents. The February letter was written to Emily Jenkins Tew approximately eight months before young Bequest arrived in Charleston and gives an account of the occupation of Mt. Pleasant by Union troops. The passages excerpted below provide an inside view to the general sensibilities of the time and describe what Bernhard Bequest would accommodate himself to when he settled in Mt. Pleasant.

> Dear Daughter,
>
> Your absence from home at the time of the evacuation by our troops and the taking possession of those of the U.S. was a great relief to our minds, as our apprehension of insults and violence had been excited by the reports of such conduct elsewhere, and I have prepared this narrative or sort of diary to put you in possession of such facts as transpired and in some of which I was an actor, as may prove of interest to you at some future time may be referred to as part of the history of these eventful times . . . .
>
> While these scenes were transpiring over here, those of Charleston must have beggared description,—to us was visible only the awful magnificence of the scene, while the terror, confusion, suffering and crime must have been appalling to the dwellers in the doomed city. The burning buildings public and private the repeated explosions, the gun boats and other vessels burning in the harbor all presented such a scene as but few ever witness in a lifetime, and surely one which none would ever desire to see repeated. Oh God! What a night of horror that memorable 17th of February was . . . .

About 12 o'clock Saturday three barges landed from the fleet and as I had been elected Intendant by the people on Friday, in that official capacity attended by some of the citizens I surrendered the town submitting to the military authority of the U.S. and was promised protection to persons and private property. The boats were commanded by Lieut. Gifford from the Flagship—they brought a small U.S. Flag ashore and hoisted it for a while on the Light house. The officers were courteous and the men quite peaceful. Many from the fleet were ashore on Saturday and Sunday but we had not yet seen any from the Army from whom we feared violence and insult. All our own blacks boisterous in their reception of the visitors but none that I am aware of had yet left their work or homes. Monday 20th we heard that the troops that had landed at Bull's Bay were marching down and about 11 o'clock the shouts of the negroes apprised us of their arrival. There were three regiments of U.S. colored troops all under the command of Col. A. S. Hartwell, who took his quarters temporarily at the light house. I called on him, told him my name and position and asked protection for the persons and property of the citizens who were mostly women and children and were greatly apprehensive at the presence of the coloured troops . . . .

Colonel Hartwell then entered into conversation with me, asked me if I was connected with the Tews of Rhode Island, and if I was favorable to secession, as he had received so many assurances from people that they were not, that he was at a loss what to think and could only judge by the manner and not the language. I told him I would reply with the upmost frankness, that if more than one man in South Carolina out of Fifty told him he had opposed secession they lied, and that for myself, tho a Union man in 1832 and in 1850, yet on the election of Mr. Lincoln I thought all hope of justice to the South in the Union was lost, and I went for secession with vote and voice. He thanked me for the frankness of my reply and said it would be better if all would be equally so . . . .

Many of the negroes from the Plantations came down in the Army train, and together with those of the village made quite a multitude of shouting wild creatures whom the thought of freedom had changed from quiet to transports of uproarious joy. I must tell you what I did for my own. A few days before I gave them $50.00 told them the money would soon be worth nothing and advised them to buy whatever they could then. I also told them that when the troops came they knew they were free to go or stay as they pleased—if they stayed, as long as I had anything to eat they should share as they always had done—Not one answered a word, and I knew of course they would go—they stayed however until Wednesday and then went off without a word of leave taking—Sary setting the example—Louis is gone also, Margaret and Zoe are still here as Elisa is with William and forbids their leaving, but I suppose they will not stay long . . . .

When orders came for the Brig. to move to the City and they left us with only six men as a guard and our negroes noisy, stealing all they could lay hands on and moving into the houses that were vacant. It was a sleepless night to us. We all sat up till 4 o'clock. Wednesday was a quiet day . . . .

March 1

The 52nd Regt. Major Hennessy Com'g now garrison Mount Pleasant. Headquarters are now established at Mr. Whilden's house and the proximity to our own dwelling is the best guaranty we can have of quiet and order. The commander seems to be determined to enforce order and maintains stricter military discipline than we have ever had over here before from the troops of *either* army. He does not appear to have much sympathy or regard for the blacks, at least he does not place them above the whites and make all claims and interest subservient to theirs . . . .

On Sunday 19th went to Church and in the pew before us was a mulatto girl with a white soldier—we heard he married her Saturday 25th. Attended the funeral of Sally Venning and on Sunday 26th that of little Eddy Royall who died of measles. The whole five of Mr. Royall's children having been taken at one time. On that Sunday the Episcopal Church was taken possession of by negro troops. Their regiment is commanded by Col. Beecher the brother of H. Ward Beecher and Mrs. H. B. Stowe, and we hear that his wife who is with him declines all acquaintance with the whites, but has called upon the colored ladies and invited them to her quarters—from this time forth until matters are settled I suppose that the Church is to be abandoned by the whites, as no one will care to subject themselves to the annoyance of having a colored gentleman or lady perhaps both walking into your pew and overpowering you with their odor or filling you with vermin . . . (Anonymous 1965, 8-14).

The idiosyncrasies of life in Mt. Pleasant in 1865 resonate with the biases, antipathies, and prejudices endemic in the South when the end of the war left a vanquished people feeling their way out of chaos and not quite used to the new rules of order. For an immigrant such as Bequest it would have been a case of new rules twice over, although with his blockade-running past he must have had a good idea of what he was getting into. If the new order called for accommodation, he was up for it—he actually had little choice. And by the time he was sufficiently acculturated that he could be elected to public office by his fellow citizens, he had slipped on new clothes and no longer acted like an outsider. One might wonder how Bernhard Bequest positioned himself when he ran for the office of mayor: in her *Historic Landscape of Mt. Pleasant*, Amy McCandless reports that "[i]n 1876, an election which overturned Black Republicanism and restored white Democrats to power in the district, state, and region so inflamed the town that black Republicans seized the streets for an entire night and fearful white Democrats along with a handful of black political allies barricaded themselves in their homes" (McCandless 1993, 41). Just how much of a role did Bequest play in "overturning" Black Republicanism and "restoring" white Democrats to power? Was he, eleven years after his immigration, elected to office because he had become a *white Democrat*? By the end of his term, his fourteen-plus years as a Mt. Pleasant citizen and his transformation from immigrant to upstanding civic leader might plausibly be read as the Book of Reconstruction—from the era's ascent, through its reign, to its demise. His holding the office of Mt. Pleasant's *Intendant* during the same years that Wade Hampton monopolized the South Carolina political scene suggests a parallel with the transformation of the German ethnic community that Jeffery Strickland describes as "how the Germans became white southerners."

Strickland's broad-stroke analysis argues that Germans were "a middleman minority community, occupying a middle tier on the racial and ethnic hierarchy below white southerners and above African Americans," who after the Civil War "increasingly exhibited their desire to become white southerners." He traces the evolution of the German immigrant dry goods merchants and grocers in Charleston from their initial openness to economic interaction with the African American community, a relationship which both found positive, to a post-war situation which put them in the middle between opposing forces.

> Middleman minorities often find themselves in conflict with the host society over economic matters, including disagreements with their clientele (in this case both black and white), native businesses (overwhelmingly white), and labor (increasingly black). First and foremost, white southerners opposed German trade with slaves, and it was a point of political debate. Second, blacks and whites clashed with German entrepreneurs over prices and credit terms. In the aftermath of the Civil War, the Germans were castigated for price gouging in the Charleston press. In 1871 African Americans rioted against German shopkeepers, in part for their refusal to extend credit to black Charlestonians. Conflict also arose because white southern businessmen, and to a lesser extent black southerners, found it difficult to compete with German grocers and dry good

> merchants because the Germans had organized vertically, owning the shipping companies, wharfs, wholesalers, banks and brokerage and commission houses (Strickland 2008, 55).

Native white southerners, however, would have acknowledged that the Germans were really the backbone of Charleston's economic revival after the war. In many ways, Bernhard Bequest could have counted himself among the backbone's successful, along with Oskar Aichel [John Hurkamp & Co., wholesale and retail grocery], Otto F. Wieters [wholesale liquor business], J. C. H. Claussen [baker], and Frederick W. Wagener [wholesaler in naval stores and cotton]. And as the Germans had gone through stages of asserting their cultural heritage on the local scene, for example, establishing the *Schutzen Gesellschaft*/Rifle Club in 1855, they had ridden a middle ground by inviting the attendance and participation of African Americans while encouraging the martial display of uniforms and guns in their exhibitionary parade—the latter supportive of the sense of white superiority held by the non-African American crowd in attendance. With their increasing social and financial ascendancy, the Germans by 1868 were becoming increasingly attuned to the platform of the Democratic Party, and by 1871 they were sufficiently politically organized to nominate one of their own, John A. Wagener, a "former Confederate general and slaveholder", for mayor of Charleston. Despite an initial hesitancy, enough white southerners could ultimately endorse Wagener's candidacy that he would win a two-year term. By then, it seemed, the Germans were operating on a different footing:

> African American Republican politicians lashed out at the Germans for their efforts on behalf of the Democratic Party . . . . Lieutenant Governor Alonzo Ransier, an African American, considered it "the basest ingratitude in General Wagener and the Germans to support a ticket in opposition to the rights of the colored people." Ransier thought the Germans had betrayed the African American community: 'So far as the negro is concerned—let the Germans remember when they came here in their blue shirts—you patronized them, traded with them, and through your patronage they are enabled to-day to raise their heads and now desire to govern us' (Strickland 2008, 62).

From the general to the specific, there are instances in which members of Bernhard Bequest's own extended family demonstrated the shift from immigrant innocent in the middle to Democratic white activist ready and willing to violate civil rights laws enacted by Reconstruction legislatures. In his 2003 dissertation, Strickland writes that "[m]any German immigrants faced scrutiny from African-Americans because of civil rights violations that Germans committed against them." He cites cases involving both Nicholas Fehrenbach, jun. and his younger brother Hermann:

> The *Daily Republican* reported that restaurant owners, many of them Germans, had pooled their money and planned to test the constitutionality of the Civil Rights Act. N. Fehrenbach, a German-American born in Charleston, Martin Meyers, a middle-aged Hanoverian, and A.D. Lorenz, a Prussian grocery clerk, all Germans, faced charges that they violated the Civil Rights Act. In each case the person discriminated against had filed charges with the magistrate. And the Germans paid bails ranging from one to two thousand dollars. N. Fehrenbach paid a twenty dollar fine for operating a barroom with four billiard tables without a license. That same day, H. H. Fehrenbach and Martin Myers (second time) faced allegations they violated the Civil Rights Act. They both posted $1,000 bail. A few days later, H. H. Fehrenbach, a young German-American liquor store owner, was arrested for charging two African-Americans $5 for two drinks of whisky. Fehrenbach claimed he charged whites the same price. The *Daily Republican* joked that Fehrenbach "must imagine himself back in the old Confederate days, when $5 dollars was the usual price for a glass of whiskey." Martin Myers and H. Fehrenbach lived in adjacent houses (Strickland 2003, 51).

On the other hand, Strickland acknowledges that "not all Germans discriminated against African-Americans" and cites the instance in which the bartender at Stelling's restaurant offered Alonzo J. Ransier and other influential blacks free drinks and cigars. (Strickland 2003, 51) Such condescension seems not to have convinced Ransier that the Germans had not "betrayed" the Negro whom they earlier had treated more equitably. Strickland suggests that by the 1870s relations between the Charleston Germans and African Americans had undergone substantial transformation. While clearly not every German could be accused of adhering to an ideology of racial supremacy, the Germans' status in the community and their expressed political and conservative leanings put them more in the camp of the white southerner than on the side of any radicals who wanted to swim against the current.

What Lincoln had started during the war with emancipation in the name of freedom and liberty for all—that tenet that was the internal drive for every immigrant lured to the United States—had indeed transformed society from top to bottom in the South as well as in the North, but most of it ultimately came to grief by the redemption of the old order. The reconstructed state was slowly dismantled, the political power of the freed people gradually but effectively diminished, and the South's legal system reshaped "in the interests of labor control and racial subordination" (Foner 1990, 248). The years during which the reconstruction of the South was processed to its ineffectual end would have been mirrored in the years during which Bernhard Bequest was processed from his immigration, through his naturalization, to his assumption of the markers of his local community in his effort to establish himself within the security of its embrace, to his *redemption* as a white Charlestonian of German birth.

Beyond the prejudices that the *pledge* would have to assume in order to become a member of the *fraternity*, the course Bequest took would not have fulfilled his every expectation. In the process of abandoning his German roots to become a white Charlestonian, there would have been times when things were less than felicitous, and success—financial and personal—not at all assured. The positives of his heritage would have been ineffective against the negatives of his new cultural place. At the zenith of his life, he would have found himself struggling in "a poverty-stricken colonial economy integrated into the national capitalist marketplace yet with its own distinctive system of repressive labor relations. While the region's upper class of planters, merchants, and industrialists prospered, the majority of Southerners of both races sank deeper and deeper into poverty" (Foner 1990, 251). "The depression of the 1870s dealt the South an even more severe blow than the rest of the nation. Between 1872 and 1877, the price of cotton fell by nearly fifty percent, and tobacco, rice, and sugar also suffered precipitous declines. The effects rippled through the entire economy, plunging farmers into poverty and drying up the region's sources of credit. The depression disrupted commerce, bankrupted merchants, seriously undermined the economic situation of artisans, and all but eliminated prospects for social mobility among unskilled laborers of both races . . . . In 1880, with a per capita income only one-third that of the rest of the nation, the South lagged farther behind the North in the total value of its agricultural and industrial output than when the decade began" (Foner 1990, 227). As evidenced by the miniscule estate settled on his death in 1899, Bernhard Bequest had not been so socially mobile during his thirty-four years in Charleston that he could think he had risen to the top and prospered. He had held his own, established a family, was successful to the degree that he owned property and a business, and had changed his orientation so that he was less a German and more a citizen of Charleston. Would he have fully understood how it had come about that it would be mostly his *Charlestonian* character that would survive in his descendants as his German origins merged with other heritages to push that ethnicity into the background?

**Charlestonians John Frederick Bequest and
Anna Charlotte Henrietta Weber at their marriage in 1904.**

XI

TOWARDS CENTURY'S END

There is reason to think that Bernhard Bequest's story is fairly representative of most of the German businessmen in the immigrant family, even though he was the only one to have held public office. With the exception of Nicholas Fehrenbach, sen., almost every one of them was successful—to be sure, some only minimally—in establishing himself, and no matter when they came to Charleston, most enjoyed some degree of status within the ethnic community. Of those who survived the war years, none amassed anything like a fortune, and despite their long struggle, some died just short of impoverishment. Many witnessed their homes and businesses affected by natural disasters and the transformation of their city into a rubble pile. Each was subsequently transformed to some degree by participating, willingly or not, in the efforts of the emancipated to right the wrongs of the past, and, with the exception of those who had died, each actively or passively became a citizen of a redeemed South once Reconstruction was declared a dead issue. Those who lived into the two decades between 1880 and 1900 would have found their lives socially and economically diminished by the slow deterioration of Charleston into a not-so-special place. And without exception, the second generation would continue the parents' transformative process into Charlestonians with little more than a sentimental regard for the original heritage. As assimilation and intermarriage with others similarly shedding immigrant status occurred, bloodlines would be diluted to form only than the gentle undertow of Charleston's ethnic origins.

On the English side, the Thompsons' post-war story indicates that for this Episcopalian family there was hardly a dull moment, a good example, perhaps, to demonstrate that the personal lives of Charlestonians continued in spite of all the political turbulence that occurred during the years of Reconstruction. With more than a half century in Charleston behind her, the post-war Jane

Thompson was separated from her husband, fulfilling by default her role as matriarch: her eldest son long gone with his family to New York, her next eldest also gone north and not returning until after the war, married, she knew, to a German immigrant who had emigrated with the intention of becoming a domestic servant [reason enough to disinherit!]; with daughters marrying successfully or not: Adeline to Greene Lewis, Sarah Jane to Albin Clifford from [Yankee!] New Hampshire, Annastatia to John Bail; younger sons George James and John G. finding their way into adulthood during years when most everything was *under construction*.

As far as Jane's pre-war role as a slave owner is concerned, it would be interesting to know how the black slave mother she owned reacted to her and her children's emancipation in the midst of those especially difficult years. Did she pick up and go when Lincoln issued his proclamation, or only when Charleston surrendered in February 1865? Did Jane's domestics abandon her to join the other African Americans cheering the arrival of Union soldiers, particularly those of the 54th Massachusetts and those in the Union army who had been slaves themselves and who now came to see to it that their fellow freedmen were indeed free? And how did she receive her first son who was mustered out of the Union army in the Charleston he had earlier left? Were they reunited at all? What indignities did she otherwise suffer as she accommodated herself to post-war Charleston?

In all likelihood Jane rejoiced at James's death in 1872 from "senile bronchitis". He had made a will on December 29, 1871, one month before he died on the following 30th of January, which stated: "First. I desire that my just debts be paid. Second. I will devise and bequeath unto Mary J. Ellis the sum of One Thousand Dollars in consideration of her kindness and attention to me for the past Sixteen years, and I desire that the said amount of One Thousand Dollars be paid to the said Mary J. Ellis at the earliest practicable moment. The rest and residue of my estate I desire shall be divided between my children as follows: my eldest son Joseph Symons Thompson and my youngest son John Thompson shall each receive double the amount that my other children shall receive, excepting my son George James Thompson, who shall only receive the sum of one dollar . . . ." He appointed his son Joseph Symons Thompson and his friend Daniel B. Gilliland as his Executors. Whatever his next-to-youngest son George had done to offend his father, the father bitterly carried a grudge up to his last day.

Roughly a month after James's decease on February 7, 1872, son Joseph Symons Thompson filed a petition with the court, saying that the estate was "inconsiderable and amounts to about the sum of fifty dollars"; further, that the real estate holdings of his father were believed to consist of several lots and houses, but that neither he nor anyone else knew the number or the value of this property; he estimated it at $10,000; further, that Daniel B. Gilliland had informed him that he declined to qualify as Executor. The court accepted the petition. The document shows a "stamp duty" of $10,000.

Mary Ellis was by no means out of the picture after James died. A legal action undertaken by Joseph E.S. Thompson in 1875 [three years after his father's death] discloses that in 1855 James Thompson had purchased property on the corner of Bogard and Sires Streets for $1,000, which he subsequently conveyed to Mary Ellis nine years later in 1864. This is the address given as James Thompson's "residence at death". In the 1875 action Joseph E.S. Thompson, as Executor of his late father's will, bought back the Bogard Street property "for valuable consideration paid to her out of the funds of the Estate of the said James Thompson and received by said Mary J. Ellis by way of compromise" and transferred it to his mother for the sum of $550 [paid by Jane Thompson]. Jane Thompson thus got back something of what her errant husband had given away. The reader may sympathize with Joseph E.S., who after his post-war return to Charleston had to negotiate the middle ground between his father and his mother in the parental estrangement that had begun during his teen-age years, while tending to his own life and family during the years of Reconstruction and its aftermath.

However Jane survived the war and the years following, she had proved tenacious in her efforts to acquire and own property. And in spite of the complexities of her inheritances and her second husband's adulterous ways, she managed to hold onto it and to pass it on to her children. If at some earlier point she might have thought of herself as among the top tier in the city—in holdings, not in name—after the war she was not much better off than most of her neighbors living on the economy of the day. By the end of her life the value of her estate had dwindled. The 1870 census put her "value" at $15,000, head of a household that included her two sons—George, a clerk in a store, and James, a machinist—and her unemployed daughter Adeline, whose husband Greene Lewis seems never to have been more than a name on her tombstone.

After Jane's death in 1877, some additional fissures in the family picture are revealed in her will. After leaving her estranged son Lawrence Michael Murray, aka Michael Lawrence, a "mourning ring" and twenty-two dollars, she bequeathed "all the rest and residue of my Estate . . . including the lot, and building thereon, on the South side of Vernon Street, and north side of Laurens Street . . . and being part of what was originally the two lots known as number One Hundred and fifteen, and One Hundred and sixteen, on Purcell's Plat of the Lands of General Christopher Gadsden, which is my property absolutely, and in severalty, unto my children, Mrs. Adeline C. Lewis, Mrs. Annastatia Bail, Joseph E.S. Thompson, George J. Thompson, and John G. Thompson in fee simple and absolutely equally between them share, and share alike." Oddly enough, the will contained no mention of the daughter Sarah Jane, born 1834. She had married Albin R. Clifford from New Hampshire, whose dental practice, according to an 1882 directory, was at 18 Washington Street, not far from Laurens and Vernon Streets. The 1880 census shows a "Sarah J." as wife of Albin R., "keeping house". Was she considered sufficiently well-off in her marriage as to not be mentioned in her mother's will, or was there some irreparable hurt between mother and daughter? Possibly she had been disinherited because she had married a Yankee from New Hampshire! If Jane purposefully omitted Sarah Jane, she purposefully included a condition specifically targeted to her son Joseph: "Provided, however, and on the express condition as to the share of my son Joseph E.S. Thompson, that he shall not claim any part of the said lot fronting on Vernon Street, or any other, or greater share or Estate in the same than such as I intend him to take equally with his aforesaid brothers and sisters as devised under and according to this my will, and that he shall not as Executor of the will of my late husband James Thompson, or in any other right under the said will or otherwise make any claim against me whatsoever, or against my Estate, or my personal representative. And provided further that the said Joseph E.S. Thompson shall not be entitled to any interest under this will, unless he shall within three months after my death by writing under his hand and seal signify that he has elected to acquiesce in the provisions of this will and to take the provision made therein for him, and to release all claims whatsoever, which it might be supposed he had a right to set up as Executor of the will of the said James Thompson . . . and in default of the execution of such declaration and release, and the delivery of the same to my Executrix, within the time above specified, then the share of my estate herein provided for the said Joseph E.S. Thompson, I hereby give, devise, and bequeath unto my other residuary devisees, and legatees, share and share alike." She appointed Adeline Catherine Lewis her executrix.

Jane's intent was clearly not to have her son Joseph receive more than his siblings, particularly as he might assume he could do as executor of his late father's estate. Her legacy was to be protected against any claims by the legatees of her husband—whose estate had excluded her, and part of which she had claimed be restored to her by her husband's agent, her eldest son by him. Joseph took the threat seriously, and on April 24, 1877 [about six weeks after his mother's death] he filed a petition with the court acquiescing to his mother's will, stipulating that he would claim nothing more than his 1/6th of the Vernon Street property and not make any further claim on her estate as the executor of the will of his father.

Some fourteen years later, in November of 1891, Jane's daughter and executrix Adeline Lewis brought a complaint against her four siblings [John G. Thompson had died three years earlier without issue] about the Laurens Street properties. The judgment on #20 Laurens went to Joseph E.S. [for $1,200]. He took out a mortgage from the Southern Mutual Building and Loan Association of Atlanta for the funds to pay for the property. The mortgage transaction was witnessed by Joseph's daughter Ida and her husband Irving L. Jones: the young couple had been married in the house in August of 1890. Joseph Thompson died there in 1894. After Jane's daughter Adeline Lewis died in 1928, the properties on Vernon and Laurens Streets that had passed to her from her mother, as well as from her brother John [John G. Thompson had died a bachelor in 1888 and owned the house and lot between his sister and brother, which on his death had reverted to Adeline] had to be sold because they were untenanted, needed repair, and in default of delinquent taxes. The several smaller dwellings were released by Adeline's executrix and executor, her niece Sarah Hopke and husband August Hopke, to the sheriff for sale in order to pay the taxes owed. #18 Vernon Street was sold to the Charleston Housing Authority. Adeline Lewis's legatees [St. Michael's Episcopal Church, St. Luke's Episcopal Church, Miss Carrie Thompson, the estate of Rebecca O'Connor, Mr. Joseph O'Connor, and Miss Mildred Hopke] each received $33.33—a rather sad end to a struggle that had begun a century earlier. Today, the entire block is commercial property, devoid of any residence.

Whether or not Jane approved of it, the English Cunliffe/Connolly/Thompson legacy had merged with a German one when Joseph E.S. met and married Rebecca Grobert in New York. Exactly when he left Charleston for New York is not known, and exactly why he left is still another question. His departure would have been subsequent to the uncomfortable rift between his parents, although it may simply have been the perceptible lack of opportunity in the antebellum city that encouraged him to seek education and/or his fortune in the North. Fraser writes of the enormous inequality in the distribution of wealth in the city and the inability of the working class to break the hegemony of slave labor that characterized pre-war Charleston. Charleston's gentry did manage to think about employment options for others when they established in 1859 the Charleston Marine School, whose students were "boys who had . . . been wandering about the streets of Charleston" (Altman 1987, 77). The founders, as well as the state in its agreement to start funding the school, were not just interested in providing employment opportunities: they were attuned to the prevailing "sectional rift" and "thought it best to form a pool of sailors whose loyalties would lie with their native state", agreeing that "the school would help replace Northern seamen with Southern sailors and 'our peculiar Institutions' [would] be protected from their evil communication with our negroes." The opportunity to enroll in this Charleston Marine School for training would have come too late for the 19- or 20-year-old young Thompson. If he was indeed looking to become a Southern sailor by going to New York, or whether he might have been caught up in the pre-secession fervor to find a way to serve his state in its efforts to establish a kind of naval defense against unfriendly elements, there is only the tenuous evidence in the 1870 New York census of a J.S. Thompson, *seaman*, whose birthpace is, unfortunately, not stated. Exactly what Joseph was trained to do through his attendance at the evening school in New York is not evident on the graduation certificate he received, and if not as *seaman*, how he earned a living while in New York is otherwise unknown. When he was back in Charleston after the war, he worked as a plumber, and his death certificate gives his occupation as "gas tender" working for the Gas Company. Nor is it known when he and Rebecca Grobert were married—whether before, during, or after the Civil War. Their first child was born in New York in 1863, and eleven others would follow. It is doubtful that Jane Thompson ever approved of this marriage, thinking it beneath the family's Episcopalian English heritage for her son to marry a German immigrant from Mecklenburg who had landed in New York intending to join relatives in Indiana, and who had immigrated with no higher expectations than to find work as a domestic servant.

Joseph and Rebecca remained in New York for the duration of the war. One of their children, John Thompson, became a long-time employee of the SC Power Co., and in an article in a company publication, *The Powerlog* [May 1937, Vol. VIII, Nr. 5], about his retirement, he reported that he was "accidentally" born in New York in 1865 "owing to the fact that his parents were visiting in New York at the outbreak of the War Between the States, and were not allowed to return south until after the war ended." Jane, another child of Joseph and Rebecca and her grandmother's namesake, is listed in the 1900 census [Charleston, Ward 9], as having been born in New York in 1870.

If something is known about Joseph E.S. Thompson's background, the early years of Rebecca Grobert's youth are much more of a mystery. That she was from Mecklenburg was part of the family lore, although that did not reveal much other than a North German heritage. The name appears only infrequently on some immigration lists: there is one listing for a Johann Friedrich Grobert from Mecklenburg-Schwerin [at the time, the Duchy of Mecklenburg was divided into Mecklenburg-Strehlitz and Mecklenburg-Schwerin], age 19, who arrived in New York in 1855 on the *Howard* from Hamburg. The family story is indeed that Rebecca came with her brother in an effort for him to avoid being conscripted into the military. Her name, however, does not appear on the same passenger list. She was born in 1842, and thus would have been thirteen years old upon arrival in 1855—old enough that she could hardly have stowed away on the ship or otherwise missed being registered as a passenger. Nonetheless, if she was indeed on the *Howard* with her brother, by 1859 she would have been old enough to marry Joseph Thompson. There is evidence that she intended to join relatives further inland—specifically, in Indiana: among the scant memorabilia passed down to the author are the wills of two individuals resident in Kendallville, Indiana—one, the will of Louis Grobert, the other, the will of Ferdinand Hellmuth, witnessed by Louis Grobert. It seems clear that these documents would have been among Rebecca Thompson's effects only if she were related in some way to Groberts who had earlier immigrated to Indiana. There are still Grobert descendants in Kendallville, but the exact relationship between Rebecca and any living or deceased Grobert family member has eluded all attempts to pin it down.

Under whatever circumstances Rebecca Grobert met and married Joseph Thompson, she must have thought marriage to a prodigal Charlestonian was a better option than domestic service in rural Indiana. Her own rural Mecklenburg origins and her young age suggest that she may have been fairly innocent of the rebellion going on in her future husband's home city and state. Life in New York during the years of the war among countless other immigrants seeking a footing, but less than directly involved in the war's causes and purposes, may have kept her innocent of the situation she would face when the couple returned to Charleston. Three of her children [Anna, James John, and Jane] were born in New York before something happened to put the return to Charleston on the couple's horizon. Whatever brought about the decision to return to Joseph's native South, the war was already five years in the past. Once back in Charleston, the E.S. Thompsons would have been newer residents in the not-yet-restored city than Bernhard Bequest and his wife. The half-German Thompson couple would have to accommodate the same host of new southern rules and ways, as well as learn to grasp the revised orientations that were part and parcel of Reconstruction that the Bequest German couple had been negotiating already for some time.

Once resident in Charleston, with Joseph all but disinherited by his mother yet not abandoned by his father, the couple had nine more children. Census records indicate that Louis was born in Charleston in 1870 [likely the year the couple returned to Charleston], Rebecca in 1872, Ida Elizabeth in 1874, Josephine in 1875, Charles in 1877, Caroline in 1879, Florine in 1884, Lillie in 1885, and James Simons in 1892. Of their twelve children, only the youngest five escaped the war years in New York and the upheavals of Reconstruction in the South. Toward the end of the Reconstruction period, Joseph was working for the Gas Company and Rebecca was operating a small store selling "fruits, etc." By the turn of the century, the large clan of Jane Thompson's grandchildren by her son Joseph E.S. and his German wife had become part of the general, non-elite, Charleston middle-class community. Anna Thompson, the eldest, was married to a John F. Jones, but was divorced from him in 1886. She subsequently married John William Mouzon, and their son Ernest A. [Dude] would later become the author's godfather. John Thompson married Mary Cleapor in 1903 and worked, like his father, for the Charleston Gas Company. They had no children. Both are buried in Magnolia Cemetery [in the same lot as his mother]. Daughter Jane married John Hammond Fedderwitz, a native of Germany [yet another English-German merger!], and moved to Ladson, SC, where he was a farmer. Both Jane and one of her sons, Ernest Henry, are buried in Charleston's St. Philip's churchyard [West portion]. Ernest died of yellow fever in 1913, and his and his mother's graves in the church cemetery suggest that Jane had maintained her Episcopal heritage through membership in the congregation while she was living in Ladson. Daughter Rebecca married James M. O'Connor. She and her husband also share the Magnolia plot with her mother Rebecca. Josephine first married Leon Grooms, then his brother Alwin; there were no children from either marriage. Caroline, the next youngest, listed as a 1-year-old in the 1880 census, never married, and became a practical nurse whose attentive care was appreciated by many. Caroline is also buried in the Magnolia lot along with her mother, with a gravestone indicating her birth date as 20 September 1882. That date is in error in view of her listing in the 1880 census: the month and day may be correct, but she was likely almost three years older than she acknowledged or that anyone else in the family was aware of. Florine died at the age of 14 of a heart problem. Lillie, born 1885, was married in 1905 to Charles Dietrich Meyer [another German!]. James Simons, the last child of Joseph and Rebecca Thompson, died of gastroenteritis when he was just 3 1/2 in 1895, preceded in death by his father.

Rebecca Grobert Thompson outlived her husband by twenty-five years. Before she was widowed, she and her husband and all their children but the last had weathered Charleston's post-war struggle to recover its place in the world against seemingly insuperable odds. Economic and natural disasters plagued the city and its residents. The Thompsons, along with everyone else, survived the terrible hurricane of 1885 that damaged or destroyed ninety percent of the city's private homes, as well as the famous earthquake of 1886. They were present to help Charleston pick up its pieces.

When she died in 1919, the former Rebecca Grobert from Mecklenburg would pass her lineage into succeeding generations through her fourth daughter, Ida Elizabeth, born 1874. It would be one of Ida's children who would connect the English Thompson heritage to an extended family of Germans that had been in Charleston almost as long as her own. The German Rebecca had taken on the Episcopalian heritage of her husband: she was buried from St. Philip's Episcopal Church. Her daughter Ida would marry someone of English origin, although not of an Anglican heritage: Ida's husband, Irving Little Jones, whom she married in August of 1890 at the house of her parents on Laurens Street, came from rural stock and was a Methodist. That couple's legacy is the other English bookend that completes this immigrant family's story in Charleston at the end of the century.

XII

Moncks Corner To Charleston

Irving Little Jones was clearly of English heritage. The village of Moncks Corner dates from about 1705, one of several rural towns that developed in the area not far from Charleston that became Berkeley County. The area was part of the original charter to the eight Lords Proprietors and was settled first by the English, Barbadians of English descent, as well as French Huguenots, followed by Dutch, German, Scotch, and Irish immigrants and a large slave population. The Jones name suggests an English/Welsh heritage, but Irving's lineage cannot be traced any further back than the mid-nineteenth century. And even that is fraught with uncertainties and, as was the case with the other immigrant forebears, is very short on written evidence. To be accurate, Irving Jones was only of immigrant stock, at best classifiable as third-generation. But he and his story nonetheless present the other English heritage to bring full circle the narrative of this immigrant family and its transition into the twentieth century.

When Irving Little Jones was born in the middle of the nineteenth century [1858], it was just after Peter Weber had died and Johann Wilhelm Friedrich Struhs had been naturalized. James Buchanan was serving as President of the United States. Bernhard Bequest's father Ludwig would die the next year in Geestendorf, and Captain Heinrich Wieting was still bringing German immigrants to Charleston. Irving's future father-in-law would have just gone to New York and was about to complete his night-school studies. South Carolina had not yet seceded from the Union, although local and national politics were on everyone's mind. When he died eight-six years later on August 7, 1944—before the end of WW II—he left little record of his past, no written or printed memorabilia, and hardly any oral history that could be passed on to succeeding generations by any of his children. There is, for example, no explanation for the middle name of *Little*. It is not inconceivable that *Little* was given to a child small in size, but that would seem to be a too-convenient explanation. Nonetheless, there is no other evidence of it being a family name of any sort. Irving Little Jones died in Columbia, SC at the State Hospital, a victim of senility.

The only pertinent written record relevant to him is a copy of the funeral arrangements made for him by his youngest son. That minimal record indicates that Irving Little Jones was born June 29, 1858 in Moncks Corner, SC of parents Solomon Jones and Bessy Taylor, both purported natives of Moncks Corner. Irving's occupation is given as "steamfitter" at the Charleston Dry Dock, where, according to the funeral home record, he had worked until 1935, having spent a total of forty-seven years working in that occupation. The funeral was on August 8th, the officiating minister was Rev. H. L. Fr. Shuler from Trinity Methodist Church. Interment was in Charleston's Magnolia Cemetery.

While the majority of this skeletal record is innocuous enough, the parentage of Irving Little Jones as given is dubious and has perpetuated a confused lineage. The birth date of 1858 is confirmed by the 1860 census record for *Jones* among the free inhabitants of St. John's Berkeley Parish in the County of Charleston [Berkeley County was separated from Charleston County only in 1882], and shows him as an infant of four months in the family of Seaborn—not Solomon—Jones, a *planter*, aged 29; Seaborn's wife is listed as Renvy, aged 25, and there are four other children: William, 9, Robert, 6, Lewis, 4, Mary, 2. The 1870 census record for the City of Charleston lists the family headed by Renvier, aged 43, "keeping home", with children William, 17, Robert, 16, Louis, 14, Irvine [*sic*], 12, Isaac, 10, and Jerome, 8. In the ten year interval between 1860 and 1870, Seaborn and Mary are both gone, Isaac and Jerome have been born, and the family has moved to Charleston.

It is the census record that makes questionable the funeral home record indicating *Solomon* as Irving's father. As for his mother, *Bessy* would have to be a variant of Renvier, Seaborn's wife. Renvier's name—in and of itself rather unusual—later gets shortened to *Renvy*, and in other records becomes *Rena*. If Seaborn was indeed Irving's biological father, his disappearance from the census record in that particular ten-year interval suggests that he was a casualty of the Civil War. Civil War records (Rivers and Anderson 1995) list a number of soldiers by that name, but only two from South Carolina. One of the two was a Private belonging to the 4th South Carolina Cavalry: that individual is listed only by a single, handwritten initial that can be read either as an *I* or a *J*, rather than an *S*. Seaborn's full Christian name, however, was Isaac [after his father] Seaborn, so that the initial can legitimately be read as an *I*. That one of his names was indeed *Isaac* is borne out by a later listing for his widow Renvy as *w[idow] Isaac* in a Charleston city directory, and further by the fact that one of his sons was named Isaac. That son Isaac, remembered by Irving's last surviving daughter as one of her father's two brothers, is known to have lived in Jacksonville, FL. His marriage to Mamie Bell Philips in June 1890 at age thirty is recorded in Susan King's record of Charleston marriages (King 2002). The 1930 census record for Jacksonville confirms Isaac Seaborn Jones at age 70, i.e. born c.1860, two years after Irving. In any case, this [Isaac] Seaborn Jones's service records show him off and on in service [active or furloughed] from September 1861 through 1864 and a casualty of the Battle of Richmond on July 22, 1864. If there were *absolute* certainty that this dead Confederate soldier was the author's great-grandfather, Isaac Seaborn Jones should take his place among the other soldiers accounted for in Chapter IX as the single individual on the English side of the family who saw action in, but did not survive, the Civil War.

Seaborn's death in the Battle of Richmond left his son Irving fatherless by the time he was 6 or 7 years old, and the mystery remains as to why in 1944 his father was thought to be *Solomon*. It happened that there was another Jones family in Moncks Corner: Jadon Jones owned a lumber business, was likely a cousin to Irving, and was prominent enough to be mentioned more than once in a short historical account (Orvin 1950) of the town of Moncks Corner. One reference reads: "The People's Bank began business in 1920, with T. J. Cottingham as the first president. Others associated with this bank were George W. Law, E. J. Dennis, J. W. Hill, J. D. Meyers, W. W. Peagler, J. S. Jones, Sr., and J. S. Jones, Jr." Another notes: "A sawmill with a daily capacity of fifty thousand feet of lumber was put in operation in August, 1927, by J. S. Jones and his sons, S. R., J. S. Jr., Charles A., and J. W. Jones" (Orvin 1950, 52). The same historical account also includes the following information:

> In June, 1897, Federal Judge Charles R. Simonton declared the dispensary law unconstitutional and that under the general liquor laws it was legal for persons to import and to sell liquors in original or unbroken packages. The constables continued to seize such liquors, however, and in July Judge Simonton granted a restraining order against the constabulary that permitted the unhindered sale of liquors in unbroken packages, but forbade drinking on the premises where it was sold. As a result, 'Original Package Stores' were opened in many parts of the State, and the Guggenheim wholesale liquor firm in Savannah, Georgia, engaged Jesse Murray to operate such a shop for them in Monck's Corner. At the time Lewis E. Jones was operating a gasoline propelled freight and passenger boat on Cooper River between Stoney Landing and Charleston. His boat, named *Beulah*, was chartered to make the trip to Savannah and return with a cargo of liquors, which was then hauled in wagons to Monck's Corner and there offered for sale by Mr. Murray in a small one-room

shop built for that purpose on the south side of Main St. about where the Bank of Berkeley is now located (Orvin 1950, 37).

In the first two mentions, the initials *J. S.* stand for *Jadon Solomon*, both sen. and jun., and their family lineage is well established: Jadon Solomon Jones, sen. [b. October 4, 1858, d. July 29, 1942] was the son of Solomon Kershaw Jones and his second wife, Rachel Catherine Murray. Solomon Kershaw Jones was born 1817 in St. Matthews, SC, and died in 1885 in Berkeley County, SC. In trying to determine possible intrafamilial connections, one might find the name *Kershaw* unusual enough to wonder about its origin: as the son of Jadon D. Jones, Solomon was named *Kershaw* for some meaningful reason. The extensive genealogical record of *The Samuel Jones Family, Kershaw County, SC, 1756-1979* by Hazel Parker Jones may be of some relevance here. Jones has traced that family's heritage back to an early Welsh settler, William Jones:

> William Jones I (1), earlier ancestry now unknown, born probably around 1700 to 1725 in Wales, came to America and settled somewhere in the coastal section of Virginia . . . . Very early, substantial family tradition is that this William Jones and his family and his two brothers and their families, if any, removed from Virginia, maybe as early as 1760 and by or before 1765, came to South Carolina . . . . Family tradition is that these 3 brothers traveled together from Virginia to South Carolina where they reached a place called the Junction, Rock Hill—Lancaster area (or between), S.C. There, for some now unknown reason, they separated, to go different ways and . . . William Jones . . . arrived at, and settled near, the present town of Kershaw, Kershaw/Lancaster Co., S.C. He did not know where his brothers settled and never heard from them again, and in time even their names were lost to his descendants. However, since family names were kept in this early Jones family, it is very probable that William named some of his sons for these two lost brothers. It was the original South Carolina settler [William]'s grandson who was Seaborn Jones. This Seaborn was the son of Major Samuel Jones I, and his third wife Elizabeth Hilton. Seaborn was a planter, born 19 October 1811 near Kershaw, SC, died there 7 June 1898, is buried in the Jones family cemetery located on his plantation about 2 miles east of Kershaw, SC., Jones Road. He had two sons, Seaborn Samuel and William J. Seaborn Samuel was born in 1858 and died in 1910. He left no children by his first or second wife.

Now none of this actually connects the upstate and Moncks Corner families. Nonetheless, it suggests a possible link through the transfer of the upstate location into the name of the Moncks Corner businessman and, as well, brings the Seaborn name into the Moncks Corner parlance. As for the account of the liquor-running operation, Lewis E. Jones was another son of Solomon Kershaw Jones and Rachel Catherine Murray, born 1865, and thus a younger brother of Jadon Solomon Jones, sen.

Without going too far afield, it is interesting to note that Solomon Kershaw Jones, in his first marriage to Catherine Way, had a daughter Jane M. Jones, born 1840, died 1882. Jane's second marriage was to Fredrick Shuler in October 1860. Their son, the Rev. Fredrick Hawkins Shuler, born 1863 [d. 1927], was father to the Rev. H. L. Fr. Shuler, who officiated in 1944 at the funeral of Irving Little Jones. The minister at Trinity Methodist Church in Charleston where Irving Little Jones was a member—and who buried him in 1944—was thus the grandson of Jadon Solomon Jones, sen.'s half-sister. This was either a matter of the proverbial *small* world, or a more substantive familial connection. The following evidence supports an actual family relationship.

The 1840 census for St. Matthew's Parish/Orangeburg District—not very far from Moncks Corner—suggests that the several relationships detailed above were the result of a small, tightly knit rural community of individuals living at a time when distances, modes of transportation, and an agricultural economy kept families close to home. This early census record attests to relationships that would normally develop in this kind of rural community. A single page of the census lists: *Solomon Jones*, head of the household, in the age bracket 30-40, with three female children under the age of 5; the very next line lists *Isaac Jones*, in the age bracket 40-50, as head of a large family: two sons under 5, two sons between 5 and 10, one son between 10 and 15, one daughter under 5, two daughters between 10 and 15. It is entirely likely that the two heads of these households are brothers, with Isaac the elder of the two. The *Solomon Jones* is likely Solomon Kershaw Jones, and the older brother *Isaac*, likely Irving Jones's grandfather. Either of Isaac's two sons between 5 and 10 years old could be Isaac Seaborn, Irving Little Jones's father whom the later 1860 census reports as the 29-year-old household head married to Renvier. Interestingly enough, on the same 1840 census page there is a listing for *Alex Shuler*, age 30-40, with five children [two sons and three daughters between the ages of 5 and 15], also *F.W. Shuler*, age 30-40 with ten children, four sons between "under 5" and 20, six daughters between "under 5" and 15, also a *Josiah Taylor*, as well as a *James R. Taylor* with two sons under 5 and three daughters between 5 and 10. Further down the page: a *James Sweat*, and a *Thomas Murray*, age 30-40, with one son, age 10-15. To make the circle complete, there is also a listing for *Jacob Way*, age 60-70, with two sons, 15-20, one daughter between 10 and 15, and another between 15 and 20.

All of these individuals were thus neighbors, and the record begs to verify what has already been stated: Solomon Kershaw Jones's first wife Catherine was likely a daughter of Jacob Way; his second, a descendant of Thomas Murray. Solomon Kershaw Jones's first marriage to Catherine Way produced Jane M. Jones, whose second marriage was to F. W. Schuler, thus establishing a familial kinship between the Jones and Schuler families. The James Sweat family is resident in the community early on [no details of family members in the census record], and paves the way for Solomon Kershaw Jones's son, Jadon Solomon Jones, sen. to first marry Ella Catherine Sweat [b. 1861, d. 1894]. The two Taylor families in the neighborhood could have provided the ancestry of the *Bessy* Taylor who was Irving's mother: if she descended from James R. Taylor, the initial *R* may be the origin of the family name *Renvier*.

The census record leaves little doubt that the two Jones lines are intertwined: accepting the two Jones household heads as brothers establishes Jadon Solomon Jones, sen. as a first cousin to Irving Jones's father, Isaac Seaborn Jones. Coincidentally, Jadon Solomon Jones, sen. and his first-cousin-once-removed Irving were born in the same year—1858.

In Orvin's historical account, the record of the sawmill operation mentions Jadon Solomon Jones's sons who were in the business with him: S. R., J. S. Jr., Charles A., and J. W.: *J. S., Jr.* is obviously Jadon Solomon, Jr.; *Charles A.* is Charles Addington Jones [b. 1887]; J. W. is John Wesley Jones [b. 1891]. These are Jadon Solomon sen.'s three sons among his eight children by his first marriage to Ella Catherine Sweat. There is no known descendant of Jadon sen. whose name matches the initials of the fourth son, *S. R.* It is tempting to wonder, however, whether this *S* stands for yet another *Solomon* or perhaps for *Seaborn*—both names prevalent in this family. In any case, there are enough generations of individuals in the Moncks Corner Jones families with the name *Solomon*—as well as specific, known kinships—to justify a semi-orphaned boy of 7, growing up in turbulent times, thinking his father was thus named. If the life of the young Confederate soldier, Isaac Seaborn Jones, was as brief as indicated, who knows what might have led his widow to suggest a paternity for her son that led back to a related, and more financially able, great-uncle Solomon Jones, or at least to tell her son that his father was Solomon rather than the Seaborn lost in the war. Such might have been the line that enabled young Irving Little to believe to the end of his life that his father was Solomon Jones.

Beyond the 1870 census record that placed the 12-year old Irving L. Jones in Charleston with his widowed mother and siblings, there is little to trace the course of his life. He would have been a child of the Reconstruction years and experienced the hardships of being a 20-year-old, minimally educated, young man looking for employment in a crippled—at best—soft economy, and trying to find his place in a redeemed southern culture that was in the process of reconstructing its earlier reconstruction. The 1880 census has an *I. L. Jones* with an approximate birth year of 1860 working on a farm in upstate South

Carolina. Charleston city directories provide some additional information on his whereabouts: his brother William is the only one listed in the 1867-68 issue, when the directories began to be published again after the war had ended, suggesting that he was the first to move to Charleston. In 1875-76, several of the brothers [Isaac, Lewis, and William] were living at 146 St. Philip Street. In 1877-78, Isaac S[eaborn?], Robert, and William were living with their mother Renvy at 6 Charlotte Street: Isaac was employed as a clerk, Robert as a boilermaker, William, as a porter for Chafee & O'Brien, and Renvy was listed as the widow of Sebron [*sic*]. According to the listing in 1881, Irving had joined them [after his farm experience] at the Charlotte Street address. The 1882 listing should not cause confusion by citing Renvey at 6 Charlotte Street as the widow of *Isaac*. In 1889, Renvey, *widow of S*, was living at 420 Meeting Street, together with Erving [*sic*], Isaac, Louis, and Robert. Renvy died in May of 1889, and on August 27, 1890, Irving married Ida Elizabeth Thompson at 20 Laurens Street, the home of her recently-relocated parents, Joseph E. S. and Rebecca Grobert Thompson—they had moved recently from 6 Reid Street.

Irving was Ida's senior by fourteen years and was employed as a boilermaker (King 2002). In 1891 Erwin [*sic*] L. was a driver for City Ry Co., but by 1895, was working again as a boilermaker for Valk and Murdoch. The couple lived at several addresses after their marriage: when their first child was born, they lived at 342 East Bay Street [across from where they would end up almost 30 years later at #339]; in 1904 they were living at 37 Washington Street, in 1911 and 1912 at 65 Washington Street. Not until 1919 did they relocate to the house at 339 East Bay Street that became the family's permanent residence. Their first child, Irving Little, jun. was born 1891 and died in infancy in 1893; Charles Randolph was born 1895 [d. 1966], followed by Evelyn Elizabeth [b. 1897, d. 1902], James Leroy [b. 1899, d. 1978], Mary Beatrice [b. 1901, d. 1973], Alston Grobert [b. 1904, d. 1987], Marguerite Adell [b. 1906, d. 1999], and Ernestine Thompson [b. 1913]. Death records at the Charleston County Library show another child, Irving Little Jones, who died July 20, 1889 at the age of 1 yr., 3 mos., 15 days, buried alone at Magnolia Cemetery. This infant was born prior to Irving's marriage to Ida Thompson at a residence at 70 ½ Reid Street. Whether this was Ida's child is not known, although it may not be incidental that her parents were at the time also resident on Reid Street.

The records of Trinity Methodist Church attest to the fact that both Irving and Ida were enrolled members of the congregation as of 1894. Marguerite Adell was baptized there on March 21, 1908, Charles married Nannie Powell there on June 7, 1919, and Mary Beatrice married Nannie's cousin, James H. Powell, there on February 17, 1925. At some point, Ida returned to her Episcopalian roots and was a member of the St. Paul's and St. Luke's congregation on Alexander Street, even though some of her children continued their affiliation with the Methodist church. It should be noted that Trinity

Methodist is described as "Charleston's Oldest Methodist Congregation", having its origin in 1786 as Cumberland Street Methodist Episcopal Church. One source states further that "it is rich in history and is a product of past dissention over the Methodist stance on the slavery issue before and during the Civil War era and the later unification of three churches who arrived at a common ground due to the ravishes of war, fire and natural disaster, as well as an eventual compromise of the controversial issues surrounding the education and ownership of blacks."[49]

At his death, Irving Little Jones was interred in Magnolia Cemetery in a plot that has no headstones and which contains the remains of eight other individuals: 1) Arthur Jones [d. August 25, 1886], resided 172 St. Philip Street; 2) Virginia G. Jones [d. September 26, 1886], resided 172 St. Philip Street; 3) Rena A. Jones [d. May 25, 1889], resided 440 Meeting Street; 4) Irine Taylor [d. June 10, 1892], resided 67 Hanover Street; 5) E. G. Phillips [d. February 25, 1895], resided City Hospital; 6) Louis C. Jones [d. May 11, 1896], resided 71 America Street; 7) William H. Jones [d. November 11, 1911], resided 70 America Street; 8) Irving L. Jones/daughter [b. December 3, 1912, d. December 4, 1912].

This cemetery record allows a couple of conclusions but adds only slightly to the life story of Irving L. Jones: (a) Arthur and Virginia are probably husband and wife who died within a month of each other; her death record shows she died in pregnancy. Arthur Jones's relationship to any of the others, however, remains a mystery; (b) "Rena" is Irving's mother Renvy/Renvey/Renvier: her record states her age as 63, that she was born in Orangeburg, SC [not in Moncks Corner as indicated in the early census record; as attested in the 1840 census, however, the Taylor family was resident in St. Matthew's Parish, *Orangeburg District*], and that she had lived in Charleston for twenty-five years. If that information is valid, it would indicate that she moved to Charleston in 1864 after the death of Seaborn in the war; (c) [Miss] Irine Taylor was doubtless a relative—perhaps a sister—of Rena; her death record indicates that she was approximately the same age, single, and born in St. Matthews, SC; (d) Mr. Phillips is a mystery: his death record indicates his age as 56, that he was married, was born in Augusta, GA, and worked as a laborer; (e) William H. is Irving's elder brother; (f) Louis C. is likely another brother [Lewis]; (g) Irving and Ida had another child—a daughter who lived for only one day—just one year before their last daughter Ernestine Thompson was born.

Very little is known about Irving's other siblings: his second eldest brother Robert and his wife lived with Irving and Ida briefly after 1913. The 1900 census lists Robert [b. 1854] married to Sarah [b. 1859], with children Robert

---

49   The church records are housed as the Avery Research Center, 125 Bull Street in Charleston.

A. [b. 1880], Marie [b. 1882], Buelah [b. 1885], and Odessa [b. 1890]. As noted earlier, Irving's younger brother Isaac, who carried on his father's name, established himself in Jacksonville, FL. Nothing is known of Mary or Jerome.

There is little evidence that Irving L. Jones's life was anything other than ordinary. If indeed, according to unattested family lore, he served Civil War troops as a water-boy at a very young age, that was probably his most exciting experience and indeed his only claim to fame. In 1890 when he and Ida Thompson wed, Ida's deceased grandmother Jane would probably have thought her granddaughter was marrying down by choosing a 32-year-old laborer from the country. Had Jane been alive for the ceremony on Laurens Street, however, she would have recognized that the family's standing was by then somewhat diminished. In fact, the plumber's daughter may already have borne a child before she was married and would have been in no position to claim that her squire from Moncks Corner was marrying up. Ida was, nonetheless, a daughter of a Charleston Episcopalian family, and Irving a Methodist from up the road. Irving fathered and helped raise ten children, six of whom survived him. His career as a steamfitter on the Charleston waterfront was honorable, if undistinguished, labor that enabled the family to live a modest existence.[50] If one was not a member of the upper echelon of Charleston society, life would not have been easy during those years after Reconstruction when Charleston was not what it had once been, nor yet what it would ultimately become. That he survived to age 86 attests to a certain tenacity during what were legitimately hard times. Still, when he died, it seems clear that Irving Little Jones was buried with *his* people. His wife survived him by six years, but she was buried in neighboring Bethany Cemetery along with three of her children who followed her a quarter to a half century later. To be sure, there was hardly room for Ida to be buried in the crowded Magnolia plot, although one can understand why she, or her children, thought it discrete to establish a different territory.

The details of Irving's heritage beyond his birth more than a hundred and fifty years ago remain unknown. By the time he entered the family picture, he would not have been considered an immigrant of any degree, but rather a member of the common stock which the other family immigrants and their offspring had become. They were all at this point common Southern blood—not English, not German, but Charlestonians.

---

[50]   When the home on East Bay Street was purchased in 1919, the mortgage was in Ida's name only. For the sum of $10, she acquired the property (a 3 ½ story brick building and a two-story brick kitchen "thereon") and assumed the mortgage of the sellers, George McF. and Catherine R. Mood.

WORKS CITED

Altman, James David. "The Charleston Marine School", *The South Carolina Historical Magazine,* April 1987, 76-82.

Anonymous. "An Eye Witness Account of the Occupation of Mt. Pleasant: February 1865", *The South Carolina Historical Magazine,* January 1965, 8-14.

Barnwell, John. *Love of Order: South Carolina's First Secession Crisis.* Chapel Hill: University of North Carolina Press, 1982.

Behrens, Rinje Bernd and Klaus-Siegfried Rothe. *Die Einwohner von Cappel im Lande Wursten 1704-1875.* Bremerhaven: Verlag Männer vom Morgenstern, 2008.

Bell, Michael Everette. ""Hurrah für dies süsse, dies sonnige Leben": The Anomaly of Charleston, South Carolina's Antebellum German-America." Ph.D. Dissertation, University of South Carolina, 1996.

—"Regional Identity in the Antebellum South: How German Immigrants became 'Good' Charlestonians", *The South Carolina Historical Magazine,* January 1999, 9-28.

Bellows, Barbara. *Benevolence among Slaveholders: Assisting the Poor in Charleston 1670-1860.* Baton Rouge: Louisiana State University Press, 1993.

Berlin, Ira and Herbert G. Gutman. "Natives and Immigrants, Free Men and Slaves: Urban Workingmen in the Antebellum South", *American Historical Review,* 88, 1983, 1175-2000.

Bernheim, G.D. *History of the German Settlements and of the Lutheran Church in North and South Carolina.* Philadelphia: Regional, 1872, reprinted Baltimore, 1975.

Boritt, Gabor S. "Lincoln and Gettysburg: The Hero and the Heroic Place", in Robert Brent Toplin (ed.), *Ken Burns's The Civil War. Historians Respond.* New York, Oxford: Oxford University Press, 1966. 81-100.

Bretting, Agnes. "From the Old World to the New", in Dirk Hoerder and Diethelm Knaus (eds.), *Fame, Fortune and Sweet Liberty.* Bremen: Temmen, 1992. 75-122.

Brooks, U.R., ed. *Stories of the Confederacy.* Columbia: The State Company, 1912.

Bullerdiek, Jörn and Daniel Tilgner, *'Was fernern vorkömmt werde ich prompt berichten': Der Auswanderer-Kapitän Heinrich Wieting Briefe 1847 bis 1856.* Bremen: Temmen, 2008.

Burns, Ken. "Four O'Clock in the Morning Courage", in Robert Brent Toplin (ed.), *Ken Burns's The Civil War. Historians Respond*. New York, Oxford: Oxford University Press, 1966. 153-183.

Butt, Winnie J.M. *100 Years of Christian Life and Service, St. Matthew's Lutheran Church, 1840-1940*. Charleston: St. Matthew's Evangelical Lutheran Church, 1940.

Capers, Ellison. *South Carolina*. Vol 5 of Clement A. Evans (ed.), *Confederate Military History: a library of Confederate States history*. Atlanta: Confederate Publishing Co., 1899. 12 vols.

Clinton, Catherine. "'Noble Women as Well'", in Robert Brent Toplin (ed.), *Ken Burns's The Civil War. Historians Respond*. New York, Oxford: Oxford University Press, 1966. 61-80.

Curti, Merle and Kendall Birr. "The Immigrant and the American Image of Europe", *The Mississippi Valley Historical Review*, 37/2 (1950), 203-30.

Dawson, J.L., M.D. and H.W. DeSaussure M.D. *Census of the City of Charleston, South Carolina for the Year 1848*. Charleston: J.B. Nixon, 1849.

"Declaration of the Immediate Causes which Induce and Justify the Secession of South Carolina from the Federal Union; and the Ordinance of Secession." Charleston: Evans and Cogswell, 1860.

Doerries, Reinhold. "Immigrants and the Church: German Americans in Comparative Perspective", in Wolfgang Helbich and Walter D. Kamphoefner (eds.), *German-American Immigration and Ethnicity in Comparative Perspective*. Madison: Max Kade Institute for German-American Studies [University of Wisconsin-Madison], 2004. 3-17.

Doyle, Don H. *New Men, New Cities, New South: Atlanta, Nashville, Charleston, Mobile, 1860-1910*. Chapel Hill: University of North Carolina, 1990.

Faust, Drew Gilpin. *Mothers of Invention: Women of the Slaveholding South in the American Civil War*. Chapel Hill & London: University of North Carolina Press, 1996.

Foner, Eric. *A Short History of Reconstruction. 1863-1877*. New York: Harper & Row, 1990.

—. "Ken Burns and the Romance of Reunion", in Robert Brent Toplin (ed.), *Ken Burn's The Civil War. Historians Respond*. New York, Oxford: Oxford University Press, 1966. 101-118.

Fraser, Jr., Walter J. *Charleston! Charleston! The History of a Southern City*. Columbia, SC: University of South Carolina Press, 1991.

Friedrichs, Erika and Klaus Friedrichs. *Das Familienbuch des Kirchspiels Geestendorf (heute Bremerhaven-Geestemünde) 1689 bis 1874*. Bremerhaven: (self published), 2003.

—. *Die Einwohner des Kirschspiels Debstedt, 1691-1875*. Bremerhaven: Verlag der Männer vom Morgenstern, 1997.

Gallagher, Gary W. "How Familiarity Bred Success: Military Campaigns and Leaders in Ken Burns's The Civil War", in Robert Brent Toplin (ed.), *Ken Burns's The Civil War. Historians Respond*. New York, Oxford: Oxford University Press, 1966. 37-59.

Gongaware, George, Adolph C. Lesemann Jr. and Kellinger R. Cotton Jr. *Two Hundred and Twenty-Five Years of American History: Taken from the Minutes and Other Records of the German Friendly Society of Charleston, South Carolina*. Spartanburg: The Reprint Company, 1999.

Goodheart, Adam. *1861. The Civil War Awakening*. New York: Alfred A. Knopf, 2011.

Gordon-Reed, Annette. *The Hemingses of Monticello: an American Family*. New York: W.W. Norton & Co., 2008.

Grob, Alexander. *Napoleon and the Transformation of Europe*. New York: MacMillan, 2003.

Grossmann, Fr. "Provinz Hannover Unter Einschluss des Kreises Rinteln (Provinz Hessen-Nassau) und des Fürstentums Waldeck", in Max Sering (ed.), *Die Vererbung des Ländlichen Grundbesitzes im Königreich Preussen*. Vol. II, Part I. Berlin: Paul Parey, 1900. 259-76.

Hallmann, Rev S.T., ed. *History of the Evangelical Lutheran Synod of South Carolina, 1824-1924*. Columbia: n.p., n.d.

Hansen, Marcus Lee. *The Immigrant in American History*. New York: Harper & Row, 1940.

Helbich, Wolfgang and Walter D. Kamphoefner (eds.), *German-American Immigration and Ethnicity in Comparative Perspective*. Madison: Max Kade Institute for German-American Studies [University of Wisconsin-Madison], 2004.

Hoerder, Dirk and Diethelm Knauf. "Internal European Migration and its Expansion to the Global Scale", in Hoerder, Dirk and Diethelm Knauf (eds.), *Fame, Fortune and Sweet Liberty*. Bremen: Temmen, 1992. 9-26.

Holcomb, Brent. *Marriage and Death Notices from the Charleston Observer, 1827-1845*. Columbia, SC: B. Holcomb, [1980].

—. "Pickens District, S.C. Naturalizations, taken from Records Now on File in [South Carolina] State Archives", *Georgia Genealogical Magazine*, 1975, 227-30.

Hoole, W. Stanley. "Charleston Theatricals during the Tragic Decade, 1860-1869", *The Journal of Southern History* 11/4 (1945), 538-47.

http://www.dmna.ny.gov/historic/reghist/civil/infantry/54thInf/54thInfMain.htm

http://www.ehistory.osu.edu/uscw/features/regimental/south_carolina/confederate/5thsccav/CoD.cfm

http://www.ehistory.osu.edu/uscw/features/regimental/south_carolina/confederate/KershawsBrigade/20thscv.cfm

http://www.lancewadplan.org/Cultural%20atlas/LS/Land%20Wursten/land_wursten.htm

http://nytimes.com/1864/06/20/news/business-at-nassau.html. 20 June 1864.

http://www.sciway3.net/proctor/marion/military/wbts/OrrReg.html

http://www.sciway3.net/sc-rangers/5th_cav_cod.html

January, Alan F. "The South Carolina Association: An Agency for Race Control in Antebellum Charleston", *The South Carolina Historical Magazine*, July 1977, 191-201.

Jervey, Clare. *Inscriptions on the Tablets and Gravestones in St. Michael's Church*. Columbia, SC: The State Company, 1906.

Jervey, Henrietta P. "The Private Register of the Rev. Paul Trapier", *The South Carolina Historical Magazine,* 58 (April 1957), 94-113 and (July 1957), 163-182.

Johnson, Michael P. "Planters and Patriarchy: Charleston, 1800-1860", *The Journal of Southern History*, 46/1 (1980), 45-72.

Johnson, Michael P. "Wealth and Class in Charleston in 1860", in Walter J. Fraser and Winfred B. Moore (eds.), *From the Old South to the New. Essays on the Transitional South*. Westport, CT: Greenwood Press, 1981. 65-80.

Jones, Hazel Parker. *The Samuel Jones Family [Kershaw County, S.C.: including allied families] 1756-1979.* Kershaw, S.C.: H.P. Jones, 1979.

Jordan, Laylon Wayne. "Education for Community: C. G. Memminger and the Origination of Common Schools in Antebellum Charleston", *South Carolina Historical Magazine*, 83/3 (1982), 99-115.

King, Susan L. *Charleston, South Carolina marriages, 1877-1895*. Columbia, SC: SCMAR, 2002.

King, Susan S. *Roman Catholic Deaths in Charleston, South Carolina, 1800-1860*. Columbia, SC: [n.p.], 2000.

Klenck, Willy. *Das Dorfbuch von Mulsum im Lande Wursten, Kreis Wesermünde in Niedersachsen*. Frankfurt am Main: Deutsche Arbeitsgemeinschaft genealogischer Verbände, 1959.

Köllman, Wolfgang and Peter Marschalck. "German Emigration to the United States", *Perspectives in American History*, VII, 1973, 499-554.

LeMay, Michael C. *From Open Door to Dutch Door: An Analysis of U.S. Immigration Policy Since 1820*. New York: Praeger, 1987.

Levine, Bruce. "'Against All Slavery, Whether White or Black': German-Americans and the Irrepressible Conflict", in David McBride, Leroy Hopkins and C. Aisha Blackshire-Belay (eds.), *Crosscurrents. African Americans, Africa, and Germany in the Modern World*. Columbia: Camden House, 1998. 53-64.

Litwack, Leon F. "Telling the Story: The Historian, the Filmmaker, and the Civil War", in Robert Brent Toplin (ed.), *Ken Burn's The Civil War. Historians Respond*. New York, Oxford: Oxford University Press, 1966. 119-140.

Lofton, John. *Insurrection in South Carolina: The Turbulent World of Denmark Vesey*. Yellow Springs, OH: Antioch Press, 1964.

Lonn, Ella. *Desertion during the Civil War*. New York: The Century Co., 1928.

Luebke, Frederick C. *Germans in the New World: Essays in the History of Immigration*. Urbana and Chicago: University of Illinois Press, 1990.

Massey, Mary Elizabeth. *Ersatz in the Confederacy*. Columbia, SC: University of South Carolina Press, 1952.

McCandless, Amy Thompson, ed. *The Historic Landscape of Mount Pleasant: Proceedings of the First Forum on the History of Mount Pleasant*. Mt. Pleasant, SC: [n.p.], 1993.

McCaslin, Richard B. *Portraits of Conflict*. Fayetteville: University of Arkansas Press, 1994.

McPherson, James M. *Battle Cry of Freedom. The Civil War Era*. Oxford, New York: Oxford University Press, 1988.

Mehrländer, Andrea. *The Germans of Charleston, Richmond and New Orleans during the Civil War Period, 1850-1870*. Berlin, New York: De Gruyer, 2011.

—. "'With more Freedom and Independence than the Yankees': The Germans of Richmond, Charleston, and New Orleans during the American Civil War", in Suzannah J. Ural (ed.), *Civil War Citizens: Race, Ethnicity, and Identity in America's Bloodiest Conflict*. New York: New York University Press, 2010. 57-97.

Miller, Kerby A. "Class, Culture and Immigrant Ethnicity", in Virginia Yans-McLaughlin (ed.), *Immigration Reconsidered*. New York: Oxford University Press, 1990. 96-129.

Mitchell, Reid. *Civil War Soldiers*. New York: Viking, 1988.

Motes, Margaret. *Migration to South Carolina, 1850 Census: from England, Scotland, Germany, Italy, France, Spain, Russia, Denmark, Sweden, and Switzerland*. Baltimore: Clearfield Press, 2005.

Münch, F. *Das fünfzigjährige Hochzeits-Jubiläum des Gold-Jubelpaares J.C.H Claussen und seiner Gattin Dorothea, geb. Fincken: feierlich begangen als Familienfest, Sonntag, den 25. April 1897, als Volksfest, Montag, den 26. April 1897, als Nachfest, Montag, den 3. Mai*. Charleston, SC: n.p., 1898.

Orvin, Maxwell Clayton. *Monck's Corner: Berkeley County, South Carolina*. Charleston: [n.p.], 1950.

Pease, Jane T. and William H. Pease. "The Economics and Politics of Charleston's Nullification Crisis", *Journal of Southern History*, August 1981, 335-362.

Pech, August F. "Bevölkerungsentwicklung und Sozialstruktur eines nordniedersächsischen Geestdorfes im 18. Jahrhundert, aufgezeigt an dem Dorf Flögeln im Landkreis Cuxhaven", *Jahrbuch der Männer vom Morgenstern*, 1981, 49-75.

Phelps, W. Chris. *The Bombardment of Charleston 1863-1865*. Gretna, LA: Pelican, 2002.

Powers, Bernard E. *Black Charlestonians: A Social History. 1822-1885*. Fayetteville: University of Arkansas Press, 1994.

Radford, John P. "Race, Residence and Ideology: Charleston, South Carolina in the Mid-Nineteenth Century", *Journal of Historical Geography*, 2/4 (1976), 329-46.

Reinert, Gertha. "'Turning my Joy into Bitterness': A Letter from John A. Wagener", *South Carolina Historical Magazine*, 100/1 (1999), 48-69.

Reports and Resolutions of the General Assembly of the State of South Carolina at the Regular Session Commencing November 28, 1893. Vol. 2. Columbia, SC, 1893.

"Reports of cases at law argued and determined in the Court of Appeals and Court of Errors of South Carolina." Vol.10: From Jan. term, 1858, to Jan. term, 1859; both inclusive (1859), 416-27.

Rivers, William J. and Judith M. Anderson. *Roll of the Dead: South Carolina Troops, Confederate States Service*. [Columbia, S.C.]: Public Programs Division, S.C. Dept. of Archives and History, 1995.

Rogers, Jr., George C. and C. James Taylor. *A South Carolina Chronology, 1497-1992*. Second Edition. Columbia: University of South Carolina Press, 1973, 1994.

—. *Charleston in the Age of the Pinckneys*. Norman, OK: University of Oklahoma Press, 1969.

Rosen, Robert N. *A Short History of Charleston*. Charleston: Peninsula Press, 1992.

—. *Confederate Charleston: An Illustrated History of the City and the People during the Civil War*. Columbia, SC: University of South Carolina Press, 1994.

Shealy, George Benet. *Walhalla: A German Settlement in Upstate South Carolina: The Garden of the Gods*. Seneca, SC: Blue Ridge Art Association, 1990.

Sheehan, James J. *German History 1770-1866*. Oxford: Clarendon, 1989.

Silver, Christopher. "Immigration and the Antebellum Southern City." Chapel Hill, 1975. M.A. Thesis.

Sinha, Manisha. *The Counterrevolution of Slavery: Politics and Ideology in Antebellum South Carolina*. Chapel Hill and London: University of North Carolina Press, 2000.

Strickland, Jeffery G. "Ethnicity and race in the urban south: German immigrants and African-Americans in Charleston, South Carolina during Reconstruction." Ph.D. dissertation, The Florida State University, 2003.

—. "How the Germans Became White Southerners: German Immigrants and African Americans in Charleston, South Carolina, 1860-1880", *Journal of American Ethnic History*, 28/1 (2008), 52-69.

Thomas, Albert Sidney. *A Historical Account of the Protestant Episcopal Church in South Carolina, 1820-1957*. Columbia, SC: [n.p.], 1957.

Toplin, Robert Brent. "Ken Burns's The Civil War as an Interpretation of History", in Robert Brent Toplin (ed.), *Ken Burns's The Civil War. Historians Respond*. New York, Oxford: Oxford University Press, 1966. 17-36.

Trapier, Paul, and John B. Adger. *The Religious Instruction of the Black Population. Extracted from the Southern Presbyterian Review*. [n.p.]: [n.p.], 1847.

Walker, Mack. *Germany and the Emigration 1816-1885*. Cambridge, MA: Harvard University Press, 1964.

Ward, Geoffrey C. "Refighting the Civil War", in Robert Brent Toplin (ed.), *Ken Burns's The Civil War. Historians Respond*. New York, Oxford: Oxford University Press, 1966. 141-152.

Whitelaw, Robert N.S. and Levkoff, Alice F. *Charleston Come Hell or High Water: A History in Photographs*. Columbia, SC: University of South Carolina Press, 1976.

Wiley, Bell Irvin. *The Life of Johnny Reb: The Common Soldier of the Confederacy*. Garden City, NY: Doubleday & Co. Inc., 1971.

Williams, George W., ed. *Incidents in My Life: The Autobiography of the Rev. Paul Trapier, S.T.D., with some of his letters*. Charleston: Dalcho Historical Society, Diocesan House, 1954.

—. *St. Michael's Charleston, 1751-1951, with Supplements 1951-2001*. Charleston: College of Charleston Library, 2001.

Wilson, Teresa E and Janice L. Grimes. *Marriages and Death Notices from the Southern Patriot, 1831-1848*. Vol. II. Easley, SC: Southern Historical Press, 1986.

Wise, Stephen R. *Gate of Hell. Campaign for Charleston Harbor, 1863*. Columbia, SC: University of South Carolina Press, 1994.

INDEX